Rx PC
The Anti-Virus Handbook

Rx PC
The Anti-Virus Handbook

Janet Endrijonas

WINDCREST®/McGRAW-HILL

FIRST EDITION
FIRST PRINTING

Library of Congress Cataloging-in-Publication Data

Endrijonas, Janet.
    Rx PC : the anti-virus handbook /by Janet Endrijonas.
        p.   cm.
    Includes index.
    ISBN 0-8306-4201-3 (pbk.) ISBN 0-8306-4202-1
    1. Computer viruses.   I. Title.
    QA76.76.C68E53 1992   92-24667
    005.8 — dc20   CIP

TAB Books offers software for sale. For information and a catalog, please contact TAB Software Department, Blue Ridge Summit, PA 17294-0850.

Acquisitions editor: Brad Schepp
Editorial team: Susan Bonthron, Editor
                Joanne Slike, Executive Editor
                Jodi Tyler, Indexer
Production team: Katherine Brown, Director
                  Rose McFarland, Layout
                  Olive Harmon, Typesetting
                  Joan Wieland, Proofreader
                  Linda King, Proofreader
Design team: Jaclyn J. Boone, Designer
              Brian Allison, Associate Designer
Cover design: Sandy Blair Design and Brent Blair Photography,
  Harrisburg, Pa.

To O and S, my faithful companions

Contents

Acknowledgments

The author gratefully acknowledges the contributions made by Nick Anis, who assembled the diskette and also shared some virus infection experiences; Jim Perra, who trusted, without asking questions, the author's ability to actually detect and remove a virus from his computer; Rob Rosenberger, whose midnight faxes kept the author interested and amused and who supplied valuable information from his and Ross Greenberg's booklet *Virus Myths*; and Aryeh Goretsky who, with grace and patience, answered a lot of dumb questions I asked. A very special thank you to Rick Cook for allowing me to reprint his clever piece on the Michelangelo scare. Thanks also to Ken Greenberg for his efforts in tracking down virus case studies, and to all those anonymous folks whose experiences with computer viruses the author was able to report. Last but not least, the author acknowledges Susan Arnold for her long suffering encouragement, and Audie, Erika, Martha, Marian, Sydney and Marilyn, for ideas and suggestions whether they were used in this book or not.

Foreword

Computer viruses are not a joke. There is nothing funny about losing programs and data—whether you are an individual, a small company, or a large corporation. Your work can come to a grinding halt through no fault of your own. A computer virus can be a devastating, frustrating experience.

Don't be lulled into a false sense of security by the media's recent lack of interest in the computer virus problem. While the press continues to cover the big events, they seem to have forgotten that computer viruses are an everyday occurrence. Viruses don't play favorites; they attack large and small computer users alike. The problem is increasing in geometric proportions. Not only are viruses continuing to arrive on the computer scene; their sophistication is increasing at a startling rate. With that added sophistication comes greater destructive characteristics.

At press times, there were over 1,200 known computer viruses. The list grows by an average of 20 new viruses each week. Unlike the earlier viruses, these newer viruses are not being created by teenage hackers motivated by youthful experimentation. They are, in the main, the products of sophisticated and experienced software engineers. And their viruses are becoming more deadly and more effective over time.

Fortunately, many major software publishers and even some smaller companies are investing the time and money required to combat the virus problem and create anti-virus solutions. The result has been more sophisticated anti-virus programs, many of which are fine products. Yet, not all anti-virus products provide an effective solution because of the enormous expense and effort involved in maintaining an exhaustive database of virus characteristics—a database vital to developing methods for detection and eradication of the latest viruses.

No matter how much computer virus awareness and education is available, it won't help the average computer user if he or she is not familiar with the best anti-virus programs on the market. I hope that this book and disk will encourage readers to learn about anti-virus programs, what they can and cannot do, and how to use them as a way to protect their computers and data.

JOHN MCAFEE

Introduction

Sick computers are like sick children—they can't tell you where it hurts, so you have to figure out the source of the infection and then decide what to do about it. Fortunately in both cases there are medications available that can eradicate the problem once the ailment is properly diagnosed. Better yet, in the case of computer viruses, there are programs that can locate the problem and diagnose the virus as well as remove it from your computer.

But these programs are your last line of defense, not your first. You are your own best defense. Using preventive measures can ensure that your computer will never become infected, and make you wonder why you invested in anti-virus software. Better to wonder than to find out why the hard way. Anyone can prevent computer virus infection, and everyone should make the effort. You don't have to be a programmer, a hacker or a computer guru. If you can turn on your computer, operate a few DOS commands, and install an application or two, you are qualified to prevent virus infection.

When you finish this book, you'll know all you need to know about how to care for your computer to avoid virus infection. You won't be bogged down with technical information you don't need. Everything in this book is in plain language with no undefined computer jargon. You'll know which anti-virus program is the right one for your needs. And you'll be able to check your computer to find any virus that may be lurking undetected by using the McAfee & Associates Shareware virus detection and eradication programs included with this book.

Don't let the fact that there have been few sensational stories about viruses appearing in the media lately give you a false sense of security. The threat is no less real—we have just become more adept at fighting the problem.

Actually, after a long quiet period, the news media broke its silence on the subject of viruses in March 1992, anticipating a catastrophic outbreak of the Michelangelo virus on March 6, a trigger date picked to honor the artist's birthday (he would have turned 517). For almost a week, reporters and commentators warned the public of the coming virus and estimated that the number of affected computers might run into the millions. This time, however, the news media also included advice on what to do to avoid letting the Michelangelo virus harm your hard drive, and as a result, very few computers suffered any damage. A week later, when the Jerusalem virus was expected to hit on Friday March 13, no one panicked—there was little if any media coverage before (and no reports of computer disaster after) that date.

This all goes to prove that viruses can be successfully detected and deleted even if you have already been infected. Remember, however, that unless you are armed with knowledge and appropriate software, you cannot fight computer viruses any more effectively than could the people who faced the very first infections. There is a reason why the market for anti-virus programs is growing at a tremendous rate, right behind the exploding market for DOS utilities. We live in an age when programs have been developed with enough intelligence to detect as yet unknown viruses if and when they appear.

Unless you are prepared to suffer the loss of data and precious hours of work, you should be ready for any virus that comes along. And you should take time to become aware of things you can do to safeguard your computer before the anti-virus software even comes into play. Consider anti-virus software to be like health insurance, and put together a preventive routine to keep your computer healthy so you'll never have to use it.

Your computer is one of some 62 million PCs in use today, any one of which could catch a virus. Viruses can pop up anywhere—not even commercial shrink-wrapped software programs are immune. This book gives you a no-nonsense, unbiased view of four major anti-virus software alternatives and starts you out with your own copy of a shareware virus detection and protection solution. In addition, three other programs are discussed.

After reading this book, you will know how to defend against virus infections in your system. You will have a good idea of what is available in the field of anti-virus programs and should be able to decide which type or brand of product you want to use. Best of all, you will have a respect for virus infections and what they can do, but you won't have an unnatural fear of getting one into your system. Panic will no longer be your mode of anti-virus operation.

1

The anatomy
of a virus

To know the nature of the enemy is the first step in combatting the problems it causes. Computer viruses are an enemy that anyone who uses computers should become knowledgeable about. You should know what they are, how to find them, and what to do about them. At the present time, some 1200 computer viruses have been identified, and more crop up with amazing frequency. You don't have to be a computer programmer or a hacker to learn how to protect yourself from computer viruses—the average computer user can become well versed in the lore of the computer virus.

If you are looking in this book to find instructions in how to beat the virus writers at their own game, put the book back on the shelf. You won't find any instructions in writing virus code here. What you will find is enough background material to help you know your enemy, and a lot of practical ways to prevent virus infections in your computer.

Because even the most assiduous prevention efforts can fail, I have included detailed discussions of many of today's finest anti-virus programs so that you can make an intelligent buying decision for your home or office. I discuss anti-virus techniques in terms of single-user computer systems, but the same prevention tactics can and should be applied to networks, which are even more vulnerable to the losses sustained in a virus attack. As devastating as a virus can be on a single-user system, multiply the damage by what a virus can destroy in a multiuser system or on a network, and the potential devastation becomes mind-boggling. You will find that most of the anti-virus programs discussed in this book are either suited to networks as well as single-user systems, or have a version specially developed for networks. To get you started, this book contains a diskette with a number of valuable virus detection and eradication shareware programs, including a network version.

As you read through the first two chapters of this book, you might feel that you are encountering a certain amount of redundancy. Well, you are. Certain points about virus prevention cannot be stressed too often. I hope that the repetition helps you understand and remember the most important aspects of virus prevention, and the need for constant vigilance.

What is a virus?

Often it seems that there are almost as many definitions of the words *computer virus* as there are viruses, but that isn't really true. Certain basics make a virus a virus. A virus is any group of unwanted programs (i.e., lines of code) that get into a computer system via a diskette or through a network. Viruses have two main characteristics: the ability to reproduce themselves, and some form of trigger that sets the virus activity in motion. A virus can and usually does replicate before it causes destruction, making detection more difficult.

Viruses are not accidental. Someone, somewhere, has purposely designed and disseminated the virus code. Propagating a virus is a crime, although—despite a few exciting cases reported in the media, such as the Internet Worm in 1988—few of the perpetrators are ever caught. Often viruses are the result of an oversized ego attached to an overactive imagination—someone's idea of a road to fame (at least within their own small circle of people who know the identity of the virus writer). Or a virus can be the result of someone's desire for revenge against real or imagined computer-using enemies.

Unfortunately, creating a virus is not difficult. You don't even have to be a programmer. All you need is one of several "how to" books that can be found at your local book store and sometimes even in the local public library.

Viruses are short programs that are set to go off when a particular situation is encountered. A virus might activate after the program in which it resides has been run a certain number of times. This means the virus, lying undetected in the program, can be copied and passed along any number of times before its host program has been run a sufficient number of times to reveal its existence.

Other triggers can be a random number or the presence (or absence) of a specific file. A date can also set off some viruses. For example, in the case of the virus known as "Jerusalem" or "Friday the 13th," the virus is set to do its dirty work whenever a computer's clock reaches a Friday the 13th. If you don't take precautions to prevent and detect them, any virus like this can lie dormant and undetected in your computer system until the appointed trigger moment. Knowing what we know about viruses these days, it is foolish not to take precautions.

Not all viruses are the same. Some infect the boot sector of an operating system, while others prey upon the executable files in applications programs. There are programs that infect the partition table, and some that can infect both programs and boot sectors or partition tables, as well as the new stealth viruses discussed below. Fortunately, most of the anti-virus programs on the market today can find all of these types of viruses.

Viruses only become active when a program is loaded. If you are going to use a diskette that has been copied on another computer, check the diskette before copying it to your hard disk, and before loading any of the programs it contains, whether from your hard disk or from the floppy. As with so many things in this world, when it comes to detecting viruses and preventing their contamination of your computer system, all it takes is a little prior effort to ward off what can become a major catastrophe. One simple precaution you can take to prevent boot sector virus transmission is always to keep the door on your primary floppy drive (Drive A) open when booting your computer, so that the computer boots from your hard drive, not from an untested floppy.

To further define exactly what constitutes a virus, there are definite attributes beyond the capability to replicate. They all have to do with the ability of a virus to modify other programs, execute those programs, and to recognize and stop other modifications in such programs. I will discuss some of these methods later on in this chapter.

Not all software diseases are viruses

Many so-called "computer viruses" are, in fact, not viruses at all, though they can be just as damaging to your computer. Fortunately, the methods for preventing and detecting these diseases are basically the same as for viruses.

Logic bombs and time bombs are short programs added to an existing program. Often they are inserted to modify a program in some way. They are set to go off when certain conditions are met. Logic bombs can be triggered by any event the programmer chooses: for example, addition or deletion of a specific file; a date and time; or a particular input sequence to the infected program.

Time bombs activate on or after a specific date. Often what looks like a time bomb can, in reality, be a date-activated virus such as the Jerusalem series. Logic and time bombs are technically not computer viruses because they do not replicate themselves. The bad news is that time bombs and logic bombs can lurk undetected in your system for the longest period of time waiting for just the right trigger event to make them "go off."

The good news is that these bombs can be detected before they are activated if you use a good scan program on a consistent basis. Time and logic bombs can be relatively benign, merely adding something like a message to your screen at the appointed time. On the other hand, they can be quite serious. They can delete and replace their host program, often by doing nothing more complicated than renaming the host program, therefore making it seem to disappear.

Trojans are named after the Trojan Horse used by the Greek Army at the siege of Troy. Just as enemy soldiers hid within the original Trojan Horse, which appeared to be a legitimate gift, computer Trojans hide within programs that appear to be legitimate. For example, a Trojan can be hidden within a word-processing program. When you load the program, the Trojan is activated and performs its appointed task—perhaps something as devastating as formatting your hard disk—while you sit watching your monitor, waiting for the program to load and wondering why the computer is so slow today.

Trojans are activated each time a program they reside in is run. The only positive side of Trojans is that they generally obliterate themselves in the process of damaging your disk. That doesn't mean they are any less dangerous to your computer; before they extinguish themselves they can do a great deal of damage.

Trojans are not true computer viruses because they do not replicate themselves. They are limited to the host program, and are only triggered when that host program is loaded. Of course, they can move from computer to computer via copies of that host program. As with logic and time bombs, Trojans can lie quietly in your computer waiting for the host program to be run. Fortunately, as with logic and time bombs, you can discover Trojans before they are activated.

Worms are computer programs designed to move through a computer's memory and disks, altering all data as it is encountered. A worm is more closely related to a virus than are Trojans and time and logic bombs because it can replicate itself. In fact, its movement through a system is managed by the worm making copies of itself over and over and filling the system with these copies. A worm can destroy or modify a lot of files before you realize what is happening and eradicate the pest. Worms do not need a host or carrier program to carry out their nasty task.

Some of the trouble that can be caused by a virus, worm, or Trojan includes relatively benign displays of a particular message on the screen (the Peace Virus was an example of this), letters melting down the display screen, or just making your computer run more slowly. Some more devastating effects include "stuffing" (using up) all the capacity on your hard drive by creating large or numerous empty files and directories. Files can be damaged directly, or the file allocation table (FAT) can be modified so that files and directories become useless. Some viruses flash a message on the monitor and then shut down your computer. Others cause your entire system to crash. Still others wipe out everything on your hard disk, through formatting or overwriting.

Debunking the popular myths about viruses

Myths surrounding computer viruses abound. Some have arisen because viruses are a mysterious, frightening subject, and people tend to fear things they don't understand. Often these myths are perpetuated by the news media because many of the reporters covering virus stories do not understand computers, but do know what makes a good story.

Rob Rosenberger, along with Ross M. Greenberg, both programmers experienced with virus detection and prevention, have written a brochure titled *Computer Virus Myths*. In their text, Rosenberger and Greenberg talk about many of the myths that bother computer users. Here are some of the more common myths, together with Rosenberger and Greenberg's explanations of why they are myths.

1. Viruses are written by hackers.

   "Yes, hackers have written viruses. So has a computer magazine publisher. Trojan horses were written for years by middle-aged men wearing business suits. We call people *wormers* when they abuse their knowledge of computers. You shouldn't be afraid of hackers just because they know how to write viruses."

2. Computer viruses are reaching epidemic proportions.

   "Wrong. Viruses might spread all over the planet but they won't take over the world. There are about 150 or so known "strains" at this time, some of which have been completely eliminated. Your chances of being infected, if you take the proper precautions, are slim."

3. Viruses could destroy all the files on my disk.

   "Yes, and a spilled cup of coffee could do the same thing. If you have adequate backup copies of your data, you can recover from any virus or coffee attack. Backups mean the difference between a nuisance and a disaster."

4. My files are damaged so it must have been a virus attack.

   "It could also have been caused by a power flux, or static electricity, or a fingerprint on a floppy disk, or a bug in your software, or perhaps a simple error on your part. Power failures and spilled cups of coffee have destroyed more data than all the viruses combined."

5. Viruses can be hidden inside a data file.

   "Data files can't wreak havoc on your computer—only an executable file can do that. If a virus were to infect a data file, it would be a wasted effort. [A file] you think is a data file might actually be an executable program file. For example, batch files are text files, yet the MS-DOS operating system treats them like a program."

6. My backups will be worthless if I back up a virus.

   "No they won't. You can restore important documents and databases without restoring the infected program. You just reinstall programs from master disks."

7. Read-only files are safe from virus infections.

"This is a common myth among IBM PC users and it has even been published... Supposedly you can protect yourself by using the DOS ATTRIB command to set the read-only attribute on program files. However, ATTRIB is software—and what it can do, a virus can undo."

8. Viruses can infect files on write-protected disks.

"If viruses can modify read-only files, people assume they can modify write-protected floppies. What [these people] don't realize is the disk drive itself (hardware) knows when a floppy is protected and refuses to write to it. You can physically disable the drive's sensor but you can't override it with a software command."

9. Viruses can spread to all sorts of computers.

"All Trojan horse [programs] are limited to a family of computers and this is especially true for viruses. A virus designed to spread on IBM PCs [and compatibles] cannot infect an IBM-4300-series mainframe, nor can it infect a Commodore C64 nor an Apple Macintosh."

10. Most BBSs are infected with viruses; BBSs and shareware programs spread viruses; my computer could be infected if I call an infected BBS.

"Very few BBSs are really infected. It is possible a dangerous file might be available on a BBS but it doesn't mean the BBS itself is infected. If a BBS were knowingly infected with a virus, it wouldn't stay open too long after word got out. Reputable BBS sysops check every file; nationwide sysop networks help spread the word about dangerous files. You should be wary of software you get from BBSs but you should also be wary of software you get from store shelves. BBSs can't write information on your disks—that's handled by the communications software you use. You can only transfer a dangerous file if you let your software do it."

11. Anti-virus software will protect me from viruses.

"There is no such thing as a foolproof anti-virus program. Trojan horses and viruses can be (and have been) designed to bypass them. Anti-virus products themselves can be tricky to use at times."

You might now be rid of erroneous thinking, but you are not rid of the possibility of a virus entering your computer and causing problems.

A short, not so illustrious history

Exactly when the history of computer viruses begins depends upon who you talk to. Some trace computer viruses back to "Creeper" in the early 1970s, although Creeper was actually more like a worm than a true virus. Creeper crawled through ARPANET, the network funded by the Defense Department that linked university, military, and corporate computers. Wherever it went, it displayed the message, "I'm the Creeper, catch me if you can," and continued replicating to fill the network's storage capacity.

Others credit the Core War game, developed at Bell Laboratories, as the starting point. Core War wasn't really a virus. It was a game with the potential to get out of hand. Here's how it worked. Players each designed a self-replicating program. Core War pitted these self-replicating programs against one another, with each program attempting to destroy the others by overwriting their program code. To do this, each Core War program reproduced itself as fast as possible in order to overwrite others before being overwritten. The game was played for a specified length of time, at the end of which the player whose program had the most copies in memory was the winner.

Core War moved from Bell Labs into corporate and university computer systems, and ultimately into networks. No one doubted the possibility that one of these self-replicating programs might get loose in a host system, and indeed that did happen, though not with any frequency. Perhaps the more unfortunate legacy of Core War was that the game served as a training ground for some programmers, who later turned their talents and knowledge from relatively harmless game playing to more destructive pursuits, and began to create viruses.

Early virus history would be incomplete without mentioning Fred Cohen. While working on his PhD at the University of Southern California (USC), Cohen designed an experimental computer program that could modify another program by including a replication of itself. As a result, Cohen created a program that could easily spread. He performed carefully controlled experiments on a USC computer system to show what his program could do. Other system users found that they could not combat the replicating program's modification of files. (Yes, when Cohen's experiment was over, all affected files were carefully removed from the system.)

The first "commercial" virus was the Pakistani Brain. This virus was ostensibly designed as a "good" virus, one that could be used to prevent piracy, but since it was designed by a couple of pirates, it soon had a more diabolical purpose. Two brothers ran a discount software operation in Pakistan at which they sold pirated copies of expensive computer programs for incredibly low prices—to foreigners. At the same time, the brothers hired out as consultants to Pakistani businesses and created customized software for their clients. Lo and behold, they discovered other people pirating their custom software. So one brother created a self-replicating virus that would be passed along in any copies made of the program and infect the unauthorized user's system. The only way a victim could get rid of the virus was to contact the brothers for the antidote. The brothers were thoughtful enough to have the virus put their telephone number on screen.

This worked so well on their customized programs, they decided to put it into the pirated copies of expensive software they were selling to non-Pakistani buyers in their store. This way, if an American bought one of their programs, he could run it, but if he allowed his friends to share it by copying it, they could not. Again, the antidote required a call to Pakistan, and again the brothers thoughtfully included their telephone number in the virus' on screen message.

After this, viruses were off and running. Once started, they began to proliferate worldwide. Each virus had its own characteristics. The virus discovered in 1987 at the library at Lehigh University modified the COMMAND.COM file so that floppy disks would not boot. The Peace Virus, a Macintosh infection, seemed quite benign since it didn't destroy anything. It just flashed its peace message on the screen on its appointed date (March 2, 1988) and disappeared. But before that time, the Peace Virus spread like wildfire, proving the capability of viruses to spread their infection far and wide. It spread via bulletin boards and disk swapping, and even managed to make it into shrink-wrapped product coming from Aldus Corporation (for only three days, however, after which the product was recalled and Aldus traced the infection back to its source).

There are endless stories about individual viruses, how they spread, the type of damage they do, and how computer users get rid of them; far too many to recount here. At first, the subject of viruses was "interesting," sort of a fun-and-games, hide-and-seek challenge for computer buffs. Viruses appeared more or less one at a time, often demonstrating a new technological aberration, and challenging programmers and hackers to crack them. In those early days, viruses were usually concocted by hackers with time on their hands and a desire to be mischievous.

In the ensuing years, however, viruses have become so prolific, so complex, and so devastating that viruses are no longer just an interesting challenge or a new game to play. Today's viruses are being designed by professional programmers. They can be extremely sophisticated. Often they are designed to suit the programmers personal purpose, one which might be destructive for the sake of revenge, as has been known to happen in the case of disgruntled employees with computer knowledge and access.

These complex virus programs are far beyond the level of expertise of people who are average computer users, i.e., those who are very familiar with the programs they use every day, but who possess only rudimentary, if any, knowledge of computer science. Such computer users are not concerned (and should not have to be) with the details of how these viruses are constructed, or the motivation of the creator. All most people want to know is how to avoid viruses and failing that, how to find them and get rid of them. Fortunately, there are "good" programmers who are just as clever as the virus designers. As fast as a new virus appears, the anti-virus sleuths are cracking its code and inventing a cure.

Anyone's computer can contract a virus

Even the most careful computer user can unwittingly pick up a virus. Floppy disks are the most common carriers, but by no means the only source of infection. CD-ROM disks and tape systems have been known to carry a virus or one of its relatives. Boot sector viruses can be carried by any floppy disk that has come into contact with an infected system.

When it comes to viruses, no one can be trusted. Even your best friend, your closest coworker and your respected computer repair technician cannot be trusted to use or give you disease-free diskettes. They won't do this on purpose; they will usually be totally unaware that their disks are infected. For example, your hard disk needs service and the technician uses a diagnostic diskette. It's easy for that diagnostic diskette to contain a virus that can be passed along, never actually changing anything on the diskette. Later—and depending upon the nature of the virus, so much later that it cannot easily be traced back to the correct source—that virus can wreak havoc in your system.

Your friend who gives you a pirated copy of a great new computer game might inadvertently give you more than either of you bargained for, depending upon his source. Any time you use a non-write-protected floppy disk in a public computer system such as at a library or in a college laboratory, you risk picking up a virus and later transferring it to your own system without realizing what has happened until the virus hits. By the way, a virus can be contained in a program transmitted over a telephone line modem to modem—downloading a friend's software rather than putting his diskette into your computer will not filter out a virus infection.

Even commercial software fresh from the shrink-wrapped package has been known to carry a virus. While these instances have been rare, there has been more than one such occurrence, and not all in the distant past either. As recently as early 1992, one company shipped virus-infected demonstration disks to its customers. At almost the same time, another company shipped a number of PCs with virus-infected hard disks.

Bulletin Board Systems (BBSs) have been given a bad rap for being virus spreaders. There is little need to be concerned about any of the commercial on-line services such as GEnie, CompuServe, or Prodigy, and little more cause for alarm on reputable private BBSs, because most system operators (sysops) are very careful about what gets uploaded to their system. One semi-reassuring fact is that boot sector viruses won't be downloaded from a BBS. Since at least half of all virus infections result from boot sector viruses, you are already a little ahead when downloading from a BBS.

But don't drop your guard; even though it won't be a boot virus, you could still encounter the one sysop who let something get by. When you download from a BBS, check for viruses before you run the program. Other communications activities—including networking, using electronic mail, and transferring files—can also spread viruses. When in doubt, check before you run any new program—as a matter of fact, always be in doubt and always check.

How viruses invade your computer
Viruses that attack executable files

A virus lives in a host program. Its code is added to that program's code, and executes each time the host program is executed. When the virus executes, it seeks at least one other program to which it can copy itself. This program (often referred to as the target program) will continue to function normally after being infected. Each time a host program is exited and reentered, the virus code repeats the infection process looking for another target program to infect. Once a target program is infected, it behaves like the original host program.

Keep in mind that just because you don't notice any change doesn't mean the virus isn't lurking there waiting for the appropriate trigger moment. This movement from target program to target program continues until all the programs on your computer that fit the target profile are infected. Eventually, when you use your computer to make a copy of a program, the virus will be passed onto your floppy along with any boot sector viruses you might have in your system. If you use this diskette in your laptop, you infect that system. Should you loan the diskette to someone else who uses it in his or her computer, that computer will then be infected as well. In each computer your diskette infects, the virus spreading process begins anew.

Viruses, other than boot sector and partition table strains, can only exist in files containing executable code that they can modify. Executable program files are the ones with one of the following extensions: .COM, .EXE, .BAT, and .SYS. They can also exist in program overlay files identified by the extensions .OVR and .OVL. This means that a virus can attack the COMMAND.COM file that your system uses to accept commands typed from the keyboard and to execute programs. Having this process disrupted by a virus can shut your system down in a hurry.

Once the virus is in a host program, it takes advantage of the fact that DOS-based PC programs each have a defined point at which the first program instruction is located. It is easy for the virus to change the instruction at this point and to transfer program control to itself instead of the next program instruction.

Some viruses make themselves memory-resident rather than continually looking for additional programs to infect. When memory-resident, the virus usually infects other programs when they are executed by intercepting a specific interrupt. An interrupt is an attention request signal that is sent either by hardware or software to the computer's microprocessor. When an interrupt occurs, the microprocessor stops what it is doing, saves its work, and transfers control to an interrupt handler that causes a specific set of instructions such as the execution of a program to be carried out. Essentially, as before, the virus is intercepting the executable program at its entry point and taking over.

Just as in program-to-program infection, memory-resident infection usually does not show up in the operation of the program, so you won't know the infection is there until it is triggered. Once in a while there might be an overt sign that the virus is there, but in most cases you won't be that lucky.

Boot sector and partition table viruses

The boot sector is an area on your hard disk that contains some small programs necessary to start (boot) your system. The boot sector is not a file and resides in its own area on disk. The only way a boot sector can become infected is from a floppy disk. When a PC boots, the ROM program automatically loads everything in the boot sector into memory and executes it. A virus might continue to give normal messages during bootup, while in the background it modifies one or more of the DOS interrupt routines. Since the boot sector is very small, often the virus cannot store itself totally in the boot sector, but must store part of its code elsewhere on the disk. Usually, to hide its whereabouts, the virus marks these additional disk sectors as "bad" in the system's file allocation table (FAT) because DOS will not store files in a bad sector and consequently will not overwrite or delete the virus.

Approximately 70 percent of all viruses are boot sector viruses, preventable merely by never booting your computer from an unknown, unchecked floppy disk. Granted, there have been cases of shrink-wrapped originals coming from the manufacturer with an embedded virus, but as you will see later in the book, today's virus detection programs can find the virus on a disk before you use it. Obviously, checking any diskette before using it in your computer is a good idea. Then, write protect the clean diskette and any copies you make of it to prevent later infection, and you should be perfectly safe.

The partition table on your disk is located at physical sector zero on your hard disk. It stores information about how the physical disk has been divided into one or more logical drives (for example, drives C and D), which operate as though they were actually separate physical entities. The same zero sector contains a partition program that ROM loads and executes to identify the logical drive from which the system can boot. A partition sector can hold a virus in exactly the same way as a boot sector.

The boot sector on a hard drive is located in sector zero of the logical drive from which the system boots. On floppies, the boot and partition sectors are the same, because floppies contain only one logical drive. While this means that a floppy cannot have an infected partition table, it can still be a carrier. Partition table viruses can infect the boot sector on a floppy and then spread back to the partition sector on a hard disk.

A few viruses can infect both boot sectors and partition tables as well as the executable files in applications programs. First they infect the partition table, and then they install themselves as memory-resident and attack each executable application file when loaded. Even though a virus that can attack in multiple ways has an opportunity to spread more rapidly, note that it also requires considerably more code, and is therefore more readily detected.

Stealth viruses

The stealth viruses arrived on the scene in 1990. Stealth viruses, as their name implies, are designed to avoid detection. Several techniques are used to create stealth viruses, and as a result, many software programs designed to detect all known viruses prior to the advent of stealth became obsolete when the stealth was unleashed on computers. Fortunately for us, the makers of virus programs are just as clever as the designers of viruses and have come up with ways in which even stealth viruses can be detected.

Stealth virus technology has, however, made one anti-virus practice essential: virus detection must be done in an environment that is safe from contamination. This means that when you are attempting to detect the presence of a virus, you must boot your computer from Drive A (not the hard disk), using a write-protected, uninfected DOS system diskette. This precaution cannot be emphasized too often.

Later in the book, as we get to the individual anti-virus programs, you will be told that before installing the program into your system, you should boot from a clean diskette (a write-protected copy of the original system disk) in Drive A. By the way, some anti-virus programs on the market will not allow hard disk access if you boot from Drive A. These are not recommended.

Stealth viruses use several different techniques to invade your computer and escape detection. The most common method involves complex code encryption where the encryption changes the virus' code with each generation. Thus, each time the program is passed from host to target, the virus code is changed so that there is no recognizable pattern established. Another stealth technique is to randomly insert "no operation instructions" (NOPs) into each succeeding generation of the virus, again in such a way as to fail to create a recognizable pattern that would give away its existence.

A third stealth practice is to alter the actual operation of DOS by intercepting functions and displaying phantom information on screen. For, example, when a .COM file has been altered (here your only clue might be a change in the file size), the infection might be from a DOS-altering stealth virus that will show you the .COM file at its original size when a DIR (directory) command is typed. Hence, your only clue, the change in file size, will be masked. And if that isn't tricky enough for you, there are stealth viruses that alter DOS so that when you call up a program—perhaps one of your applications programs—the screen display appears normal while an infected copy of the program is actually being loaded into memory. Everything appears to be fine until the program encounters the trigger and the boom lowers.

Fortunately, this never has to happen if you take care to prevent it.

Reference

Rosenberger, Rob, and Ross M. Greenberg, *Computer Virus Myths*, 8th Edition, O'Fallon, Illinois, March 1992.

2
CHAPTER

Basic prescription for anti-virus protection

Though a major portion of this book is devoted to anti-virus programs, keep in mind that such programs are your last line of virus defense, not your first. While you should always have an anti-virus program available, and you should frequently scan for viruses (a properly installed anti-virus program might automatically scan each time your system boots), you must continually use all the suggested virus prevention methods to avoid infection in the first place. If you have been careful and followed the preventive measures, your anti-virus scanning software should give you nothing but good reports of a clean computer. There is, however, always that chance that something will slip through even the most careful precautions. In that case, it's reassuring to know that you have an anti-virus program installed and performing frequent scans as a backup to your prevention efforts.

There is a long list of things you can do to prevent a virus from invading your computer. As comprehensive as the list presented here is supposed to be, someone, somewhere will know of a procedure that has been left out. Don't worry about that. If you use the preventive measures presented here religiously, no known virus will get through your net and into your computer. As a matter of fact, many as yet unknown viruses probably will be foiled as well, long before you have to worry about getting an update to your anti-virus software that can handle the latest virus or strain.

Be careful when booting your computer

Never boot your computer from a system disk that has been in anyone else's computer. If you are going to boot from a floppy, make certain that it is a write-protected, clean system disk. You might pop a diskette that you think is only a data disk into Drive A and leave it locked in there when you turn off the computer for the day. The next time you boot the computer, the system will try to boot from Drive A first, as it should. The diskette you left in the computer has a boot sector, whether or not it has bootable system files, and in that boot sector could be a virus.

The same is true if you need to "warm boot" (reset) your computer using <Ctrl>-<Alt>-<Del>. If Drive A is locked, the system will attempt to boot from there first, and pick up whatever is on the diskette, whether it can boot from the diskette or not. As mentioned earlier, it is a good practice only to lock Drive A when using it, and to make certain to unlock it as soon as you finish with it. It is also a good practice to double-check the status of Drive A regularly before you shut off your computer, so that when you start it up again, it won't go to Drive A to boot.

Some anti-virus experts go so far as to suggest that if you have more than one floppy disk drive, you disable Drive A so you can't boot from it, even by accident. These same people suggest that if you have a single disk drive, you reconfigure the system so that it thinks that the drive is B rather than A.

These suggestions are a bit extreme, especially if your two drives accommodate different media and are both required in your computer use, or if you have no hard disk. Additionally, changing Drive A might actually hinder some anti-virus activities because it can stymie the proper installation and use of anti-virus software (how can you boot from a clean system diskette in Drive A if you have no Drive A?), so unless you are willing to keep switching a drive from A to B and back again when needed, it seems far more practical just to check the door lock regularly.

Back up your computer regularly

Backing up your computer is probably one of the simplest precautions, yet because it is a tedious nuisance, relatively few people bother to do it. While backing up your computer won't prevent, detect, or destroy viruses, it is your only line of defense for restoring all of your data should a virus hit. What can seem like a time-wasting effort right now appears as a real blessing if you are ever faced with the full impact of a devastating virus. The more important the information stored on your hard disk, the more frequently you should make backup copies.

Some experts suggest using more than one set of backups. Keeping multiple sets of backups can prevent bringing a virus that you have cleaned out back onto your computer. Even if a virus slips through in making your current backups, you will hopefully have an earlier, pre-virus set to use in restoring files. Always check for a virus any time you restore from backup files. Although it might not be necessary to remind you, keep your backup diskettes in a safe place. They won't do you any good if they are lost or damaged through careless handling.

You don't have to back up everything every day. Be selective to save time and to prevent yourself from dreading the backup operation. If you back up live files daily and then back up the entire system once a week, you should be okay. By the way, if you choose to back up your files on tape, back up by file so that if a virus is detected and removed from your computer after a backup, you can omit any virus-infected files on the tape when restoring the data to your hard disk.

Remember, too, that if you are really concerned about viruses, you can restore a hard drive using the original write-protected program disks for your applications programs, and only restore data files from your backups. Even if all you are restoring from your backups is data, you must still check the diskette holding the data files before copying them back to your computer. Data files might not be susceptible to virus infection, but the diskette itself can still be a carrier of a boot sector virus.

There is a bit of good news when it comes to backing up your computer. It is no longer the tedious chore it once was. A number of new backup programs are on the market that make backing up your computer easy and fast. Most are relatively inexpensive, and the investment can be one of the best you will ever make.

Know your software source

Your best friend can be your worst enemy. If he hands you a diskette with a virus and you copy it into your computer . . . well, you know he didn't mean to do it and he feels just terrible. But if you didn't check the disk before copying it onto your system, you really can't blame him, can you? Either way, no matter who is at fault, you now have a virus and need to get rid of it.

Rule one here is know your source. Never accept software with doubtful origins and never, never run a newly copied program on your computer before thoroughly checking it for viruses using an anti-virus program. If your software allows, check the diskette the program arrived on even before you copy it to your hard drive, let alone before you run it. Don't trust anyone—everyone is vulnerable. Check, check, and double-check every diskette. It is an acknowledged fact that the most common way viruses spread is via diskette. You won't know when a friend or a coworker is giving you an infected diskette because they might not be aware their disks have been contaminated. Be careful even bringing diskettes home from the office unless your office computer and/or network is being carefully monitored for virus infection.

Software piracy is a common—if illegal—practice, and obviously pirated diskettes are a great way to pass along a virus. If you want a program, buy it and use the diskette from the shrink-wrapped manufacturer's package or a clean copy of the originals that you have made on your carefully scanned computer. No, this isn't 100 percent foolproof either; there are documented cases of viruses coming direct from manufacturers, but these instances are few and far between. Compared to the risk of accepting a pirated copy, even if you know the person who made it, the risk of shrink-wrapped originals having a virus is minuscule. If you must take a pirated copy, check it out carefully before you run the program on your computer.

Unfortunately, it is dangerous today to advise people only to buy shrink-wrapped software because of the trade-in policies of many dealers, coupled with the ease and relatively low cost of owning and operating a shrink-wrap machine. When you buy software from any dealer who accepts returns of opened software, you cannot be certain that the shrink-wrapped software you are buying is actually in the manufacturer's original wrap. By now, you know what to do—use your anti-virus program to check the disks before you copy or run the programs. You can never be too safe but you can be very sorry.

A further reminder on the subject of spreading viruses from computer to computer via floppy diskettes: It's a good idea not to let anyone else use your computer with his or her own diskettes. It doesn't matter who puts the diskette in the computer—it's what's on the diskette that counts. Even a newly formatted diskette from some other computer can carry a boot sector virus if the computer on which it was formatted has one.

The reverse of this is also true—don't use someone else's computer and then take the diskette back to your system. Also avoid using public computers, such as those found in libraries, and then taking the diskette back to your home or office for use in your computer. Any diskette passing through that computer at any time might have had one or more viruses, so the diskette you bring back to your computer can have quite a collection of infections. If you are unable to avoid using a public computer, be sure to use your anti-virus software and check the diskette thoroughly when you get it back to your home or office.

Bulletin boards aren't all that dangerous

Bulletin boards have unjustly earned a reputation for spreading virus infections, probably because viruses were passed by bulletin boards, albeit inadvertently, in the days before viruses became well documented. At that time, we had little software to make virus detection easy, and each system operator (sysop) was on his or her own, often not knowing what to look for in a file to find a virus. As a result, viruses within programs went up on the system and as they were downloaded by BBS users, spread to their computers.

Today, most sysops are extremely careful not to let viruses get onto the system—they could be out of business rather fast if it were discovered that their BBS was spreading viruses. But a BBS is never totally safe, if not from viruses, then from their cousins, the Trojan Horse programs. It's best not to be the first person to download a file newly available on a bulletin board. Let someone else go first and be the guinea pig. By now, you have figured out that you always download to a floppy disk—never directly to your hard disk—and then check for viruses before the hard disk is involved.

Choose your bulletin board carefully. Commercial online services like GEnie, CompuServe, and Prodigy are probably very safe, but more specialized BBSs that have lots of games no one else has seen or heard of, or boards that tend toward frequent discussions about computer hacking and how to do it, should be considered risky. Shareware and freeware downloaded from reputable BBSs are usually okay, but if you can, download your shareware directly from the program developer's bulletin board (most shareware developers have a private board available), to ensure you are getting it first hand.

By the way, as good as all the scanning programs are at detecting viruses, the International Computer Security Association's *Computer Virus Handbook* says that scanners do not normally detect Trojans, and suggests testing downloads on a separate test computer if possible. If this is not possible, the handbook suggests that you back up the system just before you download and test the new program or attempt to run it, from floppy or hard drive, on your computer.

Other suggestions for preventing virus infections

Those write-protect tabs that come with each package of blank floppies are useful in the fight against viruses. As I have stressed, they should be used on all clean system boot diskettes. They can also be used on all program disks and copies of those programs made directly from the originals, and they can even be used on floppy data disks. They might be aggravating and—in the case of a data disk—take a few extra seconds to put on and take off, but they can help prevent the spread of virus infections.

Computer symptoms that might tip you off

Although some symptoms can occur that should start you wondering if your computer has a virus, your computer doesn't necessarily have a virus if it starts doing unusual things. Symptoms can be caused by a hardware glitch, or a software bug. To check this out, turn off your computer system and reboot from Drive A using a clean, write-protected system disk. If you have not done a recent system backup, do one right now before you do anything else and carefully store the backup diskettes in a safe place. You can now either hunt for a virus on your own (looking for changes in executable file sizes or signatures in code if you are adept enough in programming to handle this), or you can run your anti-virus software program to scan for the problem.

It is possible that nothing will show up as a result of any tests or software you run, but your computer might still be operating strangely. At this point, the better part of valor is to shut the system down and seek help from someone with more knowledge about computers. Sometimes this is as easy and inexpensive as contacting a local users group and describing the problem to the members. If you have a dealer you can trust, take the system in for a checkup. Or, call in a consultant who can diagnose and treat the problem, whether or not it turns out to be a virus.

System changes that might indicate a virus include:

- slow program loading;
- too many disk accesses while performing a relatively simple task;
- unusual error messages, especially if they appear with any regularity or frequency;
- ghosts, such as the activity lights on a peripheral like your printer glowing when nothing is enroute;
- a noticeable lowering of available memory on your system;
- a sudden decrease in available disk space;
- mysteriously disappearing files.

While changes in executable file sizes are a good indication that an infection might be present, you might also see a change in the time and date stamp on an executable file. For example, in your directory, your COMMAND.COM file will display a date corresponding to the time when your version of DOS was written. It might say something like 1-1-90. If it suddenly says 4-15-92, your computer might have a virus.

Some viruses hide in the boot sectors of floppy disks marking those sectors as bad sectors. It is a good idea to get in the habit of running the DOS CHKDSK command on your floppies. You might be surprised to find that there are bad sectors on the disk today that were not there the last time you used the diskette. That might be an indication that a virus is hiding all or part of its code in those sectors, designating them "bad" so that DOS won't overwrite them. If your system reboots itself at odd times, like right after you exit an application, there might be a problem. Of course, there are also obvious viruses, the ones that give you an on-screen message in text or graphics.

Some techniques don't work

Several commonly touted virus-prevention techniques are not mentioned above, mainly because they don't work. You might have heard about immunization programs that put code into a file, supposedly to convince viruses that the file is already infected so the virus will ignore this file in its search for targets. This can work against the small number of viruses that look for a signature line of code before infecting a file, but only for those. It won't fool any others. Immunization code won't work against those viruses that are set up to add their own signature code to a file regardless of whether or not another signature code already exists.

You also might have been told that using the ATTRIB command to make a file read-only will prevent virus infections. This is a software solution, but one that won't foil a virus that can see through the ploy and undo the command. Changing the date in your computer to foil a date-specific virus such as Michelangelo will work only if your computer has a clock that does not restore itself to the correct date when you power down, or if you set the clock ahead and leave the computer on until the danger is over. Remember that by changing the date, you might have avoided letting the virus activate for the moment, but the virus is still in the system and still a danger that must be removed.

Power users keep trying to come up with quick fixes for virus control, and one day they might actually come up with a universal prevention method or even a universal cure. But in the meantime, consistent use of sound prevention practices, detection, and removal are the only reliable anti-virus techniques. While most computer users can handle the prevention techniques on their own, detection, identification, and eradication of a virus are probably best trusted to a properly updated anti-virus program.

Finding and destroying viruses

Before discussing the various programs available for detecting and destroying virus infections, it will be helpful to review some of the different methods these virus-fighting programs employ. Not all anti-virus programs are created equal.

Checksum or CRC

Checksum or CRC (cyclic redundancy check) comparison programs can be used to find changes in other programs. There are some minor differences between how checksum and CRC operate, but there is no need for you to be concerned with those technicalities here. As a matter of fact, checksum and CRC are terms that most people use interchangeably.

The operation of these programs is fairly simple and straightforward. The program logs all the files on your hard disk and calculates a CRC on each file. The original checksum of each file is periodically checked against the current checksum to discover any changes that might indicate a possible virus infection.

File comparison programs

File comparison programs compare two copies of the same program to see if there are any differences. If a difference is discovered, there is a possibility that a virus has caused the change. This is not a particularly reliable method for a number of reasons. First, it assumes that the original program disk you used to copy the program to your computer was uninfected. As has been shown, there is no guarantee of that. If your original is infected, chances are that the virus has also infected the copy on your disk. As a result, the two will be identical when compared, leading you to believe that no virus is present. If you are going to use this method, you must find a way to ensure that the original is virus-free, and is stored in a manner that will keep it that way.

Scanners

All anti-virus programs use scanners to detect specific patterns anywhere a virus might lurk in your system. Scanners both find and identify viruses. Not all scanners are equally effective; some can detect more viruses than others. Each manufacturer will tell you their scanner is the best, so if you are really concerned, you will have to rely on data from tests by independent organizations such as the International Computer Security Association in Washington, D.C. No one will deny that there are both pros and cons to individual scanners, and you must choose wisely.

At the same time, a scanner is critical if you are going to identify exactly which virus or viruses have infected your system. Without precise identification, you won't know which is the best and most reliable method for removing the infection. The scanner is also the only method of detection that works before an infected program has run and has had a chance to infect other programs in the process. Scanning is a method you can use to check all your new software before you run it or copy it to your system. It is the scanner that is your best commercial helper in detecting virus infections.

Scanners are not perfect, however. Most vendors will give you a list of the viruses their scanner is programmed to catch, but that list will not always be completely truthful. For example, just because the list tells you that the scanner can catch the Jerusalem virus does not assure you that it can catch every version of that virus—and there are quite a few. The scanner becomes outdated as soon as a new virus is discovered. Your scanner might have been up-to-date when you bought it, but within a month or two, it can be sadly out of touch with the newest crop of infections. Most anti-virus software vendors have procedures for keeping your scanner updated—some are monthly, some quarterly, some on an "as-needed" basis. Prices for these updates vary from a lot of money to very little, or no money at all.

The International Computer Security Association (ICSA) also warns about running more than one scanner in the same computer system—more isn't always better. They tell us that some of the scan programs fail to clear the scan codes they use in their search from memory, which might cause the second scanner to give you a false reading and indicate a virus exists in a perfectly healthy system.

When using a scanner, be certain that you have the list of the names that the scanner uses to identify various viruses. To date there is no standard convention for naming viruses, and many of the known viruses go under more than one name. If you use more than one scanner, each might tell you that your computer has a virus. The first might tell you it is virus XXX while the second scanner says your computer has virus YYY. This doesn't necessarily mean there are two viruses, or that each scanner is missing what the other is catching.

TSR programs for virus detection

Terminate-and-stay-resident (TSR) programs are also used for virus detection. A virus-detecting TSR monitors the behavior of the other software on your system. It might detect a virus in the act of attempting to spread and alert you that this was happening.

The ICSA considers TSR anti-virus programs to have a number of shortcomings. For example, many computer systems crash when TSRs are introduced, especially if there is a conflict with other TSRs already resident in the system. TSRs use up valuable RAM (random-access memory) and might interfere with the operation of other programs on your system, especially large ones like graphics and desktop publishing applications. The chance for false alarms when using TSR virus detection is great, because in detecting virus disk-writing activities, the program might also frequently report legitimate disk-writing activity as a potential problem.

As a rule, any disk-write monitors such as these TSRs slow system operation, which might be a problem for you. TSRs might also be unable to prevent boot sector infections that are present before the TSR is loaded. A TSR that resides on your hard disk, of course, will never be loaded before your system is booted from Drive A, whether intentionally or by accident, so it won't catch a boot sector virus being introduced in such a bootup process. The future for the effectiveness of the TSR as a virus detector is further limited by the fact that viruses can (and probably will) be written to evade the TSR's detection methods.

Signature detection programs

One other method of detection bears mentioning: signature detection programs. These programs maintain data files of coded disk images and let you know when a change is discovered between the disk and its stored image. Unfortunately, these programs tend to take up a tremendous amount of disk storage capacity. Their image files must be updated each time files on your disk change (for most people, this is quite frequently), and the process can be quite time-consuming. Other drawbacks include the potential for these programs to slow the boot process or conflict with other TSRs in your system.

Rule-based virus detection

Although rule-based virus detection will be discussed in depth in a later chapter, the rule-based virus detection system pioneered by Trend Micro Devices of Torrance, California, is worth noting here because it is one of the newest anti-virus techniques, and one that might be the start of a future trend in anti-virus software methodology. Rule-based virus detection can detect not only all known viruses but many as yet undiscovered strains by searching for "certain inevitable behaviors" that all viruses exhibit in their attempts to infect files. The developers of this method have formulated a list of basic rules that all viruses—regardless of strain—follow when attempting to spread infection.

Rule-based anti-virus software is more or less "intelligent," in that it can predict every possible move a virus might make while attempting to spread. While each different category of virus can be identified by its own characteristic set of rules, all strains will have a set of rules that is nothing more than its own grouping of some or all of the basic rules.

But should your computer become infected anyway . . .

When all your preventive efforts have failed, and you either fear or know that your computer has a virus, a great deal of professional help is available in the form of commercial anti-virus software. Don't wait until you suspect a virus to add anti-virus software to your system. It is the best defense to fall back on, assuming that you have carefully applied the recommended prevention methods and there is still the chance that a virus has invaded your system. Which product you choose will depend on what you want it to do, how much you want to spend, how comfortable you are with the installation and operation of a given program, and the type, frequency, and expense of updates that ensure your virus-catching software remains effective. Now it is time to look at some of the best anti-virus software currently available.

Reference

Research Center of the International Computer Security Association, *Computer Virus Handbook*, Washington, D.C.: Research Center of the International Computer Security Association, 1992.

3
CHAPTER

Microcom Virex for the PC version 2.0

Virex for the PC by Microcom consists of three programs—VPCScan, Virex, and VirexPro—all of which come on the program diskettes. VPCScan is a utility program that scans existing files and memory to locate known viruses that might be hiding in your system. Virex and VirexPro are two versions of a terminate-and-stay-resident program that monitors your system continuously. They have slightly different capabilities, and you choose which one to install.

VPCScan VPCScan contains disinfectors for certain viruses that enable the utility to repair files damaged by these viruses. When such a virus is found, the utility program will offer to repair the infected file. If VPCScan does not contain a disinfector for the virus found, it will offer instead to delete the infected file. Microcom's Virex for the PC has a file on disk that lists which viruses the program can disinfect, and claims that the list covers about 90 percent of all viruses. In addition, VPCScan can repair files with what it calls its "inoculate" feature, which can also disinfect a wide variety of viruses including both boot sector and file viruses.

As I have mentioned in earlier chapters, new viruses are constantly appearing, so you will have to update the scanner for this program frequently. The company does offer free updates for the first six months and promises to make updates available on at least a quarterly basis for a reasonable charge.

Virex   The second part of Microcom's Virex for the PC is Virex, a terminate-and-stay-resident program that monitors your system continually. Virex will alert you if an attempt is made to run an infected (known virus) program. It will also warn you if an attempt is made to run a program for which the "checksum" signature has been altered.

VirexPro   The third program component is another TSR that continuously monitors your computer system. Basically, VirexPro does everything that Virex does and more. When you install Virex for the PC, you will choose between the two. If you choose VirexPro, you will get the monitoring features listed for Virex, and in addition you will be alerted when an attempt is made to:

- format a disk;
- write directly to disk;
- make a program terminate and stay resident;
- run a program that has not been logged by VirexPro;
- run an unauthorized operation (if you customize your system).

Thus, Microcom's Virex for the PC combines a scanner, a TSR detection program, and a CRC or "checksum" comparison function in its anti-virus solution. While it is a single-user program, it is compatible with Novell NetWare and can therefore be used in a network environment. Virex for the PC can also be run with Microsoft Windows.

Getting started with Microcom Virex for the PC

Microcom's Virex for the PC runs on the IBM PS/2 system, IBM PC XTs and ATs, and 100 percent compatible computers. The operating system should be DOS 3.0 or later, and your system should have a minimum of 512K of memory.

Throughout the program, you use the Enter key to select an option, and the Escape key to continue. Continuing in Virex generally means "backing up" in the program without making a selection. This gives you the opportunity to go back to the main menu or to any screen on which you might decide to make a change in your selections.

Before you begin the installation procedure, reboot your computer from Drive A using a clean, write-protected system diskette. Next, make certain you have write-protected the original program diskettes that came in the shrink-wrapped manufacturer's package, and then make a backup copy of each. Write-protect the backup copy as well. To write-protect a 5.25-inch floppy disk, cover the write-protect notch with a write-protect tab. On a 3.5-inch floppy, slide the write-protect tab to the open position (you should be able to see through the hole this creates). Place the original diskettes in a safe place and install Virex for the PC with the backup copy.

Installation—Using VPCScan

Now you are ready to work with Virex for the PC. You will install VPCScan and your choice of either Virex or VirexPro. Before you install the program, to make certain that your system is virus-free, scan with VPCScan. To do this, change to Drive A where the Virex program is located so that you can access the scanner. Type VPCSCAN *drive:\directory\filename* to indicate the file you want to scan for possible virus infection. As is always the case with DOS syntax, you can scan a whole directory by typing VPCSCAN *drive:\directory* without indicating a filename, or you can scan an entire drive by typing VPCSCAN *drive:*. The first time through, it is advisable to scan everything on your hard disk.

As the program zooms through the drive, directory, or file(s) to be scanned, it tells you where it is working, when it finds the area clean, and when it is checking inside compressed files. If VPCScan finds a virus, you are offered several options:

- disinfect the file, which means let Virex for the PC attempt to remove the virus from the original file (if VPCScan has a disinfect routine for the virus it has detected);
- remove the virus by deleting the infected file;
- ignore the virus, leaving it as found.

Obviously, the last alternative is not acceptable, since you don't want to install Virex for the PC on an infected system. The most thorough alternative is to delete the infected file and reinstall Virex PC from a clean original. If you elect to try the disinfecting route, be sure to make a backup copy of the file (virus and all) on a floppy diskette, because disinfecting can damage or even destroy a file. Once you have completed either disinfecting or deleting the file that contains the virus, turn off your computer, count to at least 20, and then turn it on again. Do not warm boot using <Ctrl>–<Alt>–<Del>—you might leave a virus in place if you do.

Installation—Virex

To run the install program, at the prompt of the drive in which the program diskette is located, type INSTALL and press <Enter> . During the installation procedure, the scanner looks for viruses in memory. If it finds one, message screens like the ones shown in Figs. 3-1 and 3-2 appear, and your computer has the virus named in the first message screen. Turn off the computer, reboot with a clean system disk, and follow the procedures above to scan for and then disinfect or delete the virus. Most of the time, especially if you have followed the virus prevention advice in chapter 2, your computer will get a clean bill of health.

```
Virus XYZ found in memory at (place on disk)
             --Press <esc> to continue--
```

Fig. 3-1

```
What Seems To Be An Active Virus Has Been Found In This
Computer's Memory.  Cold Reboot From A Known Clean System
Floppy and Run Install From The Original Locked Virex Disk
                        --Press <Esc> to continue--
```

Fig. 3-2

```
Type of Protection to Install
   VIREX Protection
   Special VIREXPRO Protection
```

Fig. 3-3

Once you know your computer is free of current virus contamination, you can install the second part of the program, so that you are ready to detect any viruses that might attack your computer in the future. At this point, an on-screen display like the one shown in Fig. 3-3 appears, giving you the option to select either Virex or VirexPro.

You might be wondering why anyone would opt for Virex when VirexPro provides much greater anti-virus protection. The answer can be as simple as memory. You might not have enough memory to run VirexPro, which uses about 40K of RAM, at the same time as a large word-processing or even larger graphics program. Virex uses less than 1K of RAM, so it might be the only one you can run on your system. If you have limited memory available and are carefully following the virus protection procedures outlined in chapter 2, you probably won't be in serious danger of encountering an exotic virus or any virus at all. In this case, Virex is more than adequate for your needs.

Referring again to Fig. 3-3, use the arrow keys to highlight the appropriate choice and press the Enter key to select it. The next screen you see is shown in Fig. 3-4; it displays the default installation information. If this is your first installation of Virex, Drive A is the correct source, as shown. If Virex is already installed and you are updating, you will have to change the drive and directory information ac-

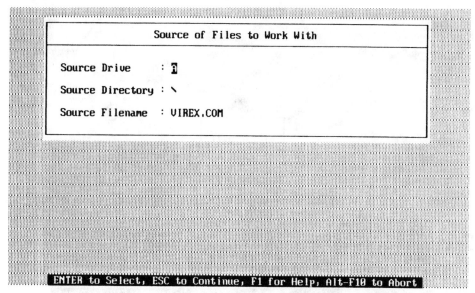

```
                    Source of Files to Work With

    Source Drive    : A

    Source Directory : \

    Source Filename  : VIREX.COM
```

ENTER to Select, ESC to Continue, F1 for Help, Alt-F10 to Abort

Fig. 3-4

cordingly, using the arrow keys to move from line to line. When you have completed any changes necessary on this screen, press <Esc>.

The next screen is the target screen. It looks just like the screen in Fig. 3-4, but instead of source, it asks for target (read it carefully). On this screen you tell the computer where to store Virex—select the drive and directory you want. Remember, according to DOS, if you want to change the target filename from the default, you have to add a .COM extension to the name you choose. When you finish with this screen, press <Esc>. If you have a protection file on your disk in the target directory, Virex will ask if you wish to use it. Answer no, since you are now updating the Virex protection program.

The program installs the Virex.DAT file, scanning and checksumming the files on your computer as shown in Fig. 3-5. When this operation is completed, you are asked whether or not you want Virex to load automatically when you boot your computer. If you say no, installation is complete and you will have to run Virex for the PC manually each time you want to check for viruses. If you choose yes, a copy of your AUTOEXEC.BAT file is displayed on-screen so you can modify it to include Virex. Position the cursor where you would like to add Virex and press <Enter>. Three lines (as shown in Fig. 3-6) are added to your AUTOEXEC.BAT file.

Microcom suggests that Virex should be placed in the AUTOEXEC.BAT file before any DOS windowing programs such as DOSShell or Menu. When you have completed this change in your AUTOEXEC.BAT file, Virex installation is complete, and you can reboot your computer to make sure that the program runs properly at boot-up. By the way, a copy of your old AUTOEXEC.BAT file is au-

```
                    ┌──────────────────┐
                    │   Please Wait    │
                    └──────────────────┘

            ┌─────────────────────────────────────┐
            │ Currently writing the protection file│
            │    ─> C:\VPC\VIREX.DAT               │
            └─────────────────────────────────────┘

Checksumming and Scanning C:\HJCUT\HJCUT.EXE .

    ENTER to Select, ESC to Continue, F1 for Help, Alt-F10 to Abort
```

Fig. 3-5

```
REM These lines inserted by Virex 2.0 Install
<drive>:\<subdirectory>\VIREX.COM
REM These lines inserted by Virex 2.0 Install
```

Fig. 3-6

tomatically stored on your disk as autoexec.vpc, should you ever want or need to return to the earlier version.

Installation—VirexPro

If you have chosen VirexPro as the program you want to install, the early steps of installation are the same as those for Virex—you indicate the correct information for the source and target files. When you have completed the target screen, press <Esc> to continue the installation process.

The program menu shown in Fig. 3-7 appears on your screen. Start with Files Protection, where you can modify the specific protection of a file or group of files on either hard or floppy disks. You have two alternatives, Wildcard Specifications and File Level Maintenance.

Wildcard specification This is a convenient way to set the protection level for a group of files of similar type. These files can be identified through their extensions such as .COM or .EXE., the executable files in which viruses hide. For example, to protect all .EXE files, you would use the wildcard * in the DOS format

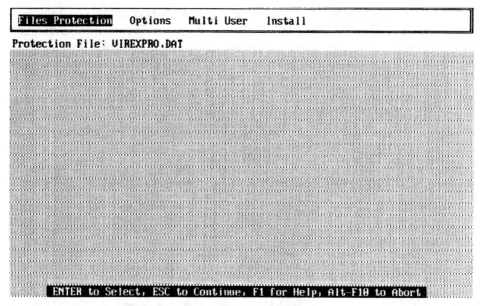

Fig. 3-7

```
┌──────────────────────────────────────────────────────────────────────┐
│ Files Protection   Options   Multi User   Install                      │
└──────────────────────────────────────────────────────────────────────┘
Protection File: VIREXPRO.DAT

┌────────────────────────────────────────────────────────────────────────┐
│ Wildcard              Read Access   Write Access   Checksum   Exceptions│
│ ┌────────────┐┌──────────────────────────────────────────────────────┐ │
│ │*.APP       ││                    Protected      Run                │ │
│ │*.COM       ││                    Protected      Run                │ │
│ │*.EXE       ││                    Protected      Run                │ │
│ │*.MOD       ││                    Protected      Run                │ │
│ │*.OV?       ││                    Protected      Run                │ │
│ │*.SYS       ││                    Protected      Both               │ │
│ │            ││                                                      │ │
│ │            ││                                                      │ │
│ │            ││                                                      │ │
│ │            ││                                                      │ │
│ │            ││                                                      │ │
│ │            ││                                                      │ │
│ │            ││                                                      │ │
│ │            ││                                                      │ │
│ └────────────┘└──────────────────────────────────────────────────────┘ │
│ <Enter> Modify Wildcard  <Ins> Add Wildcard  <Del> Delete Wildcard  <Esc> Exit│
└────────────────────────────────────────────────────────────────────────┘
```

Fig. 3-8

*.EXE. Following the on-screen instructions for choosing wildcard specifications brings you to the screen shown in Fig. 3-8. On this screen you can modify the kind of protection for each type of file, or you can add wildcards to or delete them from the file protection list. For example, you might want to add all of your .BAT files

to the default list, because .BAT files are executable. VirexPro automatically protects executable files when they are installed, write-protecting them and evaluating their checksums when they are run. You can see that these protections are there on the screen in Fig. 3-8, and that no Read Access or Exceptions have been entered.

For each group of wildcard files shown, you can set the individual protection level desired. Highlight a group line and press <Enter> to get the File Protection Edit Screen, shown in Fig. 3-9. When you highlight a protection function and press <Enter>, you are given choices of the level of protection you want for that function, also illustrated in Fig. 3-9. Highlight the protection level desired and press <Enter>. Follow this procedure for each function, and then press the Escape key to continue. You can now select File Level maintenance, or press <Esc> again to back up one more screen to the Main Menu.

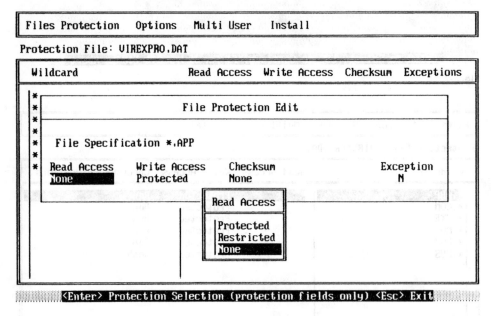

Fig. 3-9

Definition of protection levels

What are all of these protection options available in the wildcard specification? Read Access allows you to protect against viruses trying to read your files, for example, to look for virus signatures. When you choose the "protected" option, you will be warned whenever an attempt is made to read a file, and given the opportunity to approve or deny the request. If you choose "restricted," you will receive a warning whenever there is a read attempt, but you will not have the alternative of allowing the access. If you opt for "none," you will not receive any warnings, and any read request will be allowed.

Write Access operates in the same way as Read Access. The one thing you want to remember here is that you don't want to add protection to working data files until they are completed; you certainly wouldn't want to add write protection to groups of files with *.doc or *.txt extensions.

Checksum is the internal signature of a file that is almost always altered in some way when a virus hits. As mentioned earlier, VirexPro uses checksum comparison as one potent anti-virus tool. For VirexPro to properly monitor the checksums of your executable files, they must each be registered with VirexPro. Any executable programs not on the checksum list will trigger a VirexPro alert when run. VirexPro automatically protects executable files when it is installed, but nowhere in the literature or the program are .BAT files included.

You might want to add these files to the wildcard list and add protection for them as well. There are several levels of checksum available in VirexPro. If you select "Run," a file's checksum will be evaluated for changes each time the file is run, and you will see a warning should VirexPro discover any change in the checksum. Choosing "Resident" means that the checksum of each resident file will be checked whenever VirexPro is executed, whether manually, or automatically at each boot-up.

Both is the highest level of checksum protection. Files with run/resident protection will be double-checked, once each time VirusPro is started, and again each time the program file is run. As with all of these protection options, you can elect not to use checksum by selecting the "None" option.

When you have completed the wildcard setup using the standard DOS editing keys (<Ins> to insert, <Del> to delete, and the arrow keys to move around) press <Esc> to move to the next step in setting up VirexPro to meet your exact needs. The other alternative under Files Protection on the Main Menu is File Level Maintenance. File Level Maintenance is used to set protection levels for individual files.

When you choose File Level Maintenance, you are first asked to indicate the drive on which the file to be protected is located. Highlight the drive and press <Enter>. The top of your directory tree appears on the screen as shown in Fig. 3-10. Use the arrow keys to select the directory in which the file you want to protect resides. Press <Enter>. Now you should see a list of files in that directory, as shown in Fig. 3-11. Again, use the arrow keys to highlight the file you want to protect and press <Enter>. As you can see, VirexPro has automatically instituted some protection on the executable files, but you might want to add, remove, or modify the automatic protection for one or more. Figure 3-12 illustrates the File Edit Screen, where you can change the default settings for each of the file protection factors.

You are already familiar with Read Access, Write Access, and Checksum, but now there are two more items to consider. As mentioned earlier, VirexPro alerts you whenever a program attempts to terminate-and-stay-resident (TSR). This is important in detecting viruses that become memory-resident when an infected program is run. Remember that once in memory, a virus that becomes a TSR can in-

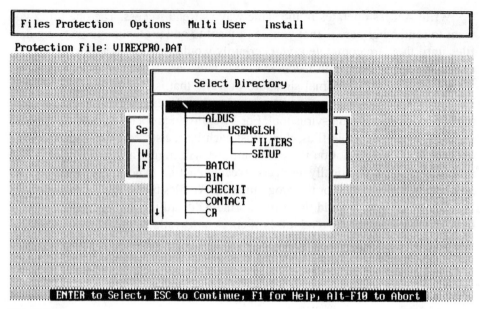

Fig. 3-10

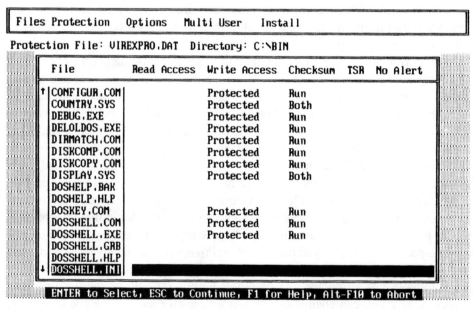

Fig. 3-11

fect every program executed thereafter. The default here is no (N), because most programs should not be allowed to terminate-and-stay-resident without warning you. If you have a program that should be allowed to terminate-and-stay-resident, this is your opportunity to have Virex for the PC allow it to do so without alerting

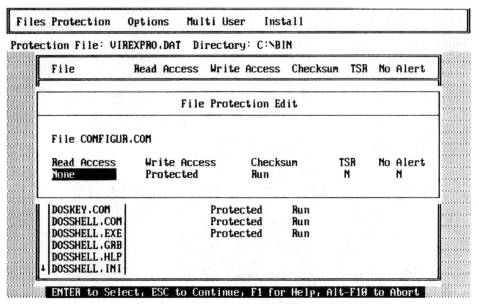

```
 Files Protection   Options   Multi User   Install

Protection File: VIREXPRO.DAT  Directory: C:\BIN

   File           Read Access  Write Access  Checksum  TSR  No Alert

                     File Protection Edit

   File CONFIGUR.COM

   Read Access      Write Access    Checksum     TSR      No Alert
   None             Protected       Run          N        N

   DOSKEY.COM                    Protected     Run
   DOSSHELL.COM                  Protected     Run
   DOSSHELL.EXE                  Protected     Run
   DOSSHELL.GRB
   DOSSHELL.HLP
 ↓ DOSSHELL.INI

     ENTER to Select, ESC to Continue, F1 for Help, Alt-F10 to Abort
```

Fig. 3-12

you every time it is run. Just change this protection factor to yes (Y) for the appropriate program file.

Choosing "No Alert" can be dangerous, but there might be times when you don't want to be alerted to the read and write activities in a particular file. To turn off the alert for a specific file only, choose yes (Y).

VirexPro installation extras

On the Main Menu, there are three more choices: Options, Multi User, and Install. Each of these choices is discussed below. Note that when you select Options, you can choose either Normal options or Advanced options.

Normal options   These options give you choices for configuring VirexPro to operate as you want it, and are shown in Fig. 3-13. Some options can be changed here or individually, as needed during normal VirexPro operation. The first option allows you to turn off the display of VirexPro status (an icon in the upper right hand corner of your screen), because the display can interfere with some graphics programs. If you run some of these programs you might want to turn off this symbol by changing the default Y to N here. If you respond yes to option two, you can interactively turn VirexPro on and off while in another program. Responding yes to option three means that you accept the default action keys, <Ctrl> and <Alt>. Answering no allows you to select your own action keys.

VirexPro can maintain a log of computer activities that tells you which VirexPro alerts were triggered and how you responded to them. The default size is 10,000

```
╔══════════════════════════════════════════════════════════════╗
║  Files Protection   Options   Multi User   Install           ║
╚══════════════════════════════════════════════════════════════╝
Protection File: VIREXPRO.DAT

        ┌────────────────────────────────────────────────┐
        │                 Normal Options                 │
        │ Display VirexPro Status at all times . . . . . . . . . . . . : Y │
        │ Allow interactive disabling of VirexPro . . . . . . . . . . : Y │
        │ Use the standard Action Keys  . . . . . . . . . . . . . . . : Y │
        │ Record actions and responses in a log file  . . . . . . . . : N │
        │ Learn . . . . . . . . . . . . . . . . . . . . . . . . . . . : 2 │
        │ Bell off  . . . . . . . . . . . . . . . . . . . . . . . . . : N │
        │ Security Level  . . . . . . . . . . . . . . . . . . . . . . : 4 │
        │ Use the standard screen colors  . . . . . . . . . . . . . . : Y │
        └────────────────────────────────────────────────┘

      ▐ ENTER to Select, ESC to Continue, F1 for Help, Alt-F10 to Abort ▌
```

Fig. 3-13

bytes. With option four, you can first select whether or not you want VirexPro to maintain a log, and then specify what its size should be. To save on memory, whenever the maximum designated size is reached, the first 5,000 bytes stored in log memory are deleted.

Action Learning Mode, option five, eliminates warning during normal operations when the warning has been displayed a certain number of times. You can turn this feature off by typing N, or you can limit the number of times it activates by typing in a number. You might be relieved to know that the warning sound emitted by the program when there is suspicious activity can also be disabled by selecting N for option six.

VirexPro offers four security levels of operation. The program default is level 4, Administrator, which allows the greatest amount of control over the program. If you are a single user, choose this option to take full advantage of the features of VirexPro. If you are on a multiuser system, you might opt to limit some users to a lower level of operational control.

Last but not least, if for some reason you want to change the screen colors or screen attributes (such as blinking or nonblinking cursor), type N here. You are presented with a screen that lets you make whatever changes you wish.

Advanced options   These options are shown in Fig. 3-14. Most of you should leave the default settings of these advanced options as is, and not bother to concern yourselves with them. It's just good to know that these options are available should you ever have a special situation that would require their reconfiguration.

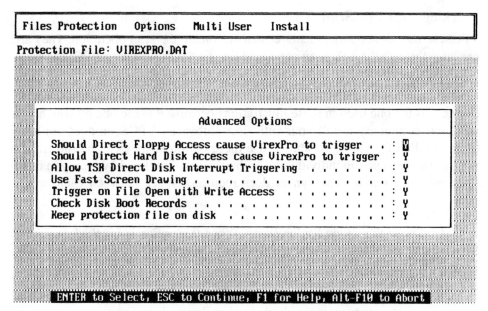

```
┌─────────────────────────────────────────────────────────────────────┐
│ Files Protection   Options   Multi User   Install                   ║
└─────────────────────────────────────────────────────────────────────┘
  Protection File: VIREXPRO.DAT

                        ┌─────────────────────────────────────┐
                        │         Advanced Options            │
                        ├─────────────────────────────────────┤
                        │ Should Direct Floppy Access cause VirexPro to trigger . . : Y │
                        │ Should Direct Hard Disk Access cause VirexPro to trigger : Y │
                        │ Allow TSR Direct Disk Interrupt Triggering  . . . . . . . : Y │
                        │ Use Fast Screen Drawing . . . . . . . . . . . . . . . . . : Y │
                        │ Trigger on File Open with Write Access . . . . . . . . . : Y │
                        │ Check Disk Boot Records . . . . . . . . . . . . . . . . . : Y │
                        │ Keep protection file on disk  . . . . . . . . . . . . . . : Y │
                        └─────────────────────────────────────┘

          ┌──────────────────────────────────────────────────────────┐
          │ ENTER to Select, ESC to Continue, F1 for Help, Alt-F10 to Abort │
          └──────────────────────────────────────────────────────────┘
```

Fig. 3-14

Multiuser   This option on the Main Menu allows you to install VirexPro for multiple users with a unique password and protection file for each user of the personal computer. VirexPro can also be installed on a Novell network.

Install   Finally, you have completed all the steps and it is time to install Virex-Pro. Highlight "Install" on the Main Menu and press <Enter>. The Install program copies VirexPro to the target disk and directory you specified at the beginning of the installation procedure. It will calculate checksums, scan for viruses, and inoculate all files on your computer.

The last installation step for VirexPro, as with the Virex installation, is deciding whether or not you want to modify your AUTOEXEC.BAT file to start Virex-Pro automatically each time you boot your computer. The procedure is exactly the same as described for Virex installation above.

Making the most of Virex for the PC

At this point you have installed and can use the VPCScan program and you have installed either Virex or VirexPro. You might want to stand pat at this point, having absorbed as much information as you can handle and feeling good about the fact that you have proven that your computer, at the moment, is virus-free. When you are ready, there are options in each part of Virex for the PC that will enable you to optimize your virus detection capability.

Working with VPCScan

VPCScan has some optional features that customize the scan operation. They are executed through the VPCScan command line on the drive where VPCScan is located; for example:

VPCSCAN C:\-*option*

(Drive C is the one used in these illustrations because it is the one on which you will most commonly install your anti-virus software.) VPCScan does not have to be installed for you to be able to use these options—they can be run from a floppy. They can be run individually, or they can be combined by typing in more than one option code. The syntax does require a space between each option code.

–L This is the option for long scan. When this option is invoked, the entire file is scanned, not just the most likely virus locations that are scanned as part of the regular scanning process.

–M This option stops the repeated searching of system memory, and can be a time saver if you are scanning multiple hard or floppy disks.

–X This option increases memory search to the entire first megabyte rather than only the 640K accessible to DOS.

–A This option instructs VPCScan to scan all files on your computer, not just executable files.

–O When you use this option, VPCScan scans only the specified directory, not any of its subdirectories.

–F This option allows you to scan a single floppy disk, but it will offer to scan another disk at its completion.

–# Using this option provides the complete list of viruses recognized by VPCScan. To print the list add >PRN to the option command line.

–R This option creates an audit file that lists all VPCScan alerts and responses.

VPCScan can be run in a batch mode if, for example, you need to have it run "in background," not interrupting you every time it suspects a possible infection. The command line syntax for this is:

VPCSCAN C:\-B*option*

It is best to use the batch function with a reviewable log file that records all warnings and the action taken. To create such a file, the command line syntax is:

VPCSCAN C:\-*option*–RVIRUS.LOG

The various batch mode options are described below.

–BD This option instructs VPCScan to disinfect all viruses it finds. Those it is unable to disinfect, it ignores.

–BR When this option is on, VPCScan will remove any file it finds infected with a virus.

–BI This option tells VPCScan to scan a volume but does not allow the program to repair or delete infected files.

–BM When you use this option, VPCScan will add a .VIR extension to any file it discovers to be infected for later identification.

Another option available with VPCScan is file inoculation. Inoculation can repair files and boot sector/partition table infections, and protect your computer against future virus infection. There are limitations to this program, however, as with any inoculation scheme. It does not work against an overwriting virus, nor does it work against a virus that uses a complex technique to insert itself into several areas of a program's code.

To take advantage of the inoculation feature, you have to build what Microcom calls an Inoculation Set. The install program produces the INOC.VRX file containing inoculation (checksum) information about all the executable files on your hard drive. Install also generates a CRITICAL.VRX file that records all important information about your hard drive, such as boot sector and partition table data. It provides protection against boot sector viruses, and saves your CMOS information on AT-type systems (XTs do not have CMOS). This file needs to be updated each time you change the partitioning on your hard disk or upgrade to a new version of DOS.

To update CRITICAL.VPX, you must remove the old version; just use the DOS RENAME command, renaming the current CRITICAL.VPX file CRITICAL.OLD. Then, in the event that a virus infection makes it necessary to replace the boot sector or partition table information (master boot sector) or CMOS information on your hard drive, you can accomplish this using the CRITICAL.VPX file with one of several options.

–P To restore the master boot sector, specify drive and filename on the VPCScan command line. For example:

VPCSCAN C:\ –PCRITICAL.VPX

–PA Use this option to restore your boot sector information and partition table data. The syntax on the VPCScan command line is:

VPCSCAN C:\ –PACRITICAL.VRX

–PC To restore your CMOS information, you do not have to specify a drive; just add the option and the filename on the command line:

VPCSCAN –PCCMOSSAVE.VRX

To create (or update) an inoculation set, add the drive name and –I+ *filename* to the command line:

VPCSCAN C:\ –I+*filename*

Specifying a filename is not required. If you do not add a filename, the program uses the INOC.VRX and CRITICAL.VRX default names. Only the INOC.VRX filename can be changed; the CRITICAL.VRX name must be used. The –I+ option is used for updating an existing inoculation set. It adds all new executable files to the set, and also warns you of any changes in current inoculation data. If a file is found to have a changed checksum, you are alerted on the screen that this has happened, the infected filename is given, and you are offered three alternative actions:

- press <Esc> to leave everything alone;

- type U to update the inoculation file to contain the new checksum signature; or

- type R to start an attempt to repair the file. You are then told whether the file can be repaired. If the system says it can, you can choose to attempt the repair or leave the modified file in place (remember that file repair is often very dangerous). If the file cannot be repaired, a screen tells you that as well.

Unfortunately, some of you might already have discovered that a virus can so severely damage your hard drive that you cannot even boot your computer from that drive. A premade VPCScan emergency disk might help you out. To make an emergency disk, first format a floppy disk and make it a DOS-bootable diskette by using the DOS command line:

FORMAT A: /S

Move to the Virex for the PC directory on your hard drive. Copy VPCScan to the formatted floppy disk. (The file you will copy is VPCSCAN.EXE.) Then copy your inoculation set to the diskette using a wildcard specification, *.VPX, to get all of the inoculation files. Now write-protect that floppy. You can copy any updated inoculation set files to the emergency diskette later by removing the write-protect tab and copying the new file over the old. Thus, when your computer won't boot because of a virus infection, you can insert the emergency disk in Drive A, boot the computer, and use VPCScan to find and disinfect your computer's hard drive.

If you are concerned about checksums, you can exercise one more option in VPCScan. Two protection files, VIREX.DAT and VIREXPRO.DAT, contain the checksums the two TSR programs use to monitor your system. You can check these checksums using VPCScan's checksum verify feature. This is a –V option with one of these filenames (or whatever filename you have substituted for the default filenames) to check the checksums. If a known virus is found, an appropriate message appears, and you are given all the usual options for removing or ignoring it. If a changed checksum is found, you are alerted and given the opportunity to update the file's checksum in the protection file (type U), or to ignore the situation by typing I. If you ignore it, Microcom does recommend that you delete the file with the problem, just in case it is not a false alarm. You can create an entirely new protection file with only Checksum information in it. To do this, use –V+. You can add a filename if you do not want to use the original default name.

Working with Virex

The Virex TSR provides constant anti-virus protection, checking for known virus signatures and using checksum changes to uncover unknown infections. There are other options you can add to Virex, but these will also add to the amount of memory the program takes up. Before you start adding these options, remember that one of the reasons you might have chosen to install Virex in the first place was to minimize the amount of memory used. If, when you installed Virex, you elected to change your AUTOEXEC.BAT file and you now wish to add some of the command line options discussed below, you will have to modify your AUTOEXEC .BAT again. One of the lines that was added to your AUTOEXEC.BAT file was C:\VPC\VIREX.COM (see Fig. 3-6). Add any command line options you want to include to this line, resave the file, and reboot your computer. If you did not add Virex to your AUTOEXEC.BAT file, you can add the options to the command line when you run Virex.

Virex only gives you two alerts: one when a checksum has been modified, and one when a known virus is detected. If you receive a checksum alert and then attempt to run the program, Virex will deny access. Use the VPCScan inoculation feature you created to disinfect the file. If the inoculation file cannot disinfect the file, it names the virus infection and gives you the option of erasing the file or exiting without any action. Should you, on the other hand, suspect that you are dealing with an unknown virus, just delete the suspect file and replace it with a copy from a clean original.

Working with VirexPro

As you have already noticed in the installation section, VirexPro is far more sophisticated and complex than Virex. As a result, using VirexPro requires far more interaction on your part. When VirexPro encounters suspicious activity, the write access attempt alert screen gives you four options: Y to allow the operation to go forward as usual this one time; G to allow the operation to go unchecked during this program only; F to stop (fail) the operation, and any other key to abort the program and return to DOS.

Keep in mind that whenever an alert message appears on the screen, you can press F1 for on-line help in responding to the alert. You will find that the alert screens are self-explanatory, so you shouldn't have any doubt as to how to proceed.

In addition to the write access attempt alert, other alert screens include one that appears when the boot sector checksum doesn't match, a file's checksum shows modification, or an actual virus that is also named on screen is detected. You are also warned when you try to run a program that you have not yet registered with VirexPro. In this case, either type F to stop the program's execution or, if you have scanned the program or are sure it is clean, type Y to run the program and add it to the VirexPro registry.

You might see a TSR alert screen. This one is letting you know that a program is about to terminate and stay resident. If this is a program that you know should not stay resident, disallow the activity by typing R as indicated on the screen. There are, however, many programs that you know are TSR and should not be a cause for alarm. VirusPro alerts you to attempts by a program other than DOS to write directly to your hard disk. It also warns you when a disk is being formatted, and gives you the opportunity to stop the format process before it begins.

Other alert messages include:

- disk parameter modification attempt;
- write access to a write-protected file;
- read access to a read-protected file;
- open file with attempt at write access on a write-protected file;
- handle access attempt on a write-protected file (similar to open file with attempt at write access);
- FCB rename of a protected file in three screens, one for a source file, another for a target file and a third for handle rename;
- attempt to delete a write-protected file.

Evaluation

Among the anti-virus programs commercially available, Virex for the PC ranks as one of the easiest to install and operate. If you opt to install VirusPro, you will have as complete a virus detection and eradication solution as is currently available.

While Virex for the PC talks about "over 200 viruses and virus strains" that it can handle, as opposed to programs that talk about numbers up to 1000 or more, remember that as was mentioned earlier, it all depends on how you count—200 viruses and strains might actually be as many or more than 1000 viruses.

Even though Microcom does offer the first six months of virus definitions free, after that you will pay a reasonable fee for additional quarterly updates. Some of you might consider quarterly updates as too infrequent, especially if the virus world starts to explode suddenly.

Virex for the PC has some definite advantages. If you are DOS-literate, all the customizing in this program is very easy because it is done at the DOS command line using DOS syntax. The emergency disk you can create using this program is one of the most comprehensive and will recover from more virus-induced problems than some of the rescue disks set up by competing programs.

Keystrokes are consistent throughout this program, so if you are a non-mouse user, you won't have to wonder about which key does what on a screen or moving from one screen to another. You can always back up while installing Virex for the PC, so that if you want to make a change, it does not involve either aborting the installation or finishing and then going back through installation to make the change. Finally, the fact that when a virus is discovered, you can press F1 for help at any time is a real comfort.

You might have noticed that there is little mention of boot sector and partition table virus infections as opposed to file-infecting viruses. Virex for the PC is sort of a "one system fits all" solution that handles all viruses without your having to make any distinctions personally. By the way, should you discover while installing Virex for the PC a boot sector virus that the inoculation feature cannot handle, the program documentation gives very clear instructions for manual removal of such a virus, operated from the DOS command line using DOS syntax.

4
CHAPTER

Norton AntiVirus version 2.0

Norton AntiVirus 2.0 from Symantec is a comprehensive program for use with DOS or with Microsoft Windows. The program can be used to detect and eliminate almost 1,000 known viruses and strains of those viruses, both program-infecting and boot sector-infecting types. With Norton AntiVirus, updates are fast and easy to obtain through bulletin board services, including a private board maintained by Symantec. You can download the complete list of viruses or just the latest release of virus definitions. If you are a CompuServe subscriber, you can find the latest virus definitions file in the NORTUTL Forum, NAV-IBM Library Section. A number of local bulletin board services maintained by user groups also have the latest virus definitions for Norton AntiVirus available for downloading.

Additionally, you can call the Virus Newsline (the READ.ME file on your Norton AntiVirus disk contains the telephone number), which provides 24-hour-a-day news about viruses, and tells how to obtain the latest virus definitions. You can also obtain the most current list of virus definitions for Norton AntiVirus with your fax machine by calling (310) 575-5018. (First call (310) 477-2707 for information about how to use this fax service, and be sure that if you call from a fax, it is properly set to receive the return transmission.) All of these virus definition update services are free. If you want the updated virus definition file on floppy disk, the company makes a new one available quarterly, at a charge of $12.00. If you live outside the United

States and Canada, you will have to contact your local Symantec distributor/dealer for update service information.

To run Norton AntiVirus 2.0 you need a system with the following minimum specifications: an IBM PC XT, AT, PS/2, or 100 percent compatible computer running DOS 3.0 or later, with a hard drive, a floppy disk drive, and 384K of RAM (minimum 1K is memory-resident at any given time). The Windows version requires Windows 3.0 or later and DOS 3.1 or later. A mouse and printer are suggested but not required. Norton AntiVirus requires about 800K of disk space for copying program and accessory files to your hard disk. If your computer has limited RAM and you are running several word-processing programs or a large graphics program, you might find that you don't have enough memory to run all of the options available with Norton AntiVirus 2.0.

Norton AntiVirus 2.0 has two main components:

- Virus Intercept loads automatically each time your computer boots, and alerts you when it detects an infected file or suspects a virus.
- Virus Clinic only runs when you type NAV at the DOS prompt, and is used to repair infected files by removing the virus.

Unless you have chosen during the setup and installation process to run Norton AntiVirus 2.0 manually, Virus Intercept runs automatically at bootup. However, you can still manually stop Virus Intercept from loading. When you turn on your computer, listen for the BIOS "beep" and immediately press and hold both shift keys until the message "Norton AntiVirus Not Loaded" is displayed. This action becomes necessary when you need to modify certain files in the program such as the NAV_.SYS file, or if you ever want to remove Norton AntiVirus from your hard disk.

Installing Norton AntiVirus 2.0

Before you install the Norton AntiVirus program, be sure to look at the large READ.ME file on program disk number one. You can do this from a word processor, from a text editor, or at the DOS prompt line. The file contains, among other information, instructions on what to do if a virus is detected during the installation procedure.

Installation without a mouse

In general, during installation, you use the spacebar to toggle options on the screen, the up and down arrow keys to move from one option to another, and the right and left arrow keys to move from one section of the screen to another. The Enter key is used to make a selection. However, keys are not totally consistent, and at times you will have to experiment to get the right key to use for a particular operation.

Starting the installation procedure

As I have stressed repeatedly throughout this book, it is best to boot your computer from a clean system diskette in Drive A when you are going to install anti-virus software. If you boot from your hard drive, you risk contamination from any virus that might already be in place. As a matter of fact, one of the first screens you see in the installation procedure, shown in Fig. 4-1, warns you to do this if you suspect a virus might be present. Do it anyway, whether or not you suspect a virus might be present.

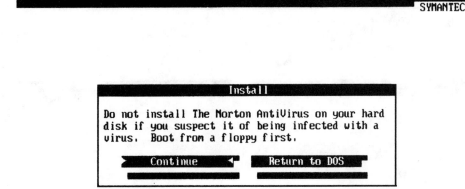

Fig. 4-1

Format an additional diskette now to use when the time comes to make a rescue disk. (I will explain how to make the rescue disk later on.)

Next make a working copy of the program diskettes and put the originals away in a safe place. Put the working copy of Disk #1 in your disk drive. (You will only use Disk #2 if you are installing for operation under Windows.) Norton AntiVirus installs from either Drive A or Drive B. At the DOS prompt, type INSTALL, <Enter>, and you're on your way. This program is menu driven and relatively easy to follow.

Select the type of monitor in your system, and then read the next screen, which summarizes the order in which installation proceeds, and keep going. Let the program scan for viruses as the screen in Fig. 4-2 requests. It doesn't take long and might turn up something you weren't expecting. As the scan runs through memory, you see the names of each virus it is scanning for flash by on screen. Then Norton AntiVirus 2.0 scans your hard disk drive(s), running through the directory tree on each disk. If viruses are found, you will have to stop the installation and repair or delete the files in which they reside. Since hopefully you won't find any viruses, discussion of the procedure for repairing or deleting files is not included until later in this chapter.

In Fig. 4-3, the program asks if the installation procedure should remove old inoculation files. You can go ahead and run this even though you know you don't

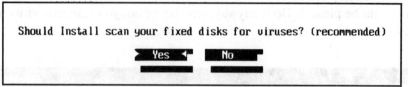

Should Install scan your fixed disks for viruses? (recommended)

Yes ◄   No

Fig. 4-2

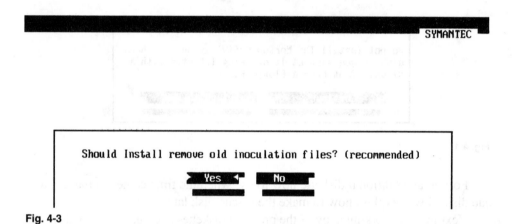

Should Install remove old inoculation files? (recommended)

Yes ◄   No

Fig. 4-3

have any Norton AntiVirus inoculation files in place. It only takes a few seconds. If you know you have no old inoculation files, you can elect to skip this operation. Next, you are prompted to select the directory in which to store Norton AntiVirus 2.0. The default directory is C:\NAV, but you can put the program anywhere you want by typing a destination in the lower box, shown on the screen in Fig. 4-4. If you happen to have an earlier version of Norton AntiVirus on your computer in a C:\NAV directory, selecting that directory again will just overwrite the older version's files with those of version 2.0.

Installing the program files is a little tricky. In Fig. 4-5, you see the instructions: "Select program to install on drive C: Press the spacebar to toggle selection." Actually, the way this works is that when you press the spacebar, you deselect an option; so what you need to do is toggle each selection you don't want (the check mark will disappear). If you happen to toggle something the Norton AntiVirus program thinks you should keep, it will warn you, as shown in Fig. 4-6.

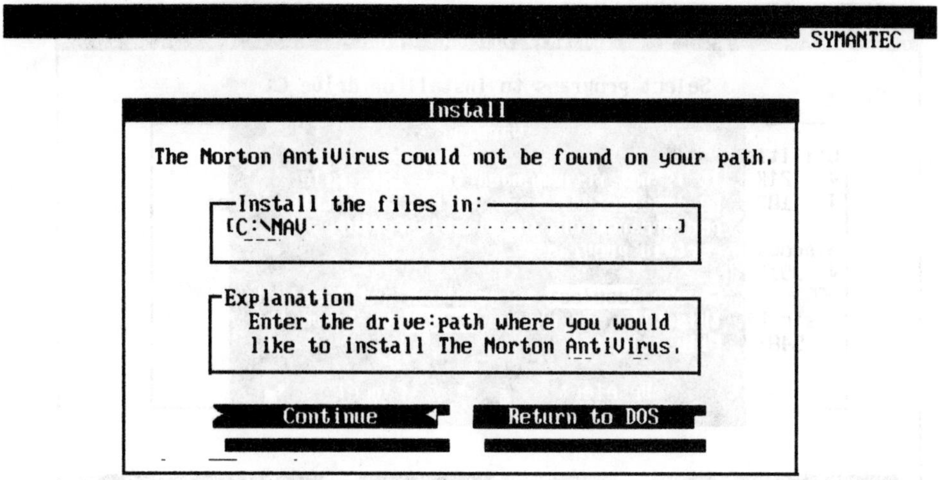

```
┌─────────────────────────── Install ───────────────────────────┐
│                                                                │
│ The Norton AntiVirus could not be found on your path.          │
│                                                                │
│       ┌─Install the files in:──────────────────────────┐       │
│        [C:\NAV · · · · · · · · · · · · · · · · · · · ·]         │
│                                                                │
│                                                                │
│       ┌─Explanation ─────────────────────────┐                 │
│         Enter the drive:path where you would                   │
│         like to install The Norton AntiVirus.                  │
│                                                                │
│                                                                │
│        ▶    Continue    ◀        Return to DOS                 │
│                                                                │
└────────────────────────────────────────────────────────────────┘
```

Fig. 4-4

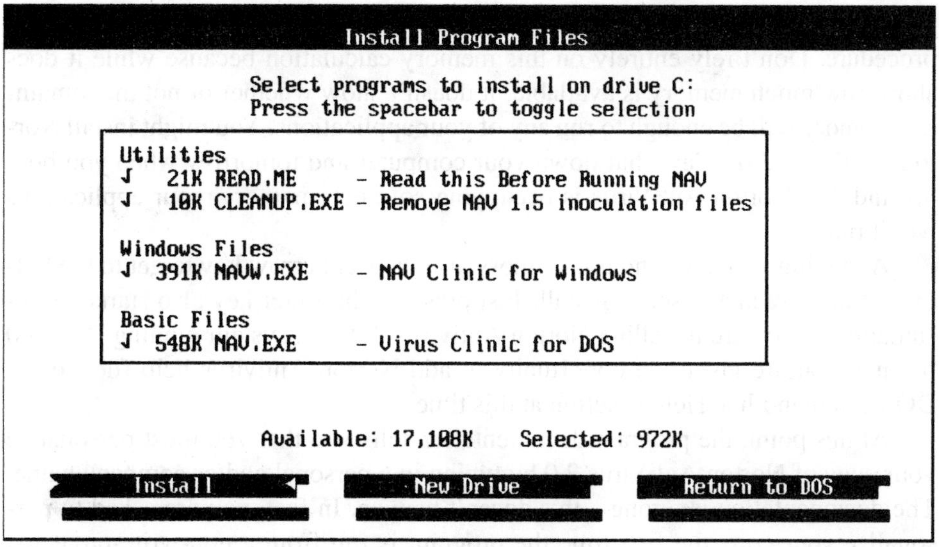

```
┌────────────────────── Install Program Files ──────────────────────┐
│                                                                    │
│              Select programs to install on drive C:                │
│              Press the spacebar to toggle selection                │
│                                                                    │
│   ┌──────────────────────────────────────────────────────────┐    │
│   │ Utilities                                                 │    │
│   │ √    21K READ.ME     - Read this Before Running NAV        │    │
│   │ √    10K CLEANUP.EXE - Remove NAV 1.5 inoculation files    │    │
│   │                                                           │    │
│   │ Windows Files                                             │    │
│   │ √  391K NAVW.EXE    - NAV Clinic for Windows              │    │
│   │                                                           │    │
│   │ Basic Files                                               │    │
│   │ √  548K NAV.EXE     - Virus Clinic for DOS                │    │
│   └──────────────────────────────────────────────────────────┘    │
│                                                                    │
│                                                                    │
│          Available: 17,108K    Selected: 972K                      │
│                                                                    │
│   ▶   Install   ◀        New Drive          Return to DOS          │
│                                                                    │
└────────────────────────────────────────────────────────────────────┘
```

Fig. 4-5

Because adding any of these programs to your disk might require more memory than you have available, the amount of memory of the selected programs (as well as the amount of RAM available) is shown at the bottom of the screen, again in Fig. 4-5. Since at the moment, everything is selected, the maximum requirement of memory is showing. If the program tells you you do not have enough space, you have two options. Either install only the programs for which you have enough room, or exit installation, make more room on your disk, and restart the installation

Fig. 4-6

procedure. Don't rely entirely on this memory calculation because while it does show how much memory is available, it doesn't show whether or not the remaining memory will be enough to run any of your applications. You might install Norton AntiVirus 2.0 today, shut down your computer and tomorrow when you boot up find that Norton AntiVirus is occupying so much memory, your applications won't run.

Assuming you have enough memory, use the right arrow key to get to the bottom of the screen and select install. Just pressing the Enter key also starts the installation. If you are installing Norton Antivirus 2.0 on a system running DOS 5.0 or later, you are given the opportunity to add Norton Antivirus help files to the DOS command line Help function at this time.

At this point, the program documentation tells you that you must personalize your copy of Norton AntiVirus 2.0 by typing in a personal and/or company name. The documentation is wrong—this doesn't happen. In fact, you are asked to personalize your copy the first time the program is run from a non-write-protected disk such as Drive C.

The next important step is to create a rescue disk. (Earlier it was suggested that you format a diskette to use for this purpose.) Creating a rescue disk is a simple procedure that can save you a lot of trouble should a virus ever destroy the boot sector, partition table, or CMOS information in your computer. Figure 4-7 shows a screen asking if you want to save rescue data. Select "OK"; the only time you might want to choose "Cancel" is if you are fastforwarding through installation at a later date to get to a specific area such as Advanced Configuration, in order to make a change.

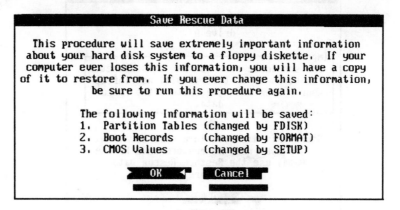

Fig. 4-7

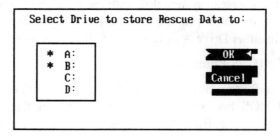

Fig. 4-8

The screen in Fig. 4-8 looks and is simple, but it can also trip you up. Be sure to have the formatted disk you prepared in the disk drive you select before you tell the system it is OK to make the rescue disk. If, for example, you are installing from Drive A and copying rescue data to the diskette in Drive B, the minute you press OK, the operation is executed. Whatever diskette is in Drive B at that moment gets the information. Because this is a diskette you are going to want to write-protect and preserve, you don't want these files in the middle of a data disk full of recipes.

The screen in Fig. 4-9 might seem like overkill on the side of "maybe there is a virus" paranoia, but unless you are absolutely positive that the diskette you used is virus free (and how can you be without checking?), you should scan it for viruses. Even a just-out-of-the-package preformatted floppy disk can contain a

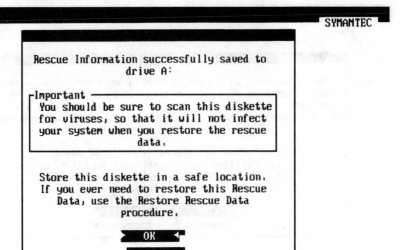

```
      Rescue Information successfully saved to
                      drive A:

     ┌Important ────────────────────────────┐
     │ You should be sure to scan this diskette│
     │ for viruses, so that it will not infect │
     │ your system when you restore the rescue │
     │                    data.                │
     └─────────────────────────────────────────┘

          Store this diskette in a safe location.
          If you ever need to restore this Rescue
          Data, use the Restore Rescue Data
                      procedure.

                  ▶  OK  ◀
```

Fig. 4-9

virus—one that would invalidate exactly the information the rescue disk is supposed to preserve.

If you ever have to use a rescue disk, here is the procedure. Turn off your computer and reboot using a clean system disk with the same version of DOS that is on your hard drive. At the DOS prompt, remove the DOS system diskette and put your rescue disk in either Drive A or Drive B. At the DOS prompt, type:

RESCUE /RESTORE <Enter>

to open the Restore System Box on screen. Check the type(s) of information you wish to restore (CMOS, boot sector, partition table). Check the drive letter of the drive containing the rescue disk and then select OK to begin restoring the information.

Configuring Norton AntiVirus

There are three configuration options, as shown in Fig. 4-10. If you elect to quit the installation at this point, the Virus Intercept device driver will not be added to your CONFIG.SYS file, and Norton AntiVirus will not automatically scan files when you boot your computer. This means you must run Norton AntiVirus manually from the DOS command line.

Easy If you opt for the Easy configuration option, the installation program will automatically update your CONFIG.SYS and AUTOEXEC.BAT files. Reboot your computer to "save" these changes. Congratulations, you have now successfully installed Norton AntiVirus 2.0, the simplest version.

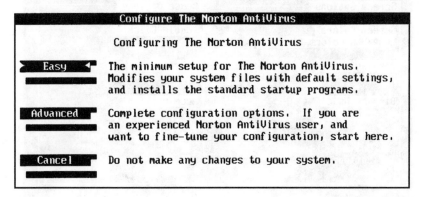

Fig. 4-10

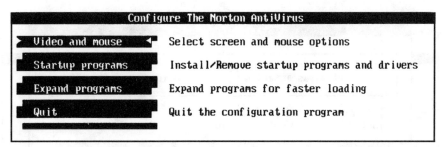

Fig. 4-11

Advanced Choosing the Advanced option lets you configure the video and mouse, and startup programs. As shown in Fig. 4-11, you can also expand Norton AntiVirus 2.0 for faster loading on older, slower machines. Most of the Advanced Configuration options are for power users; for the general user, the default factory settings in Norton AntiVirus are perfectly appropriate for optimum functioning of the program. Keep in mind that each "extra" you add to configuration adds to the amount of memory consumed by Norton AntiVirus 2.0.

Figure 4-12 shows the screen and mouse options you can configure to your liking. When you choose the startup programs option, the screen shown in Fig. 4-13 appears. The procedure for making choices is to highlight the option and press the spacebar. For example, if you highlight "Scan for viruses" and press the spacebar

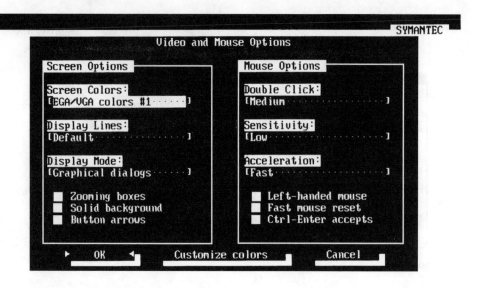

Fig. 4-12

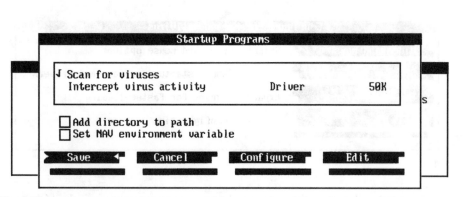

Fig. 4-13

the screen in Fig. 4-14 appears, giving you several scanning options. By selecting the scanning option in Fig. 4-13, a command is added to your AUTOEXEC.BAT file that causes the program to automatically scan in the manner you select on the screen in Fig. 4-14—either all drives or only the drives you designate. Note the two rather cryptic choices below the box on the screen in Fig. 4-13. "Add directory to path" means including a statement in your AUTOEXEC.BAT file (you can prevent that here, but then you will be operating the program manually). The second line tells the system where to find Norton AntiVirus 2.0 on your system if you have put it into a path with a long name.

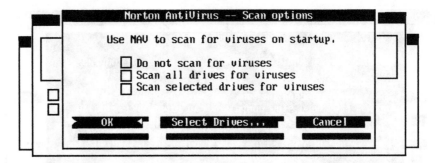

Fig. 4-14

Choosing Intercept Virus adds a device driver statement to your CONFIG.SYS file that loads Virus Intercept. Virus Intercept is a memory-resident program (TSR), and therefore must load first into memory when you start your computer. When Virus Intercept is selected and you then press the spacebar, the screen shown in Fig. 4-15 appears, so that you can configure how you want Virus Intercept to operate. The more comprehensive a group of these solutions you choose, the more RAM the program uses. When you have made your selection using the up and down arrow keys, use the right arrow key to move to the box at the bottom of the screen and select OK. When the screen shown in Fig. 4-13 reappears, select "Save" to enter your configuration selections.

Your one remaining option to consider is "Expand Program." The Virus Clinic files in Norton AntiVirus 2.0 are stored on your hard disk in compressed form. This can result in longer loading times, especially on older, slower systems. By expanding the program file on these systems, you can speed up the loading process.

```
┌─────────────────────────────────────────────────┐
│        Norton AntiVirus -- Intercept options     │
│  Use NAV to check files for viruses as you use them.│
│                                                   │
│   ☐ Comprehensive scan with system area protection│
│   ☐ Comprehensive scan                            │
│   ☐ Boot sector and execution scan                │
│   ☐ Execution scan only                           │
│   ☐ Do not check files for viruses                │
│                                                   │
│           ▶  OK  ◀      Cancel                    │
└─────────────────────────────────────────────────┘
```

Fig. 4-15

Selecting this option brings up the warning screen illustrated in Fig. 4-16, giving you a chance to change your mind about expanding the program files, along with reasons why you might want to change your mind.

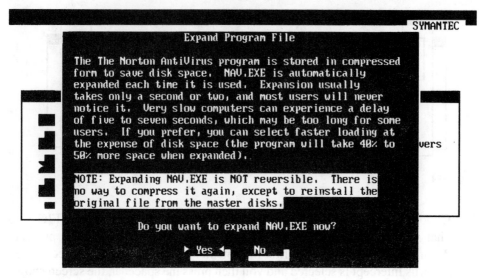

Fig. 4-16

The last option on the Advanced Configuration screen is "Quit." Once you have completed your selections, use the Quit option to return to DOS. It is suggested that you reboot your computer to "set" any changes that have been made to AUTOEXEC.BAT and CONFIG.SYS files.

Remember that nothing you do during installation is "set in concrete." You can go back through the installation process and change your selections. You can also edit Norton AntiVirus 2.0 additions to your CONFIG.SYS and AUTOEXEC.BAT files using the Edit option on the Startup Programs screen (Fig. 4-13).

A number of even more advanced setup options are available in Norton AntiVirus 2.0. These include enabling and disabling command buttons on the screen; scanning network drives; configuring Virus Intercept to beep or not to beep, and to keep a log of alerts if desired; setting global options for virus detection; establishing, entering and changing passwords; removing passwords; and configuring video and mouse options. These options are available on the Virus Clinic Options Menu, accessed by selecting Cancel on the Scan Drives menu. I discuss the Virus Clinic Options in detail later in this chapter.

Installing the Windows version

If you are installing the Windows version of Norton AntiVirus 2.0., you can add Norton AntiVirus for Windows (NAVW.EXE) to any Windows Program Manager group, or create a new program group according to the instructions in Microsoft's Windows Manual. The installation program automatically adds NAVPOPUP.EXE to the LOAD= line of your WIN.INI file to display the Virus Intercept alert boxes under Windows. This takes up 8K of RAM, and can be removed to save memory, but you will not see virus alerts on the screen, nor will you hear the "beep" and see the "file access denied" message. (If you turned off the "beep" in the setup procedure, you only see the "file access denied" message if a virus is detected.)

Deleting infected files to complete installation

Very early in the installation procedure, you were promised a discussion of what to do if a virus is discovered during the installation procedure. One alternative is to exit the installation program, delete the infected program using standard DOS procedures or a DOS shell program, and then restart installation.

You also have the option of deleting the infected files through Norton AntiVirus 2.0. If viruses are found on your hard disk, the names of the infected files will appear on the screen in a Scan Results box. Select one of the infected files: Use Shift–Tab to move to the file list, and the up and down arrow keys to highlight the desired filename, and press Enter. Mouse users can just click on the filename and then select delete. The next screen is a box that displays the name of the file. On this screen, select Yes if you are installing for DOS (if installing for Windows, the choice is "OK"). Repeat these actions for each virus named in the Scan Results box. Then, exit Norton AntiVirus by pressing <Alt>–S or by typing X (mouse users double click on the control menu box in the upper left corner of the Scan Results box). Reboot your computer and start over.

You also have the option to attempt the repair of infected files. Select one of the infected files listed in the Scan Results box. Select Repair. Use the Tab key to make this selection (mouse users can click on the Repair button). You should see a Repair Files box. If you select "Repair All" you will be informed that the files have been repaired, or that some are unrepairable and must be deleted. You know what to do with those. By the way, if you don't want to delete the unrepairables right away, make a note of the filenames and delete and replace the files at a later time. Just be certain that you do not execute an infected file before you complete the installation of the Virus Intercept part of Norton AntiVirus 2.0.

Going beyond the basics
The ins and outs of using Virus Intercept

When Norton AntiVirus 2.0 is installed, Virus Intercept is loaded into memory every time you start your computer. It works in the background, and alerts you each time it detects a possible virus. This means that depending upon how you have set up the program during installation, alarms sound, warnings flash, and a red alert screen appears whenever an activity that might be virus-related attempts to take place. This, for example, includes attempting to format a disk. You can tell that Virus Intercept has loaded because a screen to that effect appears when you boot your computer. As mentioned earlier, Virus intercept can be disabled by holding down both shift keys after the beep at bootup.

Virus Intercept comes in three versions. Here is one of the "options" that can fill up your memory and prevent your using some of the other, larger programs on your system. If you install the comprehensive NAV_.SYS file, you get a really comprehensive virus detection system. It scans when you start an application, copy or move a file, or copy a disk, and it can detect boot sector and partition table viruses. The catch is that it requires approximately 35K to 50K of memory. The NAV&.SYS/B alternative requires only 4K of memory and also scans when you start up applications. It checks for boot sector and partition table infections. NAV&.SYS requires only about 1K of memory. This installation only scans when an application is launched.

Unfortunately, even the writers of the original documentation don't seem terribly clear on how you choose one from the other. If you look at Fig. 4-14, you see that on this screen you were asked to tell the system what to do and not to do. The more you selected for it to do, the more memory you used. If you are curious about which of these programs you've put in after you install Norton AntiVirus 2.0, look at your CONFIG.SYS file either at the DOS prompt or through an editing program (DOS 5.0's Edit program is ideal for this). You will see a line that says Device=C:\NAV\NAV_.SYS if you have installed the most comprehensive version, Device=C:\NAV\NAV&.SYS/B if you have installed the middle version, and DEVICE=C:\NAV\NAV&.SYS if you have installed the 1K version. You can go back into the installation program and reinstall at a lower level, choosing fewer options on the menu shown in Fig. 4-15.

Remember that nothing takes effect until you reboot your computer. As a result, you might finish your installation, think everything is okay, turn off your computer only to boot up and discover that you no longer have enough memory to run one or more of your larger programs. Reinstall Norton AntiVirus 2.0 right away and reboot your computer to make sure you have it right this time.

A word of caution: Virus Intercept protects itself from virus infection by not allowing any application to read or write to the NAV_.SYS file. You cannot view, modify, or erase this file while Virus Intercept is active (i.e., your computer is turned on and Virus Intercept is loaded). When you back up your files, exclude the NAV.Sys file because the backup program will not be able to read this file. This only applies to the full NAV_.SYS version of Virus Intercept—the two smaller versions do not include this self-protection feature.

Virus Intercept doesn't do it all

Virus Intercept won't scan files for viruses when you are using the DOS DISKCOPY command. Scan the source and target diskettes using Virus Clinic before you make the copy. Nor can Virus Intercept scan files downloaded using a modem, or files transferred from one computer to another using a file transfer program (not even Commander Link from Norton Commander).

In order for Virus Intercept to scan compressed, packed, or archived files, they must be expanded. When using Virus Intercept with a time-sensitive communications program, the application might "crash" or lose data after a Virus Intercept alert is displayed. When an alert is displayed, Virus Intercept stops all activity on the computer. That accounts for the fact that there are no screen capture figures in this chapter showing what an alert box looks like. As soon as one appears, the system is frozen and the screen capture application program won't work.

Virus Intercept can also interfere with the operation of your backup programs. Virus Intercept might give you unexpected alerts when you back up programs (and stop the backup while you deal with the alert), or the appearance of an alert box can stop the backup program entirely. Virus Intercept is designed to work with DESQView and DOS 5.0's task switcher, but it might be incompatible with some other multitasking/TSR managers.

When Virus Intercept gives you an alert

When Virus Intercept alerts you to a possible problem, you get a warning you cannot ignore. It displays an alert box on the screen, sounds an alarm, or does both at the same time. There is a Virus Infection Alert Box and a Boot Sector Alert Box. Figure 4-17 illustrates the former. By the way, the box is red, the top line is flashing, an alarm is sounding—you'll know when an alert box pops on the scene. You now know which file has what virus, and you have two alternatives: proceed or stop. If you choose proceed, you will close the alert box and start the application despite the potential virus infection. Save this option for when you are at least 99.44 percent sure it is a false alarm. The best alternative is to stop and use the Norton AntiVirus 2.0 Virus Clinic to repair or delete the damaged file.

When a boot sector virus is detected, the alert box in Fig. 4-18 appears. This tells you that the boot sector on a floppy disk you are using has a virus, in this example, the Michelangelo. You have already scanned your hard drive and found it clean, so you know any boot sector virus has to be imported from a floppy disk. You can go ahead and run the application that is on this diskette without the boot sector virus infecting your computer, but whatever you do, don't use this diskette to boot your system or the boot sector virus will move to your hard drive. Use the procedure for restoring boot sector information on a floppy disk detailed later in this chapter.

Inoculation in this program's lingo is the word it uses to describe checking a program signature for changes. If a known virus is discovered, the virus alert screen appears, but a change in the file's "inoculation" data triggers a box similar to that illustrated in Fig. 4-19. Your choices here are to proceed with file access as though there were no alert, to let the system "reinoculate" the file (that is, store the file's current signature information), or to stop the access and return to DOS.

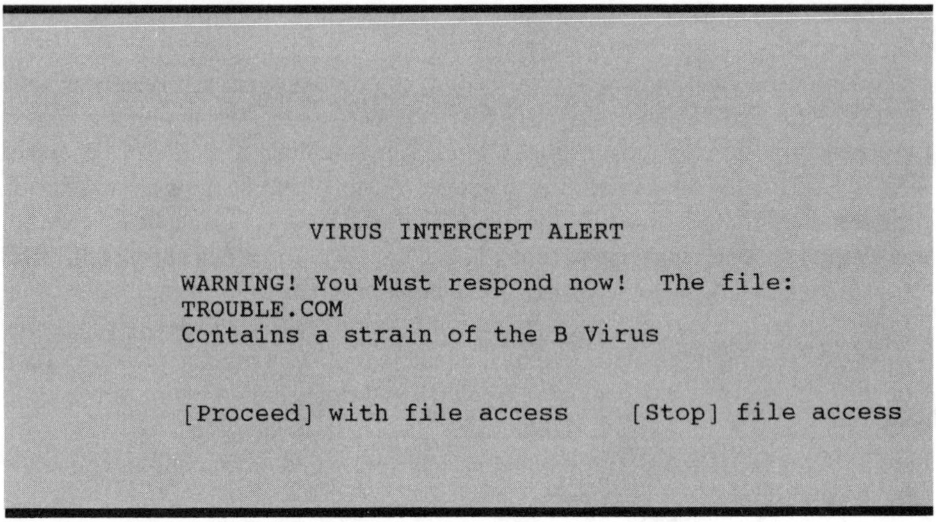

```
            VIRUS INTERCEPT ALERT

     WARNING! You Must respond now!  The file:
     TROUBLE.COM
     Contains a strain of the B Virus


     [Proceed] with file access     [Stop] file access
```

Fig. 4-17

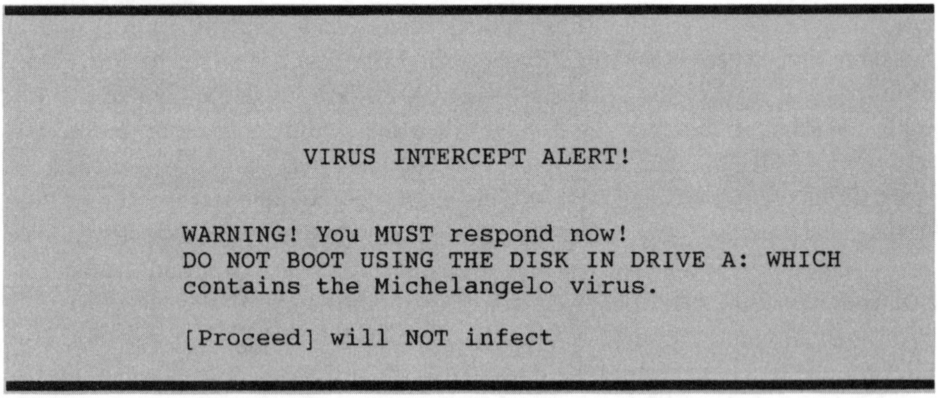

```
               VIRUS INTERCEPT ALERT!


     WARNING! You MUST respond now!
     DO NOT BOOT USING THE DISK IN DRIVE A: WHICH
     contains the Michelangelo virus.

     [Proceed] will NOT infect
```

Fig. 4-18

Using Virus Clinic

Virus Clinic does not automatically load each time you boot up the system. It must be called up by typing NAV at the DOS prompt for the drive and directory (probably C:\NAV) where Norton AntiVirus 2.0 is stored. Virus Clinic scans for all known viruses that match definitions in the program's virus definitions file. When you call up Virus Clinic, the "About Virus Clinic" screen appears, followed by a Scan Drives menu box that lets you select the drive(s) to be scanned. When you press <Enter> and begin to scan, Virus Clinic alerts you if it comes across a virus, telling you the full path name of the infected file and the name of the virus involved. You have three

```
          VIRUS INTERCEPT ALERT!

WARNING!  You MUST respond now!  The file:
C:\wp\wp.exe
has changed since it was inoculated.  If the
file has been
upgraded, then Reinoculation is suggested, other
wise this could
be an unknown virus.


[Proceed] with file access [Reinoculate] file
[Stop] file access
```

Fig. 4-19

options: repair, delete, or delete and replace the infected file. Each time you start up your computer and run Virus Clinic, it scans memory for viruses on the first pass, and does not scan on subsequent passes you might perform during a computing session.

Finding a virus in memory If a virus is detected in memory, turn off the computer, because Virus Clinic cannot eliminate a virus while the virus is resident in memory. Reboot from a clean, uninfected system disk that contains the same version of DOS as your hard disk. At the DOS prompt, use your copy of the Norton AntiVirus program diskette to run NAV.EXE, thus starting Virus Clinic. Scan all drives and repair or delete infected files.

If you do not want to scan a drive but prefer to limit the scan to certain directories or files, you can do so by pressing <Alt>–S and typing or selecting D to bring up the scan menu. Select one of these options, fill in the name of the directory or file to be scanned, and press <Enter>. You can change files and repeat, or change the directory or subdirectory and repeat. When each scan is run, a Scan Results box appears on the screen and keeps you informed of the scan's progress. It tells you what percentage of the drive/directory/file has been scanned, and lists each file that contains a virus with the name of the virus found there. You will then be able to choose your solution—scan, repair, delete, reinoc, and print.

During the scan, there is a cancel option on the screen. You can use this to cancel a file scan in progress without harming your files. You cannot, however, cancel a memory scan in progress.

Taking care of infected files

The safest alternative is always to delete an infected file. You can replace it later with a clean copy. Select the Delete option on the Scan Results screen to get to the

Delete Files screen. The only question you might have on this screen is the difference between "Delete" and "Delete all." "Delete" just deletes the file that is highlighted, while "Delete all" deletes all files shown in the Scan Results box as infected. Just follow the menu—this is a simple procedure.

On the other hand, you might choose the repair alternative from the Scan Results menu if you want to attempt to repair a file. This is not a highly recommended procedure because of the damage you can inadvertently cause. You can choose the repair option for all files infected with a virus that is recognized by the Norton AntiVirus program. If there is no repair option, it means that there are no repairable files in the scan results, and you must delete. Again you have the "Repair" and "Repair all" choice; it operates the same way as the delete choices. Here, I advise you to work with one file at a time. When all repairs have been completed, the system returns to the Scan Results box. Rescan the files you have just repaired to make certain they are clean. If they are not, repeat the repair process or delete and replace. If they seem to be okay, start up the newly repaired application and run it to make sure it is running right.

When opting to repair files, keep in mind that files stored on write-protected disks cannot be repaired. Don't be fooled by the fact that Norton AntiVirus 2.0 appears to be repairing them—it isn't. Also remember that the program needs write-access rights to be able to repair (work with) infected files whenever a program that locks a disk, or creates a logical partition mapped to a drive letter, is used. These latter two will probably only be of concern to power users—the rest of you won't get into these types of programs.

Inoculation

Inoculation is used to catch as yet undefined viruses that might have sneaked into your computer. As explained above, Norton AntiVirus stores and analyzes inoculation data for executable files and looks for any alteration to that data. You might recall that at installation the files were inoculated. There are procedures within Norton AntiVirus 2.0 for inoculating all the files on a particular drive or just a single file, when you change or add programs. When you launch Virus Clinic, choose the "Cancel" option in the Scan Drives box to get to the Options Menu, where you can press <Alt>–O and select G for Global inoculation. The Global box offers several selections: Detect Unknown Viruses; Auto-Inoculate; and Scan Executables files only. Even though auto-inoculate is checked by default, it won't be enabled unless you also select Detect Unknown Viruses. Use the OK button to save your selections. If you want to select a single file to inoculate, your next step is to press <Alt>–S to get to the Scan Menu, and choose F to get to the Scan File screen described earlier.

As you add and delete programs from your disk, your inoculate file can become too large and contain much data that is no longer needed. Press <Alt>–T from wherever you are in Virus Clinic to produce the Tools Menu, from which you can select U to get to the Uninoculate Drives screen. You can select the drive where the inoculation file is stored, or check a box that uninoculates all drives of a specific type; for example, all floppy drives. Choose OK to remove the inoculation data for all drives you have selected. Now, of course, you must reinoculate your files.

Leaving Virus Clinic

You have two choices in exiting from Virus Clinic, each of which returns you to the DOS prompt command line. Either go to the Scan Menu (press <Alt> S) and type or select X for exit, or press <Esc>. When you are asked whether you want to exit the program, you know the answer.

Evaluation

This program has a big advantage in all the ways you can obtain virus definition updates without spending additional money to do so. If you elect to go through the installation and select easy configuration at the end, you will have an adequate virus protection program that handles detection and eradication, and even some repair. On the other hand, if you venture into the more advanced configuration options, and more advanced use of Virus Clinic, don't be surprised if you get bogged down at some point unless you are a real power computer user. For the average person, Norton AntiVirus 2.0 probably has many features that will never be used or even attempted, especially because—if you carefully follow the anti-virus protection procedures discussed earlier in this book—you probably never will encounter a virus infection on your computer.

You will also find that to use this program to the fullest effect might require more room than you have to spare in memory, preventing you from running applications programs you want or need to use. An additional word of caution: The documentation that comes with this program contains some serious errors that can prove time-consuming and frustrating. Unfortunately, in addition to the mistakes, there are a number of instructions that are less than illuminating.

5
CHAPTER

PC-cillin
and PC-RX

PC-cillin 3.0 and PC-RX, both developed and marketed by Trend Micro Devices in Torrance, California, are two sides of a similar coin. PC-cillin is a hardware/software solution, while PC-RX uses only software to attack the virus problem. But both use a form of artificial intelligence not only to deal with all known viruses, but also to detect and prevent as yet undiscovered viruses. This feature means that with one of these solutions, your computer is protected against unknown viruses, and you don't have to worry about the need for updates to the software to handle newly discovered viruses as they appear. The software in PC-cillin and PC-RX will find a virus infection even if it doesn't have a definition from which to diagnose or name it.

Trend Micro's engineers have done in-depth virus analysis and classified viruses into several categories. They chose the most typical viruses as subjects in order to study the nature of viruses. To do this, they had to reverse-engineer the viruses back to the origin of their code. This is not an easy task. First the engineers had to decode the core instructions of the virus and check for encryption. Next, they had to disassemble, trace, and analyze the virus code. Finally, they had to simulate the infection mechanism of each virus to verify their analysis. You can be sure this was done under strict laboratory controls to avoid any viruses getting loose.

As a result, Trend Micro Devices was able to issue a report that explains typical virus features and characteristics that can be identified when predicting future virus development. One finding showed that certain general virus infection mechanisms exist in all viruses when they try to infect. Based on their findings, Trend Micro developed a rule-based method for catching viruses—a set of rules that look for one or more of five virus behaviors.

PC-cillin, a combined hardware/software solution, employs an intelligent viral filter that uses this rule-based method rather than other methods such as scan, checksum, and intercepting input/output interrupts to monitor suspicious or abnormal disk-write activities. Since its introduction in 1990, PC-cillin has been successful in detecting each new virus that has appeared on the scene, even the new generation "Stealth" viruses. During this time, there have been only minor adjustments to the rule base. Because people in the U.S. did not want to add even a small piece of hardware into their systems, Trend Micro took their PC-cillin technology and developed a software-only anti-virus program that employs their intelligent viral filter methodology. This program is PC-RX.

Once installed, both PC-cillin and PC-RX display a little happy face icon in the upper right hand corner of your screen to let you know the program is working.

The software portion of PC-cillin monitors virus activity in real-time to trap viruses when they try to infect clean files. Called PC-Sensor, this software is combined with the Immunizer Box to oversee the hard disk's boot area, active files, and boot sectors on diskettes. It is the software program that displays on-screen warnings and gives you the choice of rebooting from a clean system diskette or continuing on, ignoring the warning (perhaps you are sure it is a false alarm).

Several things you should be aware of:

- If you ignore a warning and continue your application, PC-cillin will no longer be able to guard against additional viruses until you reboot.

- If you reboot, don't use the warm boot (<Ctrl>–<Alt>–<Del>) option, or press your computer's reset button, or turn the computer off and on again. Instead, look at the warning screen, which displays two options: C to Continue and S for Solution. Type S to reboot and give PC-Sensor a chance to recover infected files and prevent further infection.

- Because PC-Sensor uses the intelligent virus traps described above rather than stored patterns and definitions, the program might not always identify the virus trapped by a specific name. If you are curious to know the name of the virus that's been caught, run Quarantine (see p.71) after PC-Sensor detects and clears the virus from system memory.

PC-cillin

PC-cillin is a hardware/software anti-virus system that is meant to immunize your computer system against all known as well as unknown viruses in much the same way as a shot of Penicillin works on you when you have an infection. It does more than just detect viruses; once installed it prevents further virus infection and can be used to recover a damaged boot sector. During the initial installation procedure, PC-cillin scans your system for existing viruses. If any are detected, PC-cillin identifies and deletes the infected file. The program also checks the boot sector, file allocation tables, and system RAM for infection.

Once the system has been scanned and is found to be clear of any viruses, PC-cillin loads its "intelligent viral traps" into memory and constantly monitors RAM for general virus characteristics. After installation, PC-cillin's intelligent viral traps prevent future infection by analyzing suspicious files in RAM while also monitoring DOS function call requests looking for certain virus criteria. If a virus is detected, PC-cillin holds back the file's execution, and flashes both a warning and instructions on how to clear out the virus on the monitor screen.

Boot sector protection

PC-cillin's external immunizer hardware contains a clean copy of boot sector data, so that if a boot sector virus is later discovered, PC-cillin can trap and identify the virus, and then download clean data to restore the boot sector. The hardware immunizer contains 1K of nonvolatile EPROM memory, and is isolated from the system so that it cannot be infected by a virus. It performs two special functions: disk rescue, the boot sector recovery operation mentioned above; and self-test, a function that safeguards the program integrity code of the PC-cillin file.

System requirements for PC-cillin

PC-cillin is IBM-compatible. It requires a minimum of 384K of memory, DOS 2.1 or higher and at least 1 D-Type 25-pin parallel port. Whatever peripheral you have currently occupying that port can be daisy-chained from the immunizer unit. The immunizer unit is totally transparent to your system and will not interfere with system operation. Keep in mind that if you have more than one computer and plan to move the PC-cillin Immunizer Box from one to another, each time the box is moved you must do a complete hardware/software re-installation on the new system. If not, the information recorded in the box from the previous computer will be wrong for the computer to which it is currently attached. If you change the partitioning of your hard disk or install a new hard disk in your computer, you must also completely reinstall the hardware/software to ensure the right information is recorded in the immunizer.

Important: Back up the software

With every virus protection program, you should make a backup copy of the software program, and store either the backup copy or the original carefully out of harm's way. PC-cillin is one of the few programs that instructs you to install using the original diskette, not the copy.

Turn off your computer and reboot from a CLEAN system diskette that contains the same version of DOS as your hard disk. Next, format a new diskette and include the ability to boot the system, using the DOS command FORMAT/S (/s is the parameter that tells DOS to copy the system files required for booting to the new diskette). Then put the original PC-cillin disk into Drive A, the new diskette into Drive B, and use the DOS XCOPY command to copy PC-cillin to the new diskette. The syntax is:

    A:\XCOPY A:*.* B:/S

When the copy is finished, you will have a clean backup copy of PC-cillin. Don't forget to add the write-protect tab.

Quick installation for PC-cillin

1. If your computer is on, turn it off before installing the PC-cillin Immunizer Box.

2. Simply unplug your printer or other peripheral from the 25-pin parallel port, plug the immunizer into that port, and then plug your printer or peripheral into the immunizer.

3. Put a CLEAN system disk into Drive A and boot your system.

4. After the system has booted, replace the system disk in Drive A with the original PC-cillin diskette.

5. Type PCC <Enter>

From this point on, PC-cillin installation is menu driven. As you can see from Fig. 5-1, all you have to do is select "1" to start installation, and then follow the on-screen instructions to completion. Figure 5-2 is the next screen. Here you are instructed to indicate the drive on which you want to install PC-cillin. As you can see from looking at these two screens, PC-cillin is not only menu driven and easy to follow, it contains those nice description boxes that tell what you need to know to understand what you are doing along the way. The construction of this software makes it almost impossible to make a mistake in installation and use.

Figure 5-3 is a composite. When you press <Enter> to select the installation drive, an overlay pops up that tells you the system is "scanning for known viruses." In the large box at the center of the screen, you will see every file on your computer pass by as the scan progresses. At the conclusion, assuming you have followed the instructions for virus prevention in the front of this book, you should see the message that no viruses have been found. If, on the other hand, this scan does detect a virus, abort the installation procedure here and start over, this time choosing the Quarantine option from the opening menu. (I'll explain the Quarantine option shortly).

The screen shown in Fig. 5-3 also tells you that the installation program will create or modify your AUTOEXEC.BAT or CONFIG.SYS files to include PC-cillin commands. PC-cillin is a terminate-and-stay-resident (TSR) program that

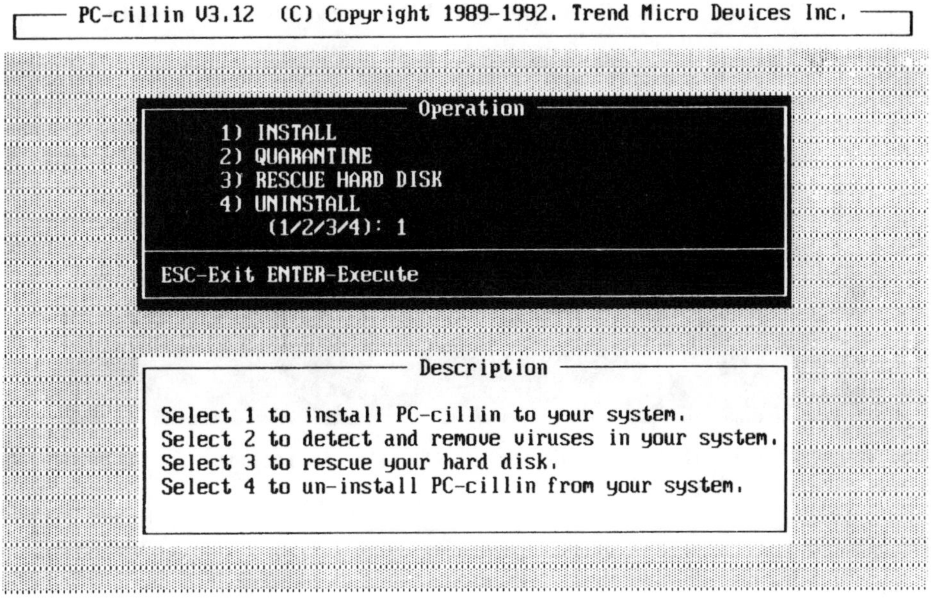

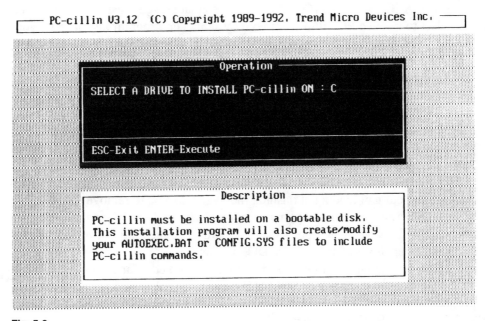

Fig. 5-1

Fig. 5-2

Quick installation for PC-cillin **69**

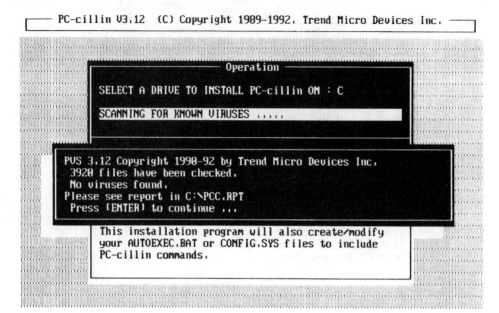

```
┌─── PC-cillin V3.12  (C) Copyright 1989-1992, Trend Micro Devices Inc. ───┐
│                                                                          │
│        ┌──────────────────── Operation ──────────────────┐              │
│        │  SELECT A DRIVE TO INSTALL PC-cillin ON : C      │              │
│        │  ┌────────────────────────────────────────────┐ │              │
│        │  │ SCANNING FOR KNOWN VIRUSES .....            │ │              │
│    ┌───┴──┴────────────────────────────────────────────┴─┴───┐         │
│    │ PVS 3.12 Copyright 1990-92 by Trend Micro Devices Inc.    │         │
│    │  3920 files have been checked.                            │         │
│    │  No viruses found.                                        │         │
│    │ Please see report in C:\PCC.RPT                           │         │
│    │  Press [ENTER] to continue ...                            │         │
│    └───────┬──────────────────────────────────────────┬───────┘         │
│            │ This installation program will also create/modify │         │
│            │ your AUTOEXEC.BAT or CONFIG.SYS files to include  │         │
│            │ PC-cillin commands.                              │         │
│            └──────────────────────────────────────────────────┘         │
└──────────────────────────────────────────────────────────────────────────┘
```

Fig. 5-3

must check your system at each bootup. When you install it on hard drive C, it will insert several lines into your AUTOEXEC.BAT file. If you do not have an AU-TOEXEC.BAT file, PC-cillin will create one. If you do have one, it will be saved as AUTOEXEC.$$$ or AUTOEXEC.@@@ so that you can restore it should you ever elect to remove PC-cillin from your system. The program also installs your hard drive partition table and boot sector information into the checksum of the im-munizer during the installation process.

If the boot sector is infected, PC-cillin will tell you during pre-installation at the end of the scan. Stop the installation procedure and remove the virus immedi-ately. There are two procedures for this, one for removing a virus from a floppy disk boot sector, the other for removing a virus from your hard disk partition or boot sector. You can also use a virus removal program. I include all these options in the discussion of the Quarantine feature below.

Once the scan is complete and you press <Enter>, the program begins to load. At the completion of loading, a flashing message asks you to remove the PC-cillin disk and press any key to reboot your computer (see Fig. 5-4). When the system re-boots, PC-cillin stores your boot sector and partition table information in its exter-nal Immunizer Box and displays the DOS prompt.

After installation is complete and you have rebooted your computer, you can always get back to the opening menu of PC-cillin to work with other aspects of the program simply by changing the directory at the DOS prompt to C:\PCCILLIN and then typing PCC and pressing <Enter>.

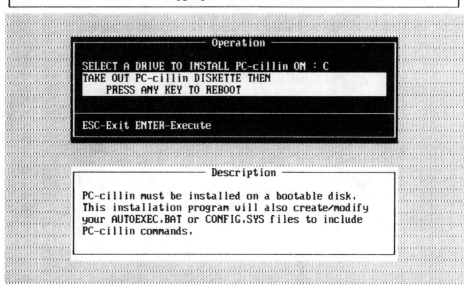

```
┌──────────────────── Operation ────────────────────┐
│                                                    │
│ SELECT A DRIVE TO INSTALL PC-cillin ON : C         │
│ TAKE OUT PC-cillin DISKETTE THEN                   │
│     PRESS ANY KEY TO REBOOT                        │
│                                                    │
│                                                    │
│ ESC-Exit ENTER-Execute                             │
└────────────────────────────────────────────────────┘

┌─────────────────── Description ───────────────────┐
│                                                    │
│ PC-cillin must be installed on a bootable disk,    │
│ This installation program will also create/modify  │
│ your AUTOEXEC.BAT or CONFIG.SYS files to include    │
│ PC-cillin commands,                                │
│                                                    │
└────────────────────────────────────────────────────┘
```

Fig. 5-4

The Quarantine feature

Quarantine is selection 2 on PC-cillin's Main Menu. It is a program that scans DOS files to see if they contain viruses, checking for viruses with code patterns that have been previously stored in its code pattern data bank. Quarantine can work with files stored on hard or floppy disks, files downloaded by modem, and files loaded from computer networks. You can and probably should run Quarantine as a routine check of all new files on a diskette before storing any of them on your hard disk.

When you select Quarantine from the Main Menu, the first screen you see is the one shown in Fig. 5-5. Use the Tab key to move from one selection to another, and type in any appropriate changes—these are not toggled options. When you move to the second selection, "Enter Directory or Files," a sub-window appears, shown in Fig. 5-6, where you can type the name and path of a directory, subdirectory, or file that you want quarantined rather than the whole drive specified. Just be sure that the smaller entity you specify in this window is, in fact, on the drive named in the first selection. You can also choose the delete option, the rename option, or the no change option as the action to take if a virus is found. These are pretty easy options to understand—rename will merely rename the file with the virus giving it a .VIR extension.

There are two ways you can set up the system to deal with a virus when one is found. You can tell it to delete, rename, or ignore (no change) automatically, without notifying you of this activity, or you can ask the system to prompt you before

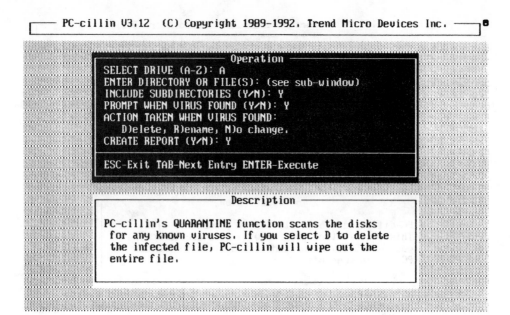

Fig. 5-5

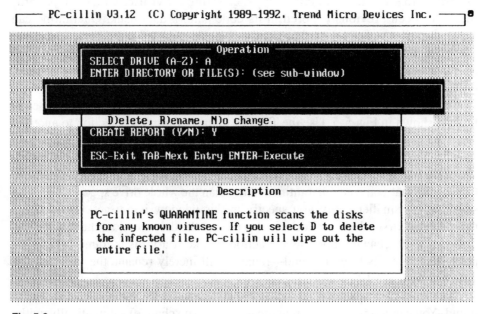

Fig. 5-6

it takes action, in case you want to change the general action you specified for one more appropriate to the current circumstance.

By the way, the Tab key works in a loop, so if you make a mistake on one of your selections, just continue to tab back to the location and type in the correction before pressing <Enter> to execute.

Assuming that you've used the virus prevention techniques talked about earlier in the book, you will find no viruses. At this point, pressing <Enter> to continue will merely bring you back to the screen shown in Fig. 5-5 so that you can scan another drive, directory, or file. When you finish and no viruses have been found, press <Esc> to return to the PC-cillin Main Menu, and press <Esc> a second time to return to DOS.

When a virus is detected, the name(s) of the files containing the virus, any newly infected file, and the name of the virus are all displayed. Quarantine handles the virus either automatically or by prompting you—whichever method you selected earlier.

Your options for handling any virus found by PC-cillin include "wiping a file" (replacing the infected file with a clean copy). You can use either Quarantine's Delete option, or a third-party utility such as the Wipe command in Norton Utilities. Merely removing the file using the DOS DELETE command will not prevent an unerase or undelete command from bringing back the file and reinfecting your computer.

If you are in a situation where wiping the file is not a practical alternative, you can use a virus removal program. These programs usually identify the infected file as well as the virus infecting it, and remove the virus code from the file based on data stored in the virus definition file. Virus removal is not always successful. If the version of the program you are using does not contain a definition for the virus you have, it cannot remove it. Nor can the program remove a mutated strain of a defined virus. Moveover, should the infected file have an internal overlay structure, chances are a removal program will not be successful.

It is hard to recommend virus removal programs because of their limitations. Using a virus removal program should, as a rule, only be attempted in cases where other anti-virus alternatives are not viable, although there are virus removal programs such as McAfee's Clean-Up (see chapter 6) that do not specify any such warnings, other than to suggest that asking for help from someone more knowledgeable might be in your best interests. PC-cillin 3.0 and higher does provide several virus removal programs in the PCCUTIL subdirectory on the PC-cillin program diskette, and also provides directions for using these programs in a file called README.DOC on the same diskette. Trend Micro Devices strongly suggests, however, that if you are not a software engineer, you should find one to perform the removal procedure. When the company that makes the product suggests you get expert help, you probably are well-advised to do so.

If Quarantine detects a virus in memory, the screen displays a message telling you to reboot your system with a clean, write-protected floppy system diskette. A word of warning: It is dangerous to continue to scan a system for file viruses when a memory virus has been detected. If a boot sector virus is found, stop the program by turning off your computer and rebooting from your clean system diskette.

Once you've rebooted, you can attempt to remove the virus from the boot sector of a diskette without too much trouble. Use the DOS COPY command to copy the uninfected files to be saved from the infected diskette to a clean, newly formatted diskette, and then use the DOS FORMAT command to reformat (clean) the infected diskette.

You can also remove a boot sector/partition table virus from your hard disk, but this procedure is not for the faint-hearted. It is not a problem with PC-cillin installed, because you have a copy of your hard disk's boot sector/partition table data stored in the Immunizer Box. However, if the virus occurred before you installed PC-cillin, even the copy in the immunizer is infected, so you have to remove the virus the hard way.

After rebooting with the clean system diskette, use Quarantine to scan all the files on your hard disk, and then use a backup utility program (either the DOS BACKUP command or a third-party program) to back up all the clean files to another storage medium. The large number of files involved in this probably make using floppy diskettes an unwieldy choice as a backup medium. If you can possibly use an external hard disk or tape or some other mass storage medium, it will be much easier.

Now run the DOS PREFORM program for a low level format on the infected hard disk. Next run the DOS FDISK command to repartition the hard disk, and then run the DOS FORMAT command to format the hard disk. Copy the clean stored files back onto the hard drive. If you are in any doubt about these commands and procedures, it is best to find someone more experienced to assist you.

PC-cillin 3.0 does contain a virus removal program for memory viruses. PART.EXE is in the PCCUTIL subdirectory on the PC-cillin program diskette. This is an extension of Hard Disk Rescue, the third feature option on the PC-cillin Main Menu. You can access this program at any time by returning to the DOS prompt, changing to the PCCUTIL subdirectory, and typing PART and pressing <Enter>.

The Hard Disk Rescue feature

Assuming you have rebooted from a clean system diskette, you put the PC-cillin program diskette back into Drive A, type PCC and press <Enter> at the A:\ prompt, and select Rescue Hard Disk (option 3 from the Main Menu). If all goes well, PC-cillin automatically recreates your hard disk's boot sector and partition table from the data stored in the Immunizer Box, and you recover your hard drive intact. But, as everyone knows, when it comes to computers, things don't always "go well."

There is a chance that the Immunizer Box will not be able to help. It might be nothing more serious than your not having plugged the Immunizer Box properly into the parallel port. Or it might be that the Immunizer Box you have plugged into this system actually belongs to another computer so it can't be used to rescue this system. In both these cases, a message appears on the screen to warn you of the problem; either one can be remedied relatively easily. Of course, it might be more serious—the data stored in the Immunizer Box might be corrupt, in which case you have to resort to more drastic measures such as the PC-cillin Hard Disk Rescue Utility.

Executing the PART program in the PCCUTIL directory brings up the Main Menu shown in Fig. 5-7. Choose the first option ("Help") to yield two screens explaining the other options. Then return to the screen shown in Fig. 5-7. Don't choose the second option ("Display partition sector") unless you are familiar with programming; you won't be able to read the screen except for a virus message that tells you your memory sector has a virus such as Stoned or Michelangelo. If the "you have XXX virus" message is displayed, you can use the next option ("Clean partition sector") to remove the virus. This option only works if your hard disk is standard formatted, but chances are 99 to 1 that it is. Once you have removed the memory virus, move to the third option ("Backup hard disk rescue data") to store your hard disk CMOS, partition, and boot sector data on a diskette. If you already have a clean backup rescue diskette, and are ready to restore that data to your system, you can go on to option 4 ("Rescue hard disk").

```
                PC-cillin Hard Disk Rescue Utility.
===============================================================
                    by Trend Micro Devices Inc.




    0. Help.
    1. Display partition sector.
    2. Clean hard disk partition sector.
    3. Backup hard disk rescue data.(A:RESCUE.RES)
    4. Rescue hard disk.(A:RESCUE.RES)
    5. Quit.

            Enter choice  :
```

Fig. 5-7

The Uninstall feature

Option 4 on the PC-cillin Main Menu is "Uninstall." This option can be used for more than just getting rid of PC-cillin. You need to uninstall an older version of the program before you can install any updated version. While PC-cillin needs fewer, less frequent updates than most anti-virus programs, there is the possibility that a new strain of virus with a different set of characteristics might be discovered. It is also possible that Trend Micro Devices will improve their Sensors to make current and future virus detection even more effective, and you will certainly want to install them.

When an update disk is issued, updating your system using Uninstall is very easy. First, turn off your system. Boot your system using the old version of PC-cillin. Put the update diskette into Drive A, change to Drive A, and type PCC <Enter> at the A:\ prompt. The Main Menu appears. Choose option 4 to uninstall the old version, and then choose option 1 to begin installation of the newer version. Install the new version onto the same drive on which the older version was stored. From here, it's the same installation procedure as before.

PC-RX—An all-software anti-virus solution

When you open up the PC-RX package, you will find, in addition to the diskette and manual, a booklet containing "Six Important Questions About Computer Viruses . . . What You Need To Know But Didn't Know To Ask." Even after reading chapters 1 and 2 in this book, reading the PC-RX booklet can provide helpful information in the form of a quick review. You will also find a Registration Card. Fill this out and return it to Trend Micro Devices immediately. This makes you eligible for the items described in the brochure, also enclosed with the software, entitled "Anti-Virus Assurance Plan." This plan includes a year of free updates to your PC-RX program, and a bimonthly newsletter free for a year that provides you with analyses of newly discovered viruses (also available through Trend Micro's BBS, 310-320-2523, and on CompuServe, GOVIRUSFORUM). In addition, Trend Micro Devices provides registered users with telephone technical support.

PC-RX consists of two parts, a virus scan pattern bank (virus definitions similar to other anti-virus programs) and a 10K TSR program that detects known and unknown viruses by looking for virus characteristics according to the Trend Micro Devices' rule-based virus detection technology, discussed at the beginning of this chapter.

A word to the wise: Many copies of PC-RX on the market have a manual that is more confusing than helpful in many ways. It refers to the Quarantine feature found in PC-cillin but not found in PC-RX under that name. In PC-RX, the feature is known as the PC-RX Virus Trap, and is described in chapter 4 of the manual— a discussion of what happens when a virus is detected, and how you can deal with it. Essentially, much of the information is the same as that for PC-cillin's Quarantine, but the nomenclature can be confusing since the book refers to Quarantine but there is no Quarantine in PC-RX.

When in doubt about how to remove a virus, go to the PCRXUTIL subdirectory and use the virus removal programs, PART.EXE and VGUARD.EXE. The subdirectory also contains a README.DOC file, but it isn't very enlightening about these utilities. PART.EXE operates exactly like its counterpart for PC-cillin, described above, and can remove boot viruses. VGUARD is a scanning program discussed below in the section on PC-RX, and can remove file viruses.

Quick installation of PC-RX

PC-RX can be installed quickly and easily without the need to read the manual word for word. You need to be an experienced PC user who is familiar with DOS to do this, though no more so than for any other program discussed in this book. The necessary lines are inserted into your AUTOEXEC.BAT file automatically, or an AUTO-EXEC.BAT file will be created by the program if you are operating without one. The PC-RX checksums are written to the PC-RX installed boot disk, so that PC-RX programs won't become infected themselves. PC-RX can be installed on a two-diskette system, a system with a hard drive, or on a local area network. In this book, the instructions will be for installing the program on a hard drive.

First turn off your computer and reboot using a clean, write-protected system diskette in Drive A. Next make a backup copy of the PC-RX program diskette on a newly formatted diskette that contains the DOS system files, to ensure that you have a working copy should any problems arise. (Do this even though it takes a bit of extra time.) Insert the original PC-RX diskette in Drive A and at the A:\ prompt, type PCRX and press <Enter>. The screen shown in Fig. 5-8 is displayed. To begin the installation process, select the top option by highlighting it and pressing <Enter>. You then see the screen shown in Fig. 5-9; once again highlight install and press <Enter>. As you can see from these first two screens, as with PC-cillin, anti-virus programs

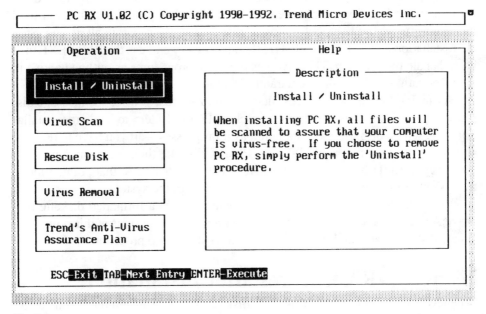

Fig. 5-8

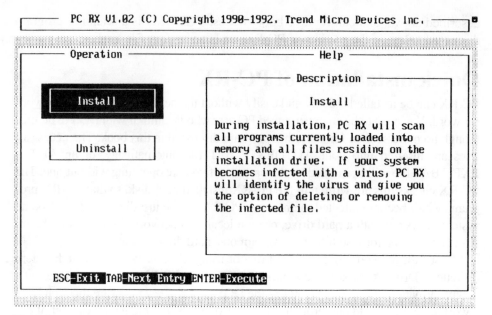

Operation ——————————— Help

———— Description ————

Install

Uninstall

Install

During installation, PC RX will scan
all programs currently loaded into
memory and all files residing on the
installation drive. If your system
becomes infected with a virus, PC RX
will identify the virus and give you
the option of deleting or removing
the infected file.

ESC-Exit TAB-Next Entry ENTER-Execute

Fig. 5-9

from Trend Micro Devices are easy to operate, and full of description boxes that let you know what is happening and why.

The next screen, shown in Fig. 5-10, asks you to designate the drive on which to install PC-RX. This drive must be bootable, which means in most cases it will be C (the default drive) on your computer. Press <Enter> to accept the default drive for program installation (or change it if necessary). The program scans your hard drive for viruses. If a boot sector virus is discovered, the program alerts you. Stop the installation and go to the PCRXUTIL subdirectory and use the PART.EXE utility to handle the problem. This involves the same procedures as outlined above in the information on PC-cillin's Quarantine feature.

Assuming that the scan process does not find a virus, you see the message displayed in Fig. 5-11 when the scan is complete. Press <Enter> to begin the installation. The screen displays the installation as it progresses—all you have to do is sit and watch until the message "Take out PC-RX diskette then press any key to reboot" begins to flash at the top of the screen (see Fig. 5-12). At that point, remove the diskette from Drive A and press any key to reboot the system.

When the reboot begins, PC-RX asks you to insert a formatted diskette into Drive A to create a rescue disk. You can press any key to continue at this point. The rescue disk is created and the system completes its bootup procedure.

Using PC-RX features after installation

Whenever you want to run a virus scan, disk rescue, or virus removal, you can go to DOS, move to the directory in which PC-RX is stored (C:\PCRX) and type

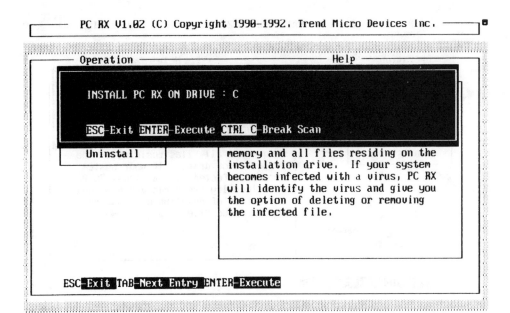

Fig. 5-10

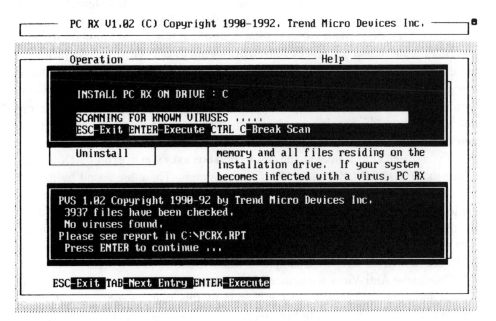

Fig. 5-11

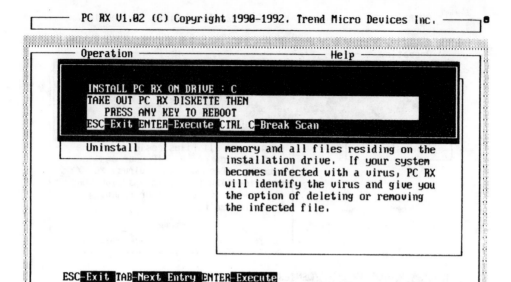

```
┌──── Operation ──────────────────────────────── Help ─────┐
│                                                          │
│   INSTALL PC RX ON DRIVE : C                             │
│   TAKE OUT PC RX DISKETTE THEN                           │
│      PRESS ANY KEY TO REBOOT                             │
│   ESC-Exit ENTER-Execute CTRL C-Break Scan              │
│                                                          │
│   ┌── Uninstall ──────┐    memory and all files residing on the   │
│   │                   │    installation drive. If your system     │
│   └───────────────────┘    becomes infected with a virus, PC RX   │
│                            will identify the virus and give you   │
│                            the option of deleting or removing     │
│                            the infected file.                     │
│                                                          │
│   ESC-Exit TAB-Next Entry ENTER-Execute                 │
└──────────────────────────────────────────────────────────┘
```

Fig. 5-12

PCRX <Enter> to bring the Main Menu in Fig. 5-8 back onto the screen. If you highlight the Virus Scan option, the description box displays the message shown in Fig. 5-13. If you press <Enter> to execute, you see the screen in Fig. 5-14, which allows you to tell PC-RX exactly what you want to scan. Once these parameters are selected and you press <Enter>, the same scan process you watched in installation will be repeated for all of the specified drives, directories and files.

Figure 5-15 shows the message in the description box if you highlight the Rescue Disk option. When you press <Enter> to execute Rescue Disk, you are instructed (as shown in Fig. 5-16) to insert the rescue disk you made as part of the installation process into Drive A and press <Enter> to use that diskette to reboot your system with clean information (assuming the system was clean when you made the rescue disk). By the way, if there is a problem with your rescue diskette, the program tells you, and provides you with the option of returning to the Main Menu.

If you select Virus Removal, the description box asks you to exit PC-RX in order to use the VGUARD.EXE and PART.EXE programs. These are found by moving from the C:\PCRX directory to the subdirectory C:\PCRX\PCRXUTIL where they are located. These programs are menu driven and easy to operate. Virus removal using the PART.EXE program with PC-RX is the same as was described in the discussion of PC-cillin virus removal programs above. VGUARD.EXE runs another scan of the disk and prints a report, a sample of which is shown in Fig. 5-18.

Choose the Anti-Virus Assurance Plan option to read (on successive screens or chosen individually by number) the details of this plan in the four categories shown in the description box in Fig. 5-19.

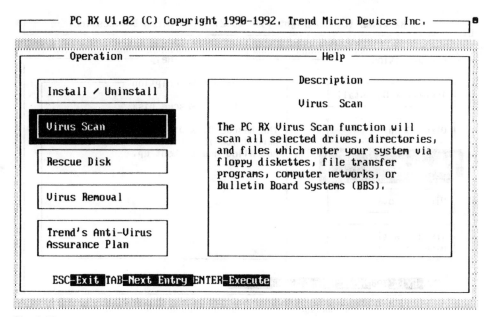

Fig. 5-13

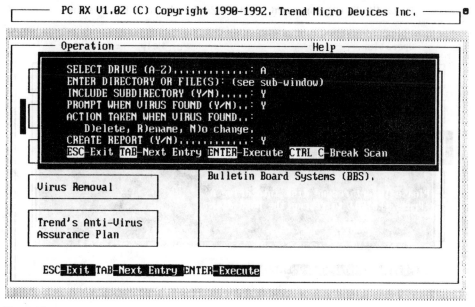

Fig. 5-14

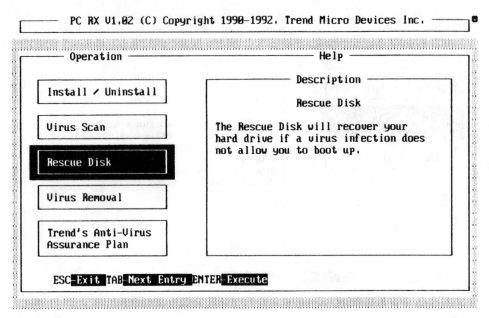

Fig. 5-15

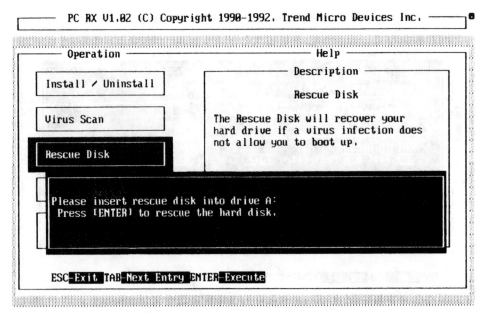

Fig. 5-16

```
┌─── PC RX V1.02 (C) Copyright 1990-1992, Trend Micro Devices Inc. ───■
│ ┌─ Operation ──────────────────────┬──────── Help ──────────────┐
│ │                                   │ ┌──── Description ────────┐
│ │ ┌─────────────────────┐          │ │                         │
│ │ │ Install / Uninstall │          │ │    Virus Removal        │
│ │ └─────────────────────┘          │ │                         │
│ │ ┌─────────────────────┐          │ │ If you choose to remove a virus from
│ │ │ Virus Scan          │          │ │ your system, VGUARD.EXE will remove
│ │ └─────────────────────┘          │ │ a file virus and PART.EXE will remove
│ │ ┌─────────────────────┐          │ │ a boot virus.  Before running either
│ │ │ Rescue Disk         │          │ │ program, please exit PC RX.
│ │ └─────────────────────┘          │ │
│ │ ┌─────────────────────┐          │ │
│ │ │ Virus Removal       │          │ │
│ │ └─────────────────────┘          │ │
│ │ ┌─────────────────────┐          │ └─────────────────────────┘
│ │ │ Trend's Anti-Virus  │          │
│ │ │ Assurance Plan      │          │
│ │ └─────────────────────┘          │
│ │                                  │
│ │  ESC─Exit TAB─Next Entry ENTER─Execute
│ └──────────────────────────────────┴────────────────────────────┘
```

Fig. 5-17

```
┌─────────────────────────────────────────────────────────────────────■
│ Virus-GUARD, ver: 4.20              (c) Pavel Baudis, ALWIL Software 1991
└─────────────────────────────────────────────────────────────────────

Serial number: 0001.420.10001

        ┌──────────┬───────────┬──────────┬──────────┐
        │          │ in memory │ at disk  │ in files │
        ├──────────┼───────────┼──────────┼──────────┤
        │ tested   │    14     │    3     │   676    │
        │          │           │          │          │
        │ infected │     0     │    0     │    0     │
        │ removed  │     0     │    0     │    0     │
        │          │           │          │          │
        │ modified │  -----    │  -----   │    0     │
        │ removed  │  -----    │  -----   │    0     │
        │          │           │          │          │
        │ destroyed│  -----    │  -----   │    0     │
        │ deleted  │  -----    │  -----   │    0     │
        │          │           │          │          │
        │ immunised│  -----    │  -----   │    1     │
        └──────────┴───────────┴──────────┴──────────┘

C:\PCRX\PCRXUTIL>
```

Fig. 5-18

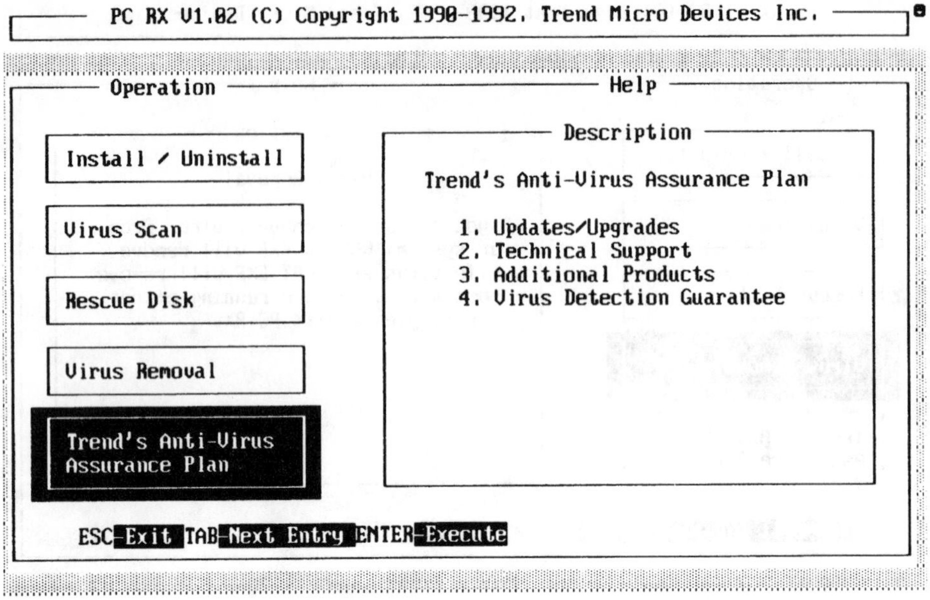

```
┌─── PC RX V1.02 (C) Copyright 1990-1992, Trend Micro Devices Inc. ───┐■
│ ┌─ Operation ──────────────────── Help ──────────────────┐ │
│ │                           ┌─ Description ─────────────┐ │ │
│ │ ┌─────────────────────┐   │ Trend's Anti-Virus Assurance Plan │ │ │
│ │ │ Install / Uninstall │   │                           │ │ │
│ │ └─────────────────────┘   │   1. Updates/Upgrades      │ │ │
│ │ ┌─────────────────────┐   │   2. Technical Support     │ │ │
│ │ │ Virus Scan          │   │   3. Additional Products   │ │ │
│ │ └─────────────────────┘   │   4. Virus Detection Guarantee │ │ │
│ │ ┌─────────────────────┐   │                           │ │ │
│ │ │ Rescue Disk         │   │                           │ │ │
│ │ └─────────────────────┘   │                           │ │ │
│ │ ┌─────────────────────┐   │                           │ │ │
│ │ │ Virus Removal       │   │                           │ │ │
│ │ └─────────────────────┘   │                           │ │ │
│ │ ┌─────────────────────┐   │                           │ │ │
│ │ │ Trend's Anti-Virus  │   │                           │ │ │
│ │ │ Assurance Plan      │   └───────────────────────────┘ │ │
│ │ └─────────────────────┘                                 │ │
│ │   ESC-Exit TAB-Next Entry ENTER-Execute                 │ │
│ └─────────────────────────────────────────────────────────┘ │
└───────────────────────────────────────────────────────────────┘
```

Fig. 5-19

Don't forget, the first option on the Main Menu is Install/Uninstall, which means that there is an uninstall feature built into PC-RX just as there is in PC-cillin. When you choose this option, and on the next screen choose Uninstall, the message shown in the description box in Fig. 5-20 appears. If you press <Enter>, an overlay screen appears that asks you to confirm the drive location of the PC-RX files. Press <Enter> again to start the removal of the files. Just follow the screen instructions to remove the program from the AUTOEXEC.BAT file as well.

Maximizing the use of PC-RX

Early in the discussion of PC-cillin, there was a brief description of the PC-Sensor feature. In PC-RX, this is known as the PC-RX Virus Trap, and is a key feature of the PC-RX virus immunization system. Like PC-Sensor, PC-RX Virus Trap is a real-time program that monitors PC activity in order to trap viruses when they try to infect files. It has the same three areas of activity: the hard disk's boot area; active files; and the boot sector on a diskette. When a virus is detected, a pop-up menu gives you the choice of rebooting and clearing away the virus or continuing on in your application if you are sure the alert is a false alarm. As with PC-Sensor, if you continue, PC-RX cannot guard against additional viruses until you reboot, and if you do reboot you should use the (S)olution option on the warning screen; you should not reboot using the warm boot (<Ctrl>–<Alt>–<Del>), the reset switch, or by turning your computer off and on.

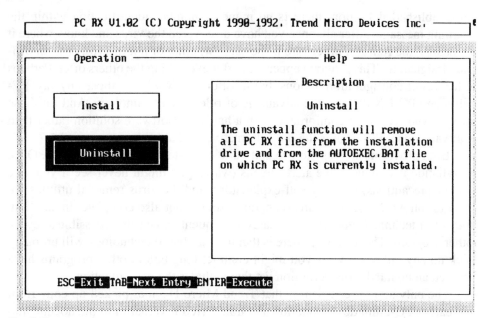

PC RX V1.02 (C) Copyright 1990-1992. Trend Micro Devices Inc.

Fig. 5-20

Thanks to the clearly-written pop-up PC-RX warning screens, when a virus is detected, you can handle the problem by reading the screen and following instructions. When there are warnings about activities such as attempts to overwrite hard disk sectors or format the hard disk, you are given two choices, the (C)ontinue and (S)olution options. If you are sure that you have encountered a false alarm, you can continue—but do so with extreme caution.

Configuring the virus trap

As with most programs, PC-RX gives you the opportunity to alter certain features to suit yourself. Unless you are an advanced computer user, it is suggested that you use PC-RX just as it comes, and do not try to customize the program.

Evaluation

Both PC-RX and PC-cillin are based on what could be the anti-virus technology of the future, the rule-based method that will be able to identify new viruses, even stealth viruses, as they appear without software updates. As this technology is refined and your program is updated to reflect the improvements, these programs should become even more effective. Rather than constantly needing virus definition updates in order to protect against newly hatched viruses, it would be nice to have a program that could catch these newcomers right away—even if, for lack of an established definition, there is no name or number identification within the warning message. After all, once you have discovered the virus and know where it is located, the removal procedure is the same whether or not the virus has an official designation. This program appears to offer everything the others offer. Perhaps it has fewer configuration options, but most of you won't use those anyway. PC-cillin and PC-RX do have the advantage of rule-based technology. And for those of you who feel more comfortable with a hardware/software solution rather than software alone, PC-cillin is the only alternative available.

Both programs are easy to use and quite consistent in their keystrokes. Once installation is complete, the alert screens (which you might never see if you take proper precautions) are very self-explanatory, and the virus removal utilities are easy to follow. These programs seem quite simple but also complete. In addition, they offer technical support and updates as frequent and easily accessible as every other program. The advantage here is that the rule-based technology will probably pick up any unknown virus you might contract long before other programs have readied an updated virus definition list that includes the new infection.

The only serious criticism is that Trend Micro Devices picked up copy from the earlier PC-cillin documentation and transferred it verbatim to the documentation for the new PC-RX program, where it doesn't fit. This would be more serious if the program weren't menu driven, with excellent descriptive boxes. There are many ways in which this copy problem could have happened and it is being corrected. Fortunately, the fact that the documentation does not match the program in no way seems to reflect on the technology—PC-RX does work and it does what it says it will.

6
CHAPTER

The shareware solution: McAfee Associates software

The programs discussed in this chapter are all found on the diskette that is included with this book. There is an additional program on the diskette, Integrity Master, that is discussed in appendix A. You can install Integrity Master along with the McAfee programs when you run the installation program on the diskette, or you can install the McAfee anti-virus programs (and the Virus Central shell to run them under), and defer installation of Integrity Master until later. You might want to wait to install Integrity Master, because it is a relatively complex process that takes up most of the installation work on the diskette.

To separate McAfee from Integrity Master and just install the McAfee programs and Virus Central at this time, make a directory called PC-Virus on the drive where you plan to store the programs (usually C). To do this at the C:\ DOS prompt, type:

MD PC–VIRUS <Enter>

When the next C:\ prompt appears, type:

CD C:\PC–VIRUS <Enter>

The next DOS prompt should read C:\PC-VIRUS. Now put the diskette from this book into Drive A and at the C:\PC-VIRUS prompt, type:

    A:\MCAFEE <Enter>

(If the diskette is in Drive B, type B:\MCAFEE instead.) The programs will self-extract into your directory on C.

For those of you unfamiliar with shareware, it can be described as a less expensive, "no frills" alternative to many software programs. Shareware can be purchased, under normal circumstances, on a "try before you buy" basis. You can get many shareware programs on diskette from a number of flourishing shareware mail-order catalogs. You can also download many shareware programs from user bulletin boards and commercial on-line services such as GEnie and CompuServe. Quite a few shareware authors maintain their own bulletin boards from which you can directly download individual programs—probably the safest way to obtain shareware without fear of virus infection.

For your information, there is an index of shareware (including software in the public domain) available on CD-ROM from:

CD-ROM Users Group
P.O. Box 2400
Santa Barbara, CA 93120
(805) 965-0265

Just in case you are thinking that shareware is a small phenomenon, the index alone takes up 120Mb and covers the shareware contained on 49 CD-ROM discs that contain somewhere between 15 and 20 gigabytes of shareware. Obviously shareware works or there wouldn't be so much of it.

John McAfee, founder and president of McAfee Associates, is a pioneer in the anti-virus field, and has been a leading virus fighter for many years. While he has been and continues to be a controversial figure in the anti-virus industry, there is no dispute as to the effectiveness of the McAfee Associates anti-virus programs that you now have, because they have been included with this book. These programs might not be the perfect solution to your anti-virus needs—one or more of the other programs described in this book might be more appropriate—but they are in your hands. Until you make a decision about which anti-virus system to buy and use, the McAfee programs will act as a solid last line of defense against virus infection.

Installing the McAfee programs

Put the program diskette into Drive A and make certain that you are at the A prompt. Type DIR to make sure that the diskette is readable on your system. (If you require double-sided double-density 3.5-or 5.25-inch media, contact Windcrest, the publisher of this book.) If you select the README file option, a screen appears with some information about the diskette and the installation procedure.

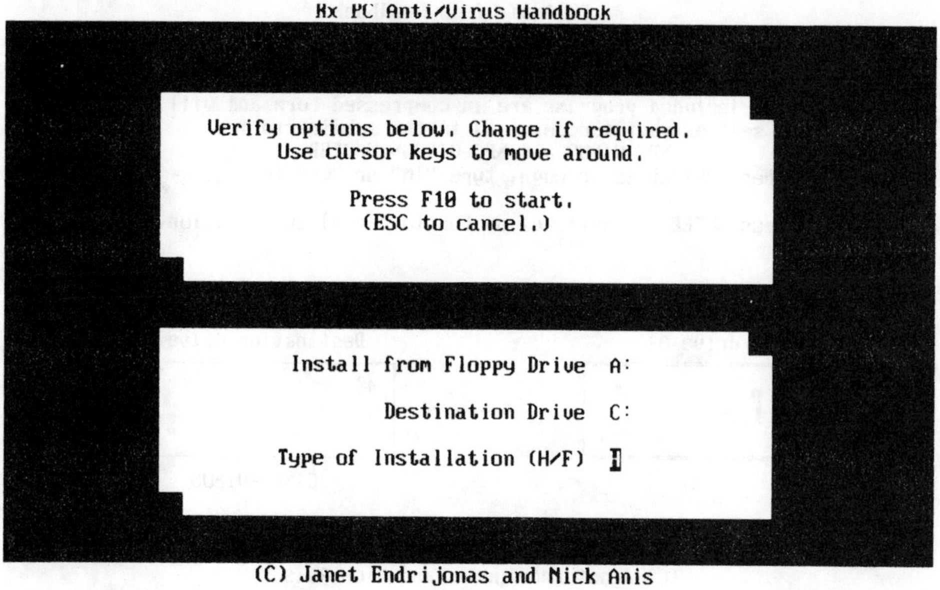

```
          Verify options below. Change if required.
          Use cursor keys to move around.

                    Press F10 to start.
                    (ESC to cancel.)



          Install from Floppy Drive  A:

               Destination Drive  C:

          Type of Installation (H/F)  ]
```

(C) Janet Endrijonas and Nick Anis

Fig. 6-1

To begin installation, type INSTALL at the A:\ prompt, and press <Enter>. The screen shown in Fig. 6-1 appears. Use the cursor keys to move up and down to change any incorrect parameter in the lower box, and when all are correct, press F10. The screen in Fig. 6-2 is displayed. The information in the top box is the same information you would have seen had you chosen to look at the README file above. When installation is complete, you will type IM to start Integrity Master or VC to begin using the McAfee programs at the DOS command line for the PC-Virus directory that installation creates. When you press <Enter> to begin the installation, you can watch the installation activity on the screen. When the extraction process is complete, the top box recommends that your AUTOEXEC.BAT file be modified to include the new directory path, as shown in Fig. 6-3. Press Y.

The next screen tells you that running SETUP will configure both Integrity Master and Virus Central (McAfee). Unless you want to abort the installation, press Y to display the screen shown in Fig. 6-4. The "Begin Update" option is highlighted when this screen appears. Unless you want to modify one of the settings on the right of this screen (remember that unless you are a programmer or a very experienced computer user, it is best to leave the defaults as they come in most anti-virus programs), press <Enter> to begin the virus list update. As soon as you do this, the list of defined viruses being entered into your system streams by, as shown in Fig. 6-5. Some have numerical designations and others—like those shown in Fig. 6-6—have names. You will also see a count of the number of virus definitions entered. At the conclusion of this procedure, the screen

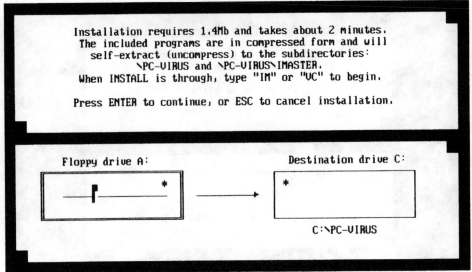

Installation requires 1.4Mb and takes about 2 minutes.
The included programs are in compressed form and will
self-extract (uncompress) to the subdirectories:
\PC-VIRUS and \PC-VIRUS\IMASTER.
When INSTALL is through, type "IM" or "VC" to begin.

Press ENTER to continue, or ESC to cancel installation.

Floppy drive A: Destination drive C:

                                   C:\PC-VIRUS

(C) Janet Endrijonas and Nick Anis

Fig. 6-2

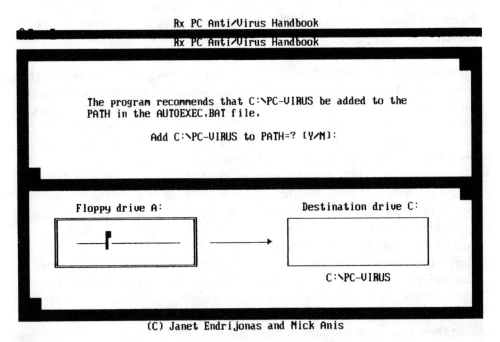

Rx PC Anti/Virus Handbook

The program recommends that C:\PC-VIRUS be added to the
PATH in the AUTOEXEC.BAT file.

Add C:\PC-VIRUS to PATH=? [Y/N]:

Floppy drive A: Destination drive C:

                                   C:\PC-VIRUS

(C) Janet Endrijonas and Nick Anis

Fig. 6-3

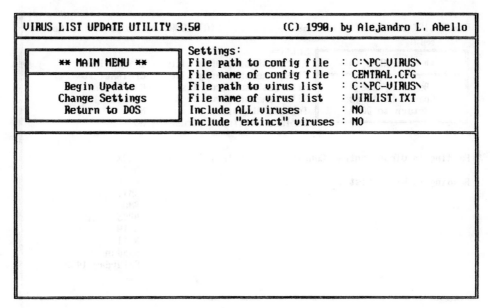

Fig. 6-4

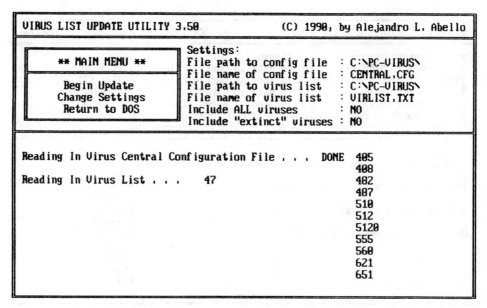

Fig. 6-5

shown in Fig. 6-7 appears, indicating that the virus list has been successfully updated. The "Return To DOS" option is now highlighted; press <Enter>.

One of the nice things about shareware is that it carries its own documentation on the diskette and all you have to do is read it on screen or print it out. You need

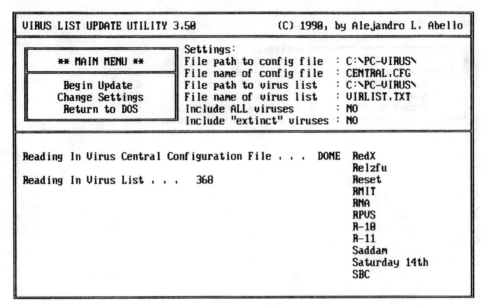

Fig. 6-6

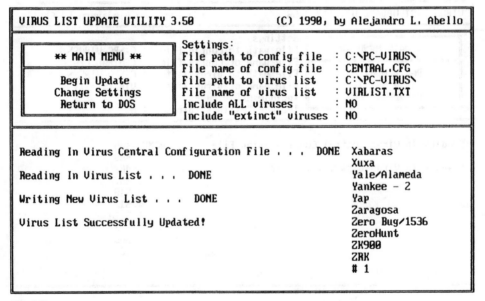

Fig. 6-7

only concern yourself with the documentation for the program you want to use at any given time. Again, these are no frills manuals—no pictures. Let this chapter act as your guide to using each of these shareware programs. There will be some screen shots in these pages for Virus Central, but beyond that, the McAfee programs use no graphics because they run directly from the DOS command line. Also missing from no frills software are some of the bells and whistles you've probably begun to take for granted in programs discussed in previous chapters.

Shareware and its documentation is provided "as is." There are no performance warranties, nor do the authors promise that their manuals won't have flaws. This isn't exactly something to worry about. While commercial publishers will replace a product if you find a legitimate bug, if you have read some of the earlier chapters in this book, you have discovered that their manuals aren't exactly error-free. These companies provide more technical support than many shareware developers, perhaps because they are in a better position to have technical staff to assist you full time. On the other hand, most shareware authors are more than happy to help you—keep trying their telephone number or leave your message on their BBSs. In the case of McAfee Associates, the exception proves the rule: This company offers its shareware users telephone, fax, BBS, CompuServe, and Internet access to their technical support.

The File Browse utility

One of the programs on your disk that has been put on your hard drive during installation is Alejandro L. Abello's File Browse utility. This program enables those of you who do not have DOS text editors, programs like X-Tree Gold that can read ASCII files, or DOS 5.0's Edit utility, to read the manuals on-line before or instead of printing. To use File Browse, type at the C:\PC-VIRUS prompt:

BROWSE <filename> <Enter>

The name you enter is the text file you want to read. This will be a file in PC-VIRUS directory that has a .DOC extension. To get familiar with the Browse utility, type BROWSE BROWSE.DOC and press <Enter> to read more about this program.

Browse is just a "look" utility. You cannot edit the file when viewing it with Browse. The cursor keys allow you to scroll up and down in the text; the Escape key is your exit. Text is displayed white on black by default. Those of you with color monitors will find instructions for changing the color scheme in the BROWSE.DOC file.

Virus Central—The shell

Now that you understand the Browse utility, look at the documentation for Virus Central (CENTRAL.DOC). Quickly read through it, but don't start to worry about much of what you read. The documentation contains quite a number of advanced options that aren't necessary to use the McAfee programs for adequate everyday anti-virus protection, detection, and removal. Virus Central is a shell program designed to simplify the use of McAfee's ViruScan, Net Scan, and Clean-Up programs. All of these programs (and more) are on the diskette that comes with this book, and were installed during the original installation process, whether you used the combination install program or the MCAfee only installation described first. The form of the program on the disk is Virus Central Lite.

Virus Central, which you start at the C:\PC-VIRUS DOS prompt by typing VC <Enter>, is menu driven with a text/graphics-based use environment that you can operate using either keyboard or mouse. The program has a built-in screen-saver that clears the screen after a prescribed amount of time (see details later in this chapter) to prevent screen image burn-in. Figure 6-8 shows the opening screen for the program; from here you move right to the copyright screen, which eventually changes to a series of displays of moving geometric designs (quite colorful if you have a color monitor).

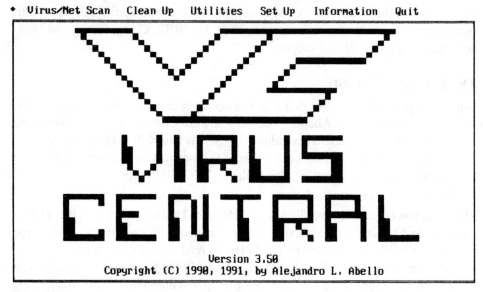

• Virus/Net Scan   Clean Up   Utilities   Set Up   Information   Quit

Version 3.50
Copyright (C) 1990, 1991, by Alejandro L. Abello

Fig. 6-8

The author of Virus Central, Alejandro L. Abello, says that the single most powerful feature of Virus Central is its Clean-Up sequence. As a disk is scanned using one of the McAfee Scan programs (either ViruScan for a single-user system or NetScan for a network), detected infections are placed in a queue. When the scan has been completed, Virus Central executes Clean-Up and passes the information in the queue to the program, automating the virus removal process.

You don't have to have a new or high-powered system to run the shareware anti-virus solutions. A PC XT or AT with 512K RAM is all that is required for Virus Central (CGA/EGA version) and 384K RAM minimum for Virus Central Lite. While it is possible to run Virus Central from a dual floppy disk drive system, the program is intended to run from a hard disk. Virus Central Lite can run with any video adapter/display and, as mentioned earlier, a mouse is optional. The program is automatically installed on your target disk (usually hard disk Drive C) once you have run the install program on the diskette that comes with this book, or used the McAfee only installation alternative. By the way, all of the McAfee programs on the disk can be run without the Virus Central shell; in fact, several of them do not even come under the umbrella of this shell program.

Figure 6-9 familiarizes you with the screen layout for Virus Central. Across the top of the screen is the menu. At the bottom of the screen are the hot keys you can use to scan a drive other than the one you have installed the programs on. The center of the screen is devoted to output from the McAfee program you are running, so you never have to leave the Virus Central screen to operate the programs or see what is happening while they are underway.

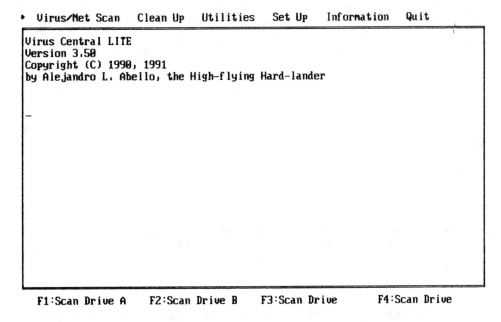

```
 •  Uirus/Net Scan    Clean Up    Utilities    Set Up    Information    Quit
┌──────────────────────────────────────────────────────────────────────────┐
│Uirus Central LITE                                                          │
│Version 3.50                                                                │
│Copyright (C) 1990, 1991                                                    │
│by Alejandro L. Abello, the High-flying Hard-lander                         │
│                                                                            │
│ _                                                                          │
│                                                                            │
│                                                                            │
│                                                                            │
│                                                                            │
│                                                                            │
│                                                                            │
└──────────────────────────────────────────────────────────────────────────┘
   F1:Scan Drive A     F2:Scan Drive B    F3:Scan Drive      F4:Scan Drive
```

Fig. 6-9

Even though the next few pages discuss many of the parameter changes you can make in the programs if you are so inclined, be aware that you do not have to make these changes to run the McAfee ViruScan, NetScan and Clean-Up programs using Virus Central. When you choose the program to run and get the pop up multifield screen, the only item to be concerned with is the first one. Make certain the drive specified is the one you want to scan or clean. If it is, press F10 to execute the program. If it is not the right drive, change the drive by pressing <Enter> to toggle the drive selection, use the cursor key to highlight the correct drive letter, and then press F10 to execute the program.

Use the cursor keys to highlight the item you want on the menu and press <Enter> to execute. If you choose Set Up, the menu seen in Fig. 6-10 pops up, and you can choose which part of the default setup you want to change. The highlight bar tells you which option you are choosing; move it with the up and down arrow keys, and press <Enter> to select. For example, when you select "Program" the screen shown in Fig. 6-11 pops up. Here you can make changes in the Virus Central program parameters. Use the cursor keys to move to the location to be changed, make the changes, and then press F10 to "okay" the screen.

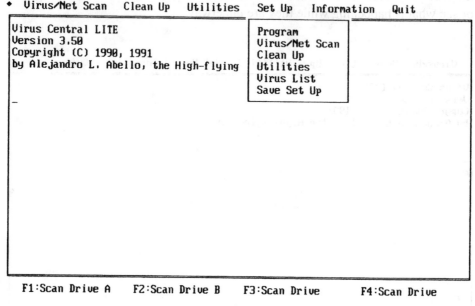

Fig. 6-10

You can work in as many or as few of the setup areas as you want—each has a pop-up screen to work with. When you have made all your changes, select "Save Set Up" and press <Enter>. This saves the changes to the CENTRAL.CFG configuration file and will take effect the next time you call up the Virus Central program. If you make any changes and forget to save them here, you are warned and given a second chance to save when you try to exit the program. To leave the set up area, press <Esc>.

You might have noticed an option on the screen shown in Fig. 6-11 called "Lock Configuration Options." If you want to make it impossible for others to access and modify the configuration options, specifically the first four choices from left to right on the Virus Central menu, you can change this option's default from no to yes. You would use this capability if you are sharing your computer with oth-

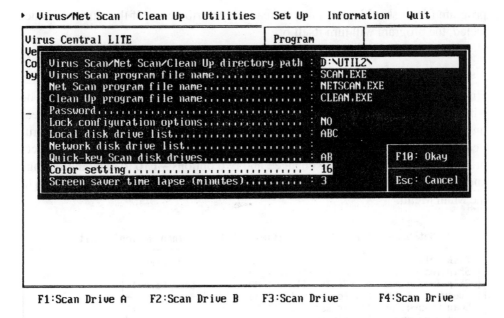

```
Virus Central LITE                          Program
Ve
Co|   Virus Scan/Net Scan/Clean Up directory path  : D:\UTIL2\
by|   Virus Scan program file name............... : SCAN.EXE
  |   Net Scan program file name................. : NETSCAN.EXE
  |   Clean Up program file name................. : CLEAN.EXE
 _|   Password.................................... :
  |   Lock configuration options.................. : NO
  |   Local disk drive list....................... : ABC
  |   Network disk drive list..................... :
  |   Quick-key Scan disk drives.................. : AB      F10: Okay
  |   Color setting............................... : 16
  |   Screen saver time lapse (minutes).......... : 3       Esc: Cancel


   F1:Scan Drive A     F2:Scan Drive B    F3:Scan Drive     F4:Scan Drive
```

Fig. 6-11

ers. When these options are in a locked state, a tiny padlock appears in the upper right-hand corner of your screen; any attempts to enter these areas will be refused without the proper password, which you can designate on this same screen. This is where you can also change the amount of time a screen stays on display before the screen-blanking takes effect.

Another option in the setup area is Virus List. This is the maintenance feature that makes updating and modifying the virus list used by the Clean-Up program easy. It is also the source for the virus list you see when you choose the Information option on the Main Menu. Using this feature, you can add, edit, or remove virus names, IDs, and individual virus information from the list. The list has a capacity of up to 16,000 viruses. By the way, since Virus Central requires a minimum of 30 viruses, you will not be able to remove the first 30 viruses listed.

One additional note about Virus Central. The program has a built-in integrity check that looks for modifications in its own code. If the program file has been modified, even slightly, Virus Central will not run and you will see a message telling you that the "Virus Central Program File Has Been Modified." While this message would normally indicate a virus in the Virus Central program itself, it will also show up if validation codes were attached to Virus Central by any virus protection program, McAfee or otherwise. This is something to watch out for if you start playing around with program parameters on the VirusScan/NetScan Menu discussed below or when adding switches on the DOS command line for either of those scan programs. And, because of the way in which Virus Central checks its program file, it should never have its read-only attribute set. If that attribute is detected, the program will turn itself off.

Using ViruScan and NetScan through Virus Central

Highlight Virus/NetScan on the Virus Central menu and press <Enter>. The Virus/NetScan menu, the top portion of which is shown in Fig. 6-12, will appear on the screen. This menu allows you to set the parameters for both McAfee ViruScan and NetScan and execute these programs. The menu has 29 fields that affect program operation and can be changed and two options—F10 to okay the settings and execute the programs and <Esc> to cancel any changes made and to return to the Main Menu.

```
 ◆  Virus/Net Scan    Clean Up    Utilities    Set Up    Information    Quit
┌─────────────────────────────────────────────────────────────────────────
│ ┌─────────────────────────────────────────────────────────────────┐
│ │ Disk drive........................ : [-A-]     F10: Okay          │
│ │ Skip inside scan of LZEXE files.. : NO                           │
│ │ Skip inside scan of PKLITE files. : NO        Esc: Cancel        │
│ │ Overwrite & delete infected files : NO                           │
│ │ Scan memory for all viruses...... : NO                         ↑ │
│ │ Scan high memory for viruses..... : NO                         ■ │
│ │ Scan all files................... : NO                          │
│ │ Scan listed overlays............. : NO                          │
│ │ Scan DOS 4.0X damaged boot sector : NO                          │
│ │ Skip memory scan................. : NO                          │
│ │ Scan multiple floppies........... : NO                          │
│ │ Scan using DOS error handler..... : NO                          │
│ │ Scan subdirectories.............. : NO                          │
│ │ Beep when virus is detected...... : NO                          │
│ │ Add validation codes............. : NO                          │
│ │ Remove validation codes.......... : NO                        ↓ │
│ └─────────────────────────────────────────────────────────────────┘
│
│
└─────────────────────────────────────────────────────────────────────────
   F1:Scan Drive A    F2:Scan Drive B    F3:Scan Drive    F4:Scan Drive
```

Fig. 6-12

The fields on this menu each correspond to a command line option that is found in the ViruScan and NetScan programs (see above), but instead of having to deal with DOS syntax, here you can work in plain English. You can click on a selection if you are using a mouse, or use the cursor keys to move to a field and use the Enter key to toggle a change. Use the up and down arrow keys or the PgUp/PgDn keys to move to the rest of the fields not shown on the first screen.

The only field that is not a straight toggle change is the first one. When you toggle this field, you will see a list of disk drives from which to choose by using the left/right arrow keys to position the cursor over the correct drive letter and then pressing <Enter>. You don't have to worry about whether to use ViruScan or

NetScan. Virus Central makes this determination for you automatically based on the drive specified in the first field.

The on-line documentation for Virus Central explains each of the choices you can make for the 23 fields, and also gives you a list of how each parameter compares to the ViruScan or NetScan command line parameters. If you are either curious or truly interested in these details, you can look at or print out the documentation (CENTRAL.DOC) if you haven't already done so. For the most part, except for choosing the drive to be scanned, you will normally want to leave the default parameters as they are.

Using Clean-Up through Virus Central

Highlight Clean-Up on the Virus Central Menu and press <Enter>. The Clean-Up Menu shown in Fig. 6-13 pops up on screen. This menu, with only 13 fields, works the same way as the one discussed above for ViruScan and NetScan. For details on each option and its corresponding command line syntax, refer to the on-line documentation for Virus Central (CENTRAL.DOC).

```
•  Virus/Net Scan    Clean Up    Utilities    Set Up    Information    Quit
┌────────────────────────────────────────────────────────────────────────┐
│Virus Central LIT│ Disk drive......................... : [-A-]   F10: Okay │
│Version 3.50     │ Check all files................... : NO                │
│Copyright (C) 199│ Clean listed overlays............. : NO     Esc: Cancel│
│by Alejandro L. A│ Check high memory for viruses..... : NO                │
│                 │ Check DOS 4.0X damaged boot sector : NO                │
│                 │ Skip memory scan.................. : NO                 │
│_                │ Clean multiple floppies........... : NO                │
│                 │ Generate CleanUp report........... : NO                │
│                 │ Pause on full screen.............. : YES               │
│                 │ Virus name........................ : Stoned            │
│                 │ Overlay extension list............ : .OVL .OVG .OV1 .OV2│
│                 │ Report file name.................. : NUL               │
│                 │ File path to clean................ :                   │
│                 └───────────────────────────────────────────────────────│
│                                                                          │
│                                                                          │
│                                                                          │
└────────────────────────────────────────────────────────────────────────┘
    F1:Scan Drive A    F2:Scan Drive B    F3:Scan Drive    F4:Scan Drive
```

Fig. 6-13

The major difference in using Clean-Up through Virus Central and using the program directly is the Virus Central Clean-Up sequence that places detected viruses in a queue as disks are being scanned and passes the queue information to the Clean-Up program when the scanning is finished. The queue process is automatic when you scan through Virus Central with either ViruScan or NetScan and, if you are working with a very large single-user system or a multiuser network, can prove quite a timesaver. There are several important things to know about this feature:

- The queue can hold up to 150 individual infections (hopefully you'll never have that many to deal with, especially if you follow the virus prevention practices outlined in Chapters 1 and 2 of this book). Should you have more than 150 viruses, ViruScan or NetScan continues the scanning, but Virus Central ignores subsequent finds.

- Virus Central always puts the viruses into the queue, even when you are running ViruScan or NetScan with the "overwrite and delete infected files" switch (/D) in place.

- The Virus Central Clean-Up sequence works on each individual file in which a virus is found, even if the same virus is found in multiple files— there is no "batch removal process" for a given virus.

- If the "attempt automatic clean up" option is off, Virus Central asks if you want to initiate the Clean-Up sequence for any infections that have been detected by ViruScan or NetScan. If you decline, the virus queue is not cleared and you are prompted to initiate the sequence, should you attempt to scan or clean another disk.

- To stop the Clean-Up sequence, press <Ctrl>–C. You can later restart the sequence. Be aware, however, that the virus being worked on at the time of the interruption will be removed from the queue whether or not it actually has been cleaned from your disk.

The Virus Central Utilities menu

Highlight Utilities on the Virus Central Menu and press <Enter>. The rather cryptic-looking menu shown in Fig. 6-14 pops up. This menu allows you to invoke a DOS shell to run a user-defined utility program, and return to Virus Central when the utility program terminates, while Virus Central remains in memory.

You can have as many as six options on this menu. One is defined by default but even that one can be changed. Obviously, before you can select an option, it must be defined—you cannot select a line of <<<<< >>>>> symbols. To define these options, back out using the <Esc> key to the Virus Central menu, move the highlight to Set Up and press <Enter>. Now move the highlight bar to select Utilities and press <Enter>. The screen shown in Fig. 6-15 appears.

Defining a utility is a two-step procedure. First, you give the utility a name; second, you specify the command line to run the utility. Whatever name you give it then replaces <<<<< >>>>> in the Utilities menu when it is next called up. When you have added your utilities, press F10 to accept or, if you don't like what you have done,

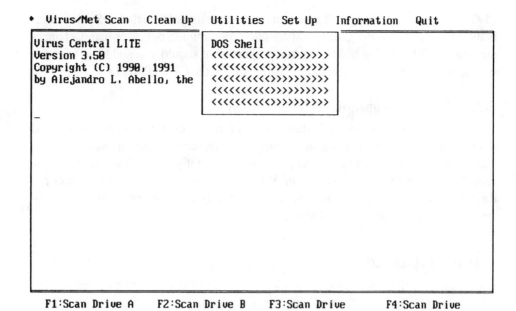

Fig. 6-14

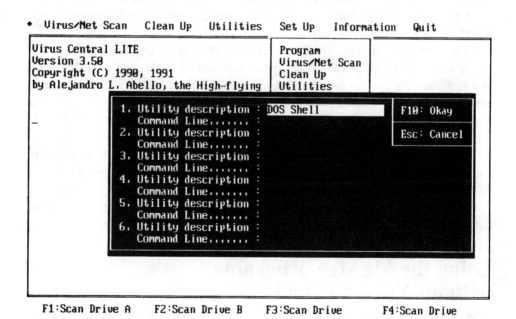

Fig. 6-15

<Esc> to cancel the changes. The command line designation tells DOS what command will start the utility. Unless you are into programming or power-using, chances are you won't be adding utilities to this program, but should you suddenly have the urge to do so, there are more detailed instructions in the CENTRAL.DOC file.

Other features to optimize Virus Central

Virus Central has a number of other features that are useful to some but beyond many users. These are detailed in the program's documentation in easy-to-understand language that should cause no problems—even if you are a curious neophyte rather than an experienced power user. Whether the switches and other features not discussed here are useful or necessary for everyday use remains up to you to determine, based on your individual needs.

Virus Update

On the diskette that came with the book is another utility program by Alejandro L. Abello (UPDATE.EXE) for updating the Virus List. This utility provides a faster way to update your on-line virus list than the virus list feature within the Set Up area in Virus Central.

Abello suggests that this program be installed in the same directory as the CENTRAL.CFG file and the VIRLIST.TXT file; this has been done automatically if you used the installation procedure on the diskette. When you start this program by typing UPDATE and pressing <Enter> at the DOS prompt (C:\PC-VIRUS), you see a main menu screen that is very familiar (see Figs. 6-4 and 6-5), since you saw it early in the installation process.

There are three options. The Begin Update option is the one you used to install the virus list in the first place. This program will read the version of VIRLIST.TXT you have on your system into the Virus Central CENTRAL.CFG file. When you get an updated virus list, all you have to do is copy it to replace the old list on your hard disk and then run this utility to update Virus Central and have the list ready for use by ViruScan, NetScan, and Clean-Up. As explained earlier, the first 30 viruses on the list will not change because of the program's minimum requirement and normally, the only viruses that Update includes are those that are marked as removable by the Clean-Up program. You can, however, reset this parameter (select the "Change Settings" option to do so), so that all viruses are included, even those that require a special disinfector and cannot be handled by Clean-Up.

Using the McAfee programs
without Virus Central

Aryeh Goretsky writes the documentation for the McAfee programs. He has done an excellent job, as you will quickly see when you use the BROWSE program described above to read the .DOC files that belong to the McAfee programs on the diskette. Naturally, since this is shareware, Goretsky has had to paint pictures with words, because the no frills approach doesn't allow for fancy graphics. He has written a quick-start guide for ViruScan and Clean-Up that is not on the diskette, but bears inserting in this book for your convenience. This is not meant to replace either the full documentation for each McAfee program, nor the discussion of the McAfee programs to follow.

I recommend that you print out each of the .DOC files to keep as handy reference if you are going to work with the McAfee programs individually, without Virus Central. These documents are clear and do not waste words. However, you need a basic understanding of the DOS command line to use these programs.

I have not stressed reading through the documentation before starting the other programs in this book, but with the McAfee programs, it is wise to read through the documentation before trying to run each program, so that you understand how to optimize the program at the command line. If you are the least bit in doubt about using the DOS command line, you will find the sample command lines provided by Goretsky in each .DOC file to be of invaluable assistance.

QuickStart for ViruScan and Clean-Up

Running ViruScan There are five steps to running ViruScan. Some of those steps are going to be familiar; none are in the least bit difficult.

1. Assuming you have installed ViruScan from the diskette that came with this book, copy the program files to a floppy disk in Drive A. It shouldn't be necessary at this time to tell you to make certain that this disk is clean and newly formatted.

2. Write-protect the diskette.

3. Put the disk into the infected PC and type:

    A:\SCAN C: (You can add D: E: if those drives exist)

    Note: If you are scanning the same computer on which you have installed these programs, skip steps 1 and 2 and at the DOS prompt (C:\PC-VIRUS), type SCAN with the letter(s) followed by a colon of the drive(s) to be scanned as in Step 3.

4. If infected files are found, they can be erased by running ViruScan with the /D (overwrite and delete) switch. With the ViruScan program in Drive A, the syntax for this is:

    A:\SCAN C: /D

    Be aware that running ViruScan with this switch in place deletes files in a nonrecoverable manner. Use this switch only if you do not want to recover the infected file(s)—otherwise use the Clean-Up program.

5. Turn off your computer to remove the virus from memory.

Running Clean-Up Before getting started using Clean-Up, it would be a good idea to print out the file called VIRLIST.TXT. This contains the list of viruses that can be removed using Clean-Up and their ID codes, which you will need. You will probably find this list very interesting reading, because it not only gives you a full list of viruses by name or number designation, it also tells you what each virus will infect, the increase in the infected program's size that will occur when it is infected (remember back in chapters 1 and 2, one of the instant recognition signs for possible infection was a change in the size of a program file), and the types of damage each virus can inflict.

Again, the QuickStart method involves five steps:

1. Copy all the Clean-Up files you installed on your hard disk to a clean, newly formatted diskette in Drive A.

2. Write-protect the diskette.

3. Power down the system and reboot from a clean write-protected system diskette that contains the same version of DOS as the infected computer. This reboot must be done to remove any viruses from memory that might interfere with the virus removal process. If you cannot access your hard disk after this reboot, double-check to make certain that any special drivers your system requires for hard disk access are on the floppy and being run from the CONFIG.SYS or AUTOEXEC.BAT file.

4. Insert the Clean-Up diskette into Drive A of the infected PC and type:

   A:\CLEAN C: [virus–ID–code] <Enter>

   You can add D: and E: if those drives exist and viruses were found to be on them as well. In the above syntax, consult the VIRLIST.TXT file you printed out earlier to find the virus ID code, and be sure to type the square brackets with that code. For example, the code for the Jerusalem virus is [JERU] so the Clean-Up syntax would be A:\CLEAN C: [JERU]. When you are cleaning out a file virus (as opposed to a memory infection), Goretsky suggests that you use the /A switch on the command line to check all files, especially those with overlay files that do not use the overlay extension recognized by the Clean-Up program. If more than one type of virus was discovered during the scan, Clean-Up will have to be rerun for each type of virus (this is where the Clean-Up sequence in Virus Central might be a better alternative than running Clean-Up standalone).

5. Turn off the computer and reboot from the hard disk.

Using the full
ViruScan version 8.4B89 program

As you have probably figured out by now, the SCAN89.DOC file on the diskette included with this book is the documentation for ViruScan. To get full details on the program, you can print this document. ViruScan works on any PC with 320K RAM running DOS 2.0 or above.

When you execute ViruScan, the program runs a self-test, and if it has been modified in any way, displays a warning. ViruScan continues to scan, but it is probably a good idea to obtain a clean copy of the program. The diskette with this book also contains the Validate Program (see p.109) to ensure the integrity of the ViruScan program.

ViruScan searches a PC for known computer viruses on hard disks and diskettes. It identifies the infection and tells you where the virus is located: in memory, boot sector, or file. As explained in the quick start section on p.105, by running the program with the /D switch, infected files can be removed with the overwrite and delete option. Or, you can go on to use the Clean-Up program.

This version of ViruScan identifies all 534 known computer viruses along with their mutations and variations. Counting all variations, McAfee Associates says there are 1,263 known virus variants, including the 20 most common viruses that account for over 98 percent of all reported infections on personal computers (see that VIRLIST.TXT file you printed earlier). When ViruScan finds a virus, it identifies the infector by name and Clean-Up ID code as well as location.

ViruScan also checks for unknown viruses using the Add Validation and Check Validation options. This is accomplished using the checksum method, calculating a checksum for the file and appending to the end of the file, and later comparing the file against it. If the file has been modified there will be no match. When run in the enhanced mode, the validation codes save information that can be used to restore whatever has been damaged by the infection of an unknown virus. You can also update ViruScan to look for new viruses by using the External Virus Data File option, which can provide ViruScan with new search strings for viruses. This latter is beyond what most of you probably know or care to know about viruses.

Several other features of ViruScan you should know about include the fact that ViruScan is trilingual. The program can display its messages in English (default), French, or Spanish. The program works on both standalone or networked PCs, but not on file servers; there you have to use NetScan. And, an aging notice is built into the program that warns you at the end of seven months that the program might be outdated, and you should be contacting McAfee Associates' BBS or the Virusforum on CompuServe to obtain updates.

ViruScan continues to function normally even after the message begins to appear, and if the message bothers you, you can turn it off by using the /noexpire switch. The default file extensions that are checked by ViruScan include .APP, .BIN, .COM, .EXE, .OV?, .PGM., .PIF, .PRG, .SWP, .SYS and .XTP. Additional extensions can be added or all files can be checked.

To start ViruScan once it is installed on your hard drive, at the DOS prompt (C:\PC-VIRUS), type SCAN. Don't expect a fancy graphic screen to pop up. You will see a list of switches you can use to tell the system what to scan. Use the PgDn key to see the full list. At the bottom of the list, it is suggested that you refer to the documentation (SCAN89.DOC) for additional options. To start the program's scanning operation, type SCAN followed by the drive designation with a colon, followed by the appropriate switch. To scan your entire C drive, the syntax is:

    C:\PC–VIRUS>SCAN C:/A

One of the features you can add is a bell to sound each time a virus is detected (/bell). This would make the syntax C:\PC-VIRUS>SCAN /A /BELL. You'll have to refer to the documentation, which contains a complete description of each switch, to learn all the possible switches and put together the combination that optimizes the program for your use. Each time you run ViruScan you can change these options to suit your current needs. In the documentation, you will also find a number of examples of possible combinations and the DOS syntax for each.

    If a virus is found, you can move on to the Clean-Up program to remove it.

Using the McAfee Clean-Up
program version 8.4B89

Clean-Up is a virus disinfection program that searches through the partition table, boot sector, or files and removes whatever virus you have specified. In most cases, Clean-Up is able to repair the damaged area of your system and restore it to normal usage. As I stated before, Clean-Up works on all viruses identified in the virus list that you printed earlier. The program runs on any PC with 320K RAM and DOS 2.0 or higher.

    When you start Clean-Up, the program runs a self-test and warns you if it has been modified. Clean-Up continues to remove viruses, but you should get a new clean copy of the program as soon as possible.

    As with ViruScan, the Validate program included on the diskette ensures the integrity of the Clean-Up program file. For the version of Clean-Up you will be using, the validation results should read:

    FILE NAME: CLEAN.EXE
        SIZE: 92,579
        DATE: 3-26-1992
    FILE AUTHENTICATION
    Check Method 1: CD93
    Check Method 2: 0769

    Clean-Up isolates and removes the detected virus, and in most cases, repairs the file and restores it to normal operation. There are times when a file is infected with one of the less common viruses that Clean-Up is not able to repair or restore, and the program will ask your permission to overwrite and delete, which, as you know, removes the file from your disk without possibility of recovery.

    The only trick to running Clean-Up is to remember to include the square brackets when entering the virus ID code. The documentation in the CLEAN89.DOC file includes a list of the viruses that Clean-Up can successfully remove while also repairing and restoring the damaged programs.

Before starting the Clean-Up program, it is important to turn off your system and then reboot from a clean, write-protected system diskette containing the same version of DOS as your infected computer. After you finish using Clean-Up, repeat the power down and reboot procedure using the clean system diskette, and then re-run ViruScan to make certain Clean-Up got all the viruses. When you run Clean-Up, it displays the name of the infected file and the virus found in it, and reports a "successful" disinfection when the virus is removed.

To execute this program, at the DOS command line, type CLEAN C: [virus ID] and press <Enter>. You can check one or more drives, so if you are looking for the Jerusalem virus on C and D drives and want Clean-Up to check all the files on those drives at the same time to be absolutely sure you got all the infections, the command line syntax would be:

C:\PC–VIRUS>CLEAN C: D: [JERU] /A <Enter>

The CLEAN89.DOC file has a list of the switches that can be used to optimize the operation of this program for your system and circumstances. It also contains some examples of the syntax for frequently used options.

About the Validate version 4.0 program

As you have learned, the diskette contains Validate version 4.0 from McAfee Associates, a file-authentication program that can be used to check other programs for signs of tampering, and is in fact used to check the other McAfee programs. Validate uses a dual cyclic redundancy check (CRC) system to provide a high degree of security. To confirm that any program is in its original state, run the Validate program on the original program disk, and record the validation data produced. Next run Validate on the copy that is on your hard disk, or the working copy you are using in floppy format. If the information matches, chances are very good that there has been no modification and the program is clean.

To run Validate, at the DOS prompt type VALIDATE along with the drive, path, and filename of the program you are checking. Assuming you installed Validate on your hard drive, the syntax is C:\PC-VIRUS>VALIDATE C:\WP51\WP.EXE to check the executable file in WordPerfect 5.1 as an example. The validation screen report resembles the one shown above for Clean-Up.

```
FILE NAME:     (name of file you specified)
        SIZE:     (# of bytes)
        DATE:     (file creation date)
File Authentication
        Check Method 1:  (a four digit CRC)
        Check Method 2:  (a four digit CRC)
```

The two methods for checking CRC comprise the dual CRC method. They are separate and distinct from one another. You can even validate the Validate program itself. The correct validation figures for the Validate program are given in the VALIDATE.DOC file on disk. This is a short document you might want to look at using the BROWSE utility rather than bothering to print it.

The McAfee NetScan program

Despite the fact that this book concentrates on single-user systems, there is a bonus on the diskette for those of you who also work on networks. McAfee's NetScan, the network-compatible version of ViruScan, is a virus detection and identification program for local (LAN) and wide area (WAN) networks. The program scans any DOS-accessible network drive for known viruses by searching the system for instruction sequences or patterns that are unique to each virus, and reporting any that are found. NetScan, like the other McAfee programs, runs from the DOS command line and offers a list of switches that can be used to customize the program to your exact needs. Details are found in the NETSCN89.DOC file.

The McAfee Associates VShield program

VShield is a virus prevention program. When first loaded, VShield searches your PC for known computer viruses in memory, the partition table, the boot sector, system files, and its own files, and then installs itself as a terminate-and-stay-resident program. After this, VShield scans all programs before allowing your system to run them, and if any contain a virus, VShield refuses to allow the infected program to execute. Additionally, VShield does not allow a warm boot from any diskette that contains a boot sector virus.

VShield can optionally check files that have been validation-coded by ViruScan for unknown viruses as well as for viruses as they are copied or accessed. The program monitors your system for viruses by checking programs for virus signature code, by checking the validation code added by ViruScan, or by doing both. Another program called VShield1, which only checks validation codes, is also included.

The VShield programs monitor programs run from any hard or floppy disk automatically. If you are in doubt as to whether you have the VShield programs installed in memory (after you install each by merely running their .EXE files at the DOS prompt), you can use yet another program—ChkShld, also on the diskette included with this book—to check if VShield is resident in memory. ChkShld, however, is mainly intended for network administrators to check various user's systems for VShield before allowing network log on. It is not recommended for single-user systems. If you are involved in a network and have reason to use ChkShld, you can find detailed instructions for its operation VSHLD89.DOC file on your disk.

VShield, like the other McAfee programs, can be run on any PC with 256K RAM (slightly less than the amount required by the other McAfee programs) and DOS 2.0 or higher.

VShield can be placed in your AUTOEXEC.BAT file so that it runs each time the computer boots up. You can place VShield in AUTOEXEC.BAT without a long list of switches and still get adequate protection. It monitors all program loads for viruses after having checked all the places where viruses usually lurk.

VShield has four levels of protection, and you can choose the level best suited to your needs. Level I is the VShield1 program. It uses the least amount of system memory and provides only minimal protection. VShield1 checks the CRC validation code values added to the programs by running VirusScan with the /AV switch. If the validation codes don't match, VShield1 does not allow the program to run. While this program also checks the partition table and boot sector validation codes, it might not provide enough protection in the long run. If your system can handle the larger, more complete VShield program, you are better off moving at least to Level II.

Level II is the VShield program. This program checks each program file for virus signature code or for a pattern unique to a virus strain. VShield checks memory, partition table, boot sector, and system files, and also runs a self-check before installing itself as a TSR. Once it is memory-resident, VShield checks each program as it is loaded, and if a virus is found, VShield does not allow the infected program to run. It also prevents a computer from being warm-booted with a diskette that has a virus in its boot sector.

Level III protection is a combination of Level I and Level II. To get this protection, run VShield with the /CV switch at the DOS command line.

Level IV protection has everything in Level III plus access control, allowing you to specify which programs can and cannot be run. For example, Level IV can be set up only to allow programs that are listed in the certification table to run; or perhaps, only to allow programs that have been validated by VirusScan to run. To get Level IV protection, run VShield with the /Certify switch at the DOS command line.

Level II, VShield without any switches at all, is probably adequate for most of you. Those of you prone to optimizing each program can study the switches listed in VSHLD89.DOC and choose those that you want or think you need for any given situation.

If VShield or VShield1 find a virus, you can use Clean-Up to remove it, or call in an expert in virus removal to do the deed.

Evaluation

Since you already have the McAfee anti-virus programs, they can act as a strong last line of defense as well as offering good anti-virus protection. They are certainly better than not having any anti-virus protection, detection, and eradication capability on your computer. With the VShield program, you have anti-virus protection along with the detection and removal capabilities of ViruScan and Clean-Up. Fortunately, despite the large number of programs involved, they each take up a reasonably small amount of RAM even when counted together. When taken all together the McAfee programs do just about everything most of the other programs do, but in a manual rather than automatic way.

These programs are limited, however. They are each individual programs, and aside from running ViruScan and Clean-Up through the Virus Central shell that is included here, each program must be run individually—a time-consuming effort that might cause many of you not to bother with virus-protection activities after the novelty of this book and these programs wear off.

Another limitation is that ViruScan does not provide automatic scanning capability from either AUTOEXEC.BAT or CONFIG.SYS at bootup. VShield, the virus protection program in the McAfee group that also performs scanning, can be automated. It can be placed in AUTOEXEC.BAT so that it installs itself each time the computer is booted, giving you detection capabilities and virus protection equal to any of the more expensive commercial programs.

Some of you might know how to write a batch file to automate ViruScan, but most of you are not able to do this, so you have to run each program in a manual sequence (except where you can use Virus Central, or if you put VShield into your AUTOEXEC.BAT file). Unfortunately, the more manual the operation, the greater the chance that you will not remain truly "virus vigilant" after a while.

Perhaps, for many of you, the most problematical drawback to the McAfee programs is that you have to have a fairly solid understanding of the DOS operating system in order to optimize these programs. Because these programs are no frills, they make the most of the capabilities of DOS.

It is suggested that you use these programs until you have evaluated other commercially available products and selected the one that best fits your needs. In all fairness, Clean-Up does seem to be one of the most efficient programs for removing a virus and restoring files to normal operation. Frankly, the graphics, color, and automation found in many of the other programs are more appealing to most computer users, and going beyond the basics of the quick start operation, most programs are much easier to operate and configure. On the other hand, if you are a closet hacker or someone who enjoys spending time at the keyboard, or very frugal, these McAfee anti-virus programs can be as effective as any others.

7
CHAPTER

Anti-virus programs worth a second look

In making the decision to cover a limited number of the commercially available anti-virus programs in depth, I had to bypass other anti-virus programs of merit, three of which are discussed in this chapter. Even with the addition of this chapter, this book still covers only a representative sample of the programs commercially available. I expect, however, that from the array of programs presented in the pages of this book, you will be able to make an informed buying decision and not have to search further to find excellent virus protection for your computer.

ViruCide Plus

ViruCide Plus is the latest version of the virus removal program from Parsons Technology. This program allows you to find and easily remove viruses from your computer system, as well as from any new programs you are introducing to your computer through network links or diskettes. ViruCide Plus includes both the ViruCide and ViruCide Shield programs.

Like some of the McAfee programs in the preceding chapter, ViruCide does not run continuously, and has to be invoked each time you import a file from an outside source. ViruCide also cannot restore files destroyed by viruses, and cannot reverse virus damage to files. On the other hand, ViruCide Shield, which is the virus prevention part of ViruCide Plus, is a memory-resident program that you can enter into your AUTOEXEC.BAT file so that it is loaded as soon as you boot your computer.

ViruCide Plus works on any IBM or compatible PC, XT, or AT. It requires 512K of RAM and DOS 3.0 or higher. As with all programs, before you begin to look at installation, make that all-important clean working copy of the ViruCide Plus diskette, write-protect it, and then store the original in a safe place. Put the working copy into Drive A and at the A:\ prompt, type INSTALL <Enter>.

The installation program is menu-driven, so you shouldn't have any problem. At the outset, you are offered the opportunity to read a file containing some additional information about the program—if you are installing ViruCide Plus under Windows 3.0 or on a Novell network, you should definitely read this file. Also, if you want to install ViruCide Shield so that a small face icon in the upper right hand corner of your screen is displayed whenever the program is active, this same file explains how to turn on this feature. Press <Esc> to exit this README file and begin installation.

The installation menus for ViruCide Plus are text, not graphics, and black and white, not color. The first screen asks you to designate the drive on which to install ViruCide Plus. This is most likely Drive C. Type C <Enter> The second screen shows you the default directory that will be created on Drive C during the installation. Press <Enter> to accept. You are then notified that said directory does not exist but can be created. Press <Enter> again to create the directory. Now the automatic installation procedure begins. Within a minute, the screen tells you that installation is complete—but there is one more step. You still have to add the program to your AUTOEXEC.BAT file in order for it to run at bootup. Use any ASCII text editor program, the EDIT program in DOS 5.0 (or if nothing else is available, the DOS EDLIN editing utility) to edit the AUTOEXEC.BAT file by adding these three command lines:

```
CD\ViruCide
VS
CD\
```

before any other executable files to be sure all executable files are scanned at each bootup. Remove the working diskette from Drive A and put it away carefully. Turn off your system, count to twenty and start it up again. ViruCide Shield will run a scan at the end of which, assuming no viruses were detected, it displays the screen shown in Fig. 7-1, and the program continues to run in background checking on all executable files as they are introduced to the system.

Using ViruCide Shield

If a virus was detected in that initial scan (or any subsequent scan), ViruCide Shield tells you whether it is in the boot sector or a file, and immediately stops your

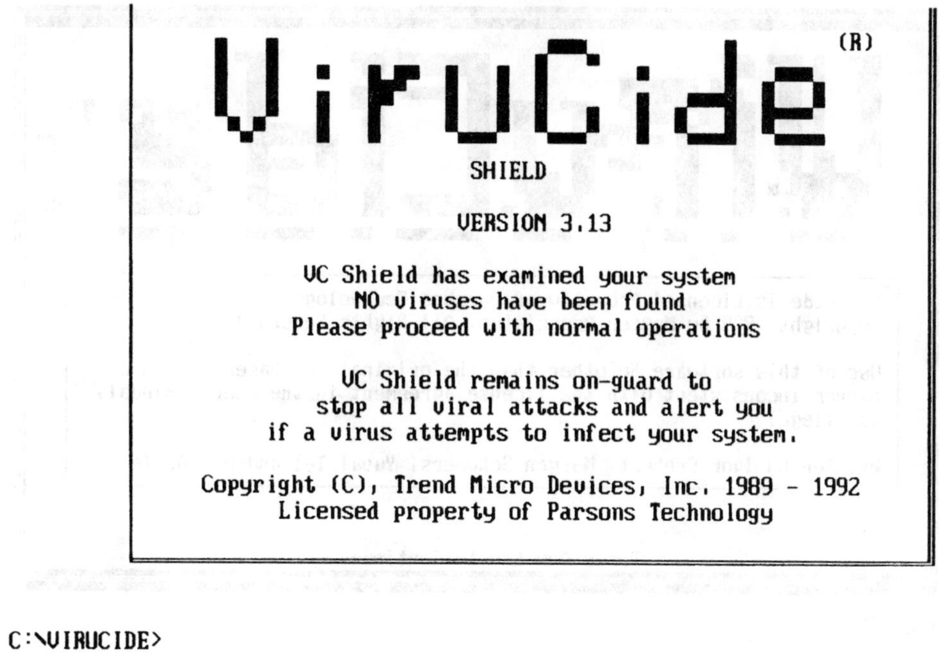

```
         ViruCide (R)
         SHIELD

       VERSION 3.13

  UC Shield has examined your system
     NO viruses have been found
  Please proceed with normal operations

       UC Shield remains on-guard to
     stop all viral attacks and alert you
   if a virus attempts to infect your system.

 Copyright (C), Trend Micro Devices, Inc. 1989 - 1992
    Licensed property of Parsons Technology
```

C:\VIRUCIDE>

Fig. 7-1

computer's operation. The manual that comes with the program has screen shots of
each of the warning screens you might see. Each screen tells you what to do about
the particular problem that has been detected, the most frequent solution being to
run ViruCide to remove the virus. This menu-driven program is one of the easiest
to work with in the event a virus is found.

Using ViruCide

To start ViruCide on your hard drive, change to the DOS prompt for the directory
that was created during installation (C:\VIRUCIDE), and type VIRUCIDE <Enter>.
If you are running ViruCide from a floppy diskette, put your working ViruCide Plus
diskette into Drive A and at the A:\ prompt, type VIRUCIDE <Enter>. When starting
ViruCide Plus from the DOS command line, you can optimize the program by using
one or more of a list of switches [/switch] in much the same manner as you learned
to do with the McAfee programs in chapter 6. All of the available switches are listed
in an appendix in the ViruCide Plus documentation, a much shorter list than the one
available for the McAfee programs.

When you start ViruCide, the program information screen shown in Fig. 7-2 is
the first to appear. Press any key to move into the program and bring up the screen
in Fig. 7-3. Before you enter a directory to search, press F10 to select your options.
The screen changes to offer what ViruCide Plus calls the "Options Menu" across

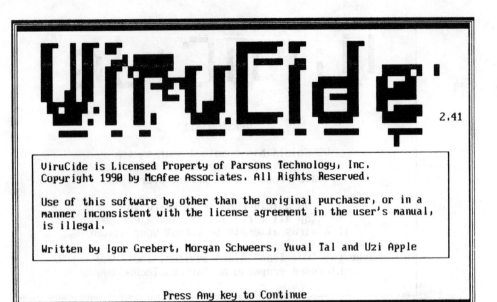

Fig. 7-2

ViruCide V 2.41

Currently checking:

Enter search directory
C:\..

N
Number of COM files scanned: 0   Number of infected files: 0
Number of overlays scanned: 0   Percentage of infected: 0%

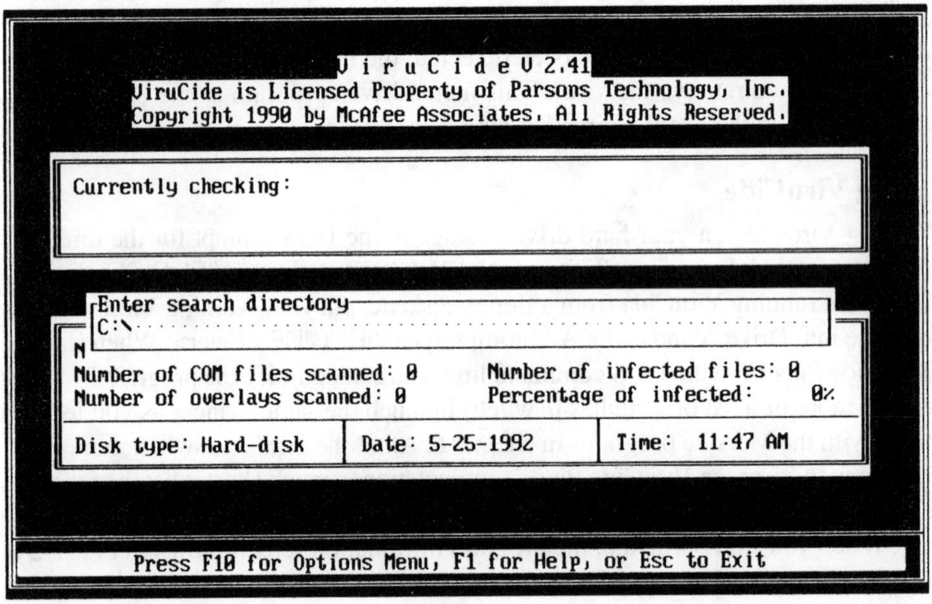

Disk type: Hard-disk   Date: 5-25-1992   Time: 11:47 AM

Press F10 for Options Menu, F1 for Help, or Esc to Exit

Fig. 7-3

the top, as seen in Fig. 7-4. Use the right and left arrow keys to highlight your selection, in this case Options. Press <Enter> and the menu shown in Fig. 7-5 pops up. On this menu, you use the up down arrow keys to move from one selection to another, pressing either the highlighted letter or <Enter> to toggle between yes and no and set each item.

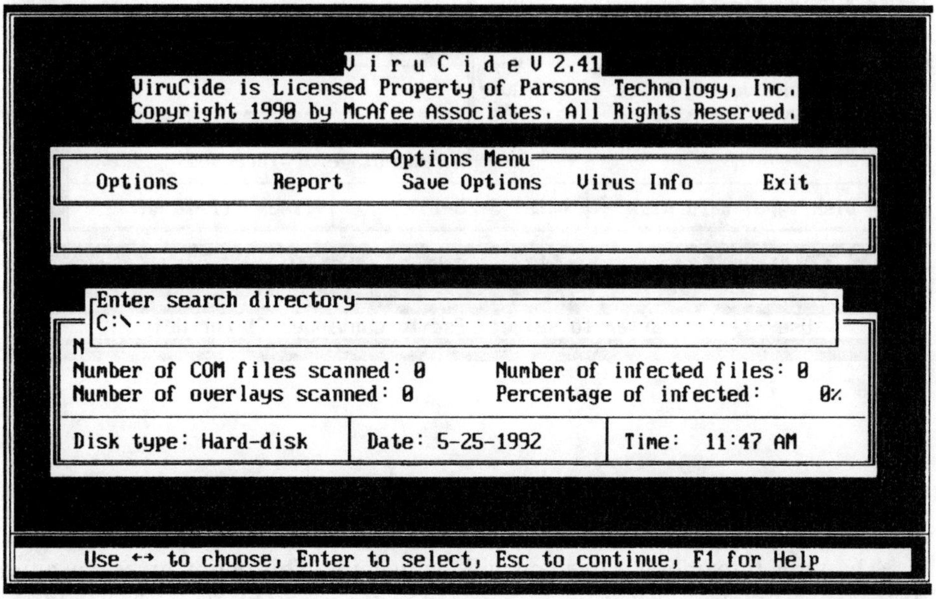

```
                    V i r u C i d e V 2.41
           ViruCide is Licensed Property of Parsons Technology, Inc.
           Copyright 1990 by McAfee Associates. All Rights Reserved.

        ┌────────────────────Options Menu────────────────────┐
        │  Options       Report     Save Options   Virus Info      Exit │
        └─────────────────────────────────────────────────────┘

        ┌Enter search directory─────────────────────────────┐
        │ C:\..............................................│
        N└────────────────────────────────────────────────┘
        Number of COM files scanned: 0      Number of infected files: 0
        Number of overlays scanned: 0       Percentage of infected:      0%

        Disk type: Hard-disk    Date: 5-25-1992      Time:  11:47 AM

           Use ↔ to choose, Enter to select, Esc to continue, F1 for Help
```

Fig. 7-4

After all are set, press <Esc> to return to the menu in Fig. 7-4. By the way, if you are in doubt about any of these settings, press <Esc> to return to the main Options Menu and press F1 for Help. ViruCide offers some of the most complete context-sensitive on-line help available in an anti-virus program.

Another option on this menu is Report. This option lets you specify the type of report you want, and the destination for that report (either out to the printer or to a file on your hard or floppy drive). To set up your report, highlight Report Type and press <Enter> three times to view the choices. Then continue to press <Enter> until the type of report you want is displayed, after which you can use the down arrow key to select the destination.

Here you have two choices: to the printer or to a file on hard or floppy disk. When you select Printer, you get a list of four printer ports where you can send the report. In most cases the LPT1 port is where your printer is located. Then press <Esc> to return to the Options Menu. When you choose File for the destination, you specify a path and name for your report file, and then press <Esc> twice to exit

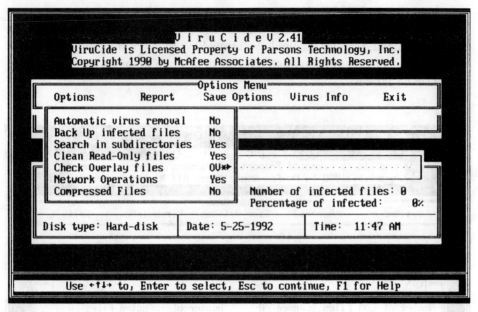

Fig. 7-5

back to the Options Menu. You can save what you have done so that in the future all reports will be printed or filed in the manner specified by using Save Options.

The Virus Info option is one you will really enjoy. This option gives you a full description of each virus that can be detected and removed by ViruCide. Highlight Virus Info on the Options Menu and press <Enter>. Two boxes appear, the one on the left contains ViruCide virus removal statistics, the one on the right contains the list of viruses. This is shown in Fig. 7-6.

Now, use the cursor keys to scroll through the list of viruses and select a virus you want to learn more about. When that selection is highlighted (in this instance, the Frere Jacques virus was highlighted even though the highlight could not be captured for reprinting here), press <Enter>, and a full description of this virus— along with words to the wise about cleaning this virus from your system with Viru-Cide—is displayed, on as many screens as it takes (see Figs. 7-7 and 7-8).

The Exit option is exactly what it seems to be, and takes you back to the original screen shown in Fig. 7-3. (You can also back out using the Esc key, which takes you all the way back and out to DOS if you desire.)

Now you can enter the search directory using standard DOS naming conventions. As ViruCide searches the specified path for viruses (this can be as broad as an entire directory or as narrow as a single file or anything in between), you see the search as it is conducted in the top window on the screen under "currently checking." At the end of the scan, you are given the opportunity to specify another path to be scanned or to quit scanning. At the same time, unless you have specified otherwise

```
┌────────────────────────────────────────────────────────────┐
│                    V i r u C i d e V 2.41                    │
│        ViruCide is Licensed Property of Parsons Technology, Inc.  │
│        Copyright 1990 by McAfee Associates. All Rights Reserved.  │
│                                                              │
│  ┌─────────────────────Options Menu─────────────────────┐   │
│  │   Options      Report    Save Options   Virus Info    Exit │
│  │                                      ┌───Viruses───┐       │
│  │                                      │F - Word      │       │
│  │                                      │Father Christmas     │
│  │                                      │Fellowship    │       │
│  │  ┌─── Version's Statistics───┐       │Finger in ears│       │
│  │  │List Version:    2.41      │       │Fingers       │       │
│  │  │Created on:      4-1-1992  │       │Fish          │       │
│  │  │Known Viruses:   920       │    Nu │Flash         │  0%   │
│  │  │Discrete Strains: 417      │    Pe │Flip          │       │
│  │  │File Viruses:    796       │       │Form          │       │
│  │  │Boot Viruses:    124       │ 5-25-19│Frere Jacques │       │
│  │  │Stealth Viruses:  25       │       └──────────────┘       │
│  │  └───────────────────────────┘                             │
│  │                                                            │
│  └────────────────────────────────────────────────────────┘  │
│      Use ←↑↓→ to, Enter to select, Esc to continue, F1 for Help │
└────────────────────────────────────────────────────────────┘
```

Fig. 7-6

```
┌────────────────────────────────────────────────────────────┐
│                    V i r u C i d e V 2.41                    │
│        ViruCide is Licensed Property of Parsons Technology, Inc.  │
│        Copyright 1990 by McAfee Associates. All Rights Reserved.  │
│                                                              │
│  ┌─────────────────────Options Menu─────────────────────┐   │
│  │   Options      Report    Save Options   Virus Info    Exit │
│  │                                   ┌───Viruses───┐          │
│  │                                   │F - Word      │          │
│  │  ═════════════ The Frere Jacques Virus ═══════════         │
│  │  -- General Description --                                 │
│  │                                                            │
│  │  The Frere Jacques virus is a COM and EXE file infector virus.  It │
│  │  infects executable files by attaching itself to those files, │
│  │  increasing their size by 1811 bytes.  This virus is memory resident, │
│  │  but is not encrypted.  Infection from the Frere Jacques virus occurs │
│  │  by executing any infected program.  After a system is infected, the │
│  │  virus transfers itself to any COM or EXE file that is executed. │
│  │                                                            │
│  │                                                   (More)   │
│  └────────────────────────────────────────────────────────┘  │
│                  Press Any key to Continue                     │
└────────────────────────────────────────────────────────────┘
```

Fig. 7-7

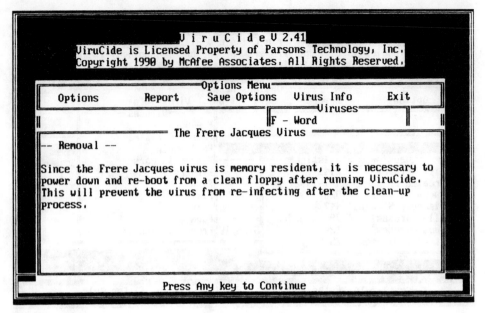

Fig. 7-8

in the Options area, a report is printed automatically. If you say no to additional scans, you are returned to DOS.

ViruCide can scan compressed files but cannot detect viruses when they are in compressed format. You must explode the file first. When the network option is set to Yes, ViruCide is able to scan and detect viruses in files on a network. By the way, if the network option is on, ViruCide does not scan the boot sector on local drives.

Removing a virus using ViruCide

ViruCide responds to a virus in the way you specified on the Options Menu. As with any other anti-virus program, ViruCide can detect viruses, but there might be side effects from removal attempts. This means that you might not want to set the program to do automatic virus removal when a virus is detected in a scan. Make certain again that the options you chose while in the Options Menu are correct, or go back and change them now. When you have finished searching a specified area and either found it clean or removed the viruses (remember that you can use methods like deleting a file and replacing it with a clean copy, rather than relying upon ViruCide or any other removal program), you can answer the questions on the screen, enter another search path, and start the process over again.

Optimizing the ViruCide Plus program

In addition to the use of switches on the DOS command line as mentioned above, you can configure ViruCide Shield in a number of ways to make yourself more comfortable working with the program—changing display features, customizing warning messages, and more. The program's documentation also includes instructions for creating an emergency disk with the files needed to start up your system should a virus shut down your hard drive.

Evaluation

This program is just about the simplest to install and operate of all of them. It doesn't take up much room on disk, can run in background, is as simple as the McAfee shareware, but contains well-done graphics to make using it even easier. While a little knowledge of DOS is helpful, each time you need to use the DOS command line (for example, for switches), the DOS syntax is carefully explained in the documentation.

The help screen and virus descriptions are particularly nice features, easy to access and use. For those of you who liked the McAfee virus list on the diskette with this book, you will find that this program is based on that list. In fact, if you look in the program's directory, you will find the VIRINFO.TXT file that contains the McAfee list. Technical support for the program is as good as any. You can reach Parsons Technology directly on telephone technical support lines, through CompuServe at GO PCVENC (you can get a free introductory CompuServe membership, thanks to Parsons Technology, as detailed in the beginning of the ViruCide Plus documentation), through GEnie, or by fax through Parson's Smartfax system.

Parsons Technology says that ViruCide Shield is equipped with artificial intelligence techniques that enable the program to detect as yet unknown viruses, which means you do not have to be worried about frequent updates. It is notable, however, that while the documentation for ViruCide Plus talks about two types of viruses, boot sector and executable file viruses, nowhere does it refer to viruses in memory, or how this program deals with such viruses.

VirusSafe version 4.5

VirusSafe version 4.5 is marketed by the same people who developed and sell the XTree line of file, disk, and information management software. The program is a collection of modules that offer a number of features, most of which should be familiar to you by now. VirusSafe can find and eliminate hundreds of known viruses in memory, boot sector, and executable files on both hard and floppy disks. The program can find viruses it has never seen before and recognize them again in the future, neutralize or remove most viruses, reconstruct any of its component programs in case of virus infection, and immunize memory against future viral attacks.

The program is menu-driven for easy use and has context-sensitive help for every command. The program can be used for automatic virus protection or run manually. You can search part or all of your system for viruses, and you have the choice of automatic virus removal or just a warning when a virus is found.

ViruSafe requires DOS version 3.0 or later and is fully compatible with DOS 5.0, Windows, GEM, and DESQview. Your system can be a PC, XT, AT, PS/2 or compatible with 256K RAM, a hard disk with a floppy drive, or dual floppy drives. For local area networks, there is a special version of ViruSafe available.

If you suspect your computer has a virus before you start installation, you know that you should power down, wait for a count of 20, and then reboot from a clean, write-protected floppy diskette with system files that match the DOS version on your computer. The steps for virus removal before installing ViruSafe (but using the ViruSafe program) are covered in the "First Aid" section of the documentation. They are also included on a "First Aid" card that comes in the package, a very handy guide that also covers standard virus removal after installation (which I will discuss later).

Installation

Make a working copy of the ViruSafe disk and put the original in a safe place. Place the copy in your floppy drive (ViruSafe can be installed from either Drive A or Drive B), change to the appropriate drive, and at the DOS prompt, type INSTALL and press <Enter>. The first screen you see is the one shown in Fig. 7-9, asking you to indicate the drive on which to install ViruSafe. As usual, the default value is C, so most of you will simply have to press <Enter> to accept the default. When you press <Enter>, a line to establish the \VS directory on the default drive is added to the screen. Press <Enter> to accept this default as well.

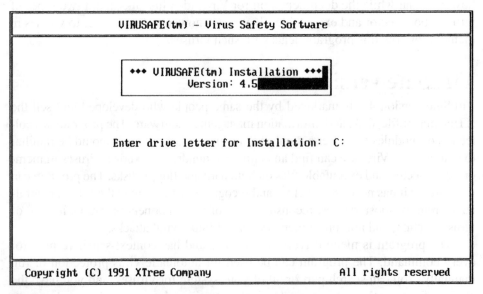

Fig. 7-9

It is time now for ViruSafe to scan your computer for viruses, as indicated in the screen shown in Fig. 7-10. Press <Enter> and let the scan begin. As with so many of the more graphical programs, you see the scan in progress, including a statistical report down the right hand side of the screen. At the conclusion of the scan, you see a report, hopefully telling you that no viruses have been found in your system (as shown in Fig. 7-11). After you press a key to exit the scan, ViruSafe copies its files to the C:\VS directory on your computer, and gives you a list of the files copied along with their definitions (see Fig. 7-12).

```
┌──────────────────────────────────────────────────────────────────┐
│           VIRUSAFE(tm) - Virus Safety Software                     │
├──────────────────────────────────────────────────────────────────┤
│                                                                    │
│          ┌──────────────────────────────────────────┐             │
│          │  ♦♦♦ VIRUSAFE(tm) Installation ♦♦♦█       │             │
│          │           Version: 4.5█                   │             │
│          └──────────────────────────────────────────┘             │
│                                                                    │
│                                                                    │
│          Enter drive letter for Installation:  C:                  │
│                                                                    │
│          Enter directory to install to:  \VS                       │
│                                                                    │
│  ┌──────────────────────────────────────────────────────────────┐ │
│  │ IMPORTANT:███████████████████████████████████████████████████ │ │
│  │ Before installing, VIRUSAFE(tm) will check for viruses in the computer.│ │
│  └──────────────────────────────────────────────────────────────┘ │
│                                                                    │
├──────────────────────────────────────────────────────────────────┤
│ Copyright (C) 1991 XTree Company            All rights reserved    │
└──────────────────────────────────────────────────────────────────┘
```
Press <Enter ◄─┘> to continue ...

Fig. 7-10

At this time, pressing <Enter> brings up the screen in Fig. 7-13. You can have ViruSafe modify your AUTOEXEC.BAT file so that the program runs automatically each time your computer is booted, or you can decline this modification. While I strongly recommend that you always accept these automatic run options in order to maintain your anti-virus vigilance without having to think about it, you can say no at this point and later change your mind and add ViruSafe to your AUTOEXEC.BAT at a future time.

As with any additions to AUTOEXEC.BAT, manually adding ViruSafe at a later time involves using a text editor program, a word processor that can handle ASCII text, the EDIT utility in DOS 5.0, or the DOS Edlin utility. ViruSafe, however, has made it easy by including its own text editor in the PCC.EXE file that has been installed to your disk. Run PCC.EXE and after choosing the Files option, press <Enter> when the cursor reaches the AUTOEXEC.BAT file, and insert the

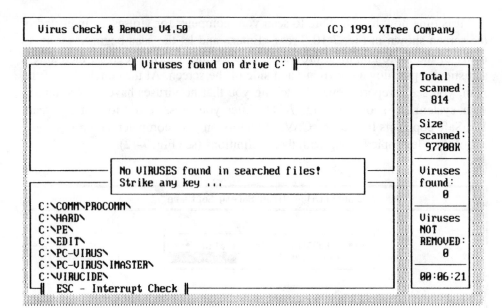

```
┌─────────────────────────────────────────────────────────────────┐
│ Virus Check & Remove V4.50              (C) 1991 XTree Company    │
└─────────────────────────────────────────────────────────────────┘

    ╣ Viruses found on drive C: ╠                    Total
   ┌────────────────────────────────────────┐        scanned:
   │                                         │         814
   │                                         │
   │                                         │        Size
   │                                         │        scanned:
   │                                         │        97700K
   │     ┌──────────────────────────────┐   │
   │     │ No VIRUSES found in searched files! │  Viruses
   │     │ Strike any key ...           │   │        found:
   │     └──────────────────────────────┘   │          0
   ├────────────────────────────────────────┤
   C:\COMM\PROCOMM\                                  Viruses
   C:\HARD\                                          NOT
   C:\PE\                                            REMOVED:
   C:\EDIT\                                            0
   C:\PC-VIRUS\
   C:\PC-VIRUS\IMASTER\                              00:06:21
   C:\VIRUCIDE\
   ╣ ESC - Interrupt Check ╠
```

Fig. 7-11

```
┌─────────────────────────────────────────────────────────────────┐
│           VIRUSAFE(tm) - Virus Safety Software                    │
│                                                                   │
│      Copying programs to your hard disk ...                       │
│                                                                   │
│      VSMENU.EXE      -  ViruSafe(tm) Main Menu                     │
│      VS.EXE          -  ViruSafe Resident Monitor                  │
│      VC.EXE          -  Memory Virus Check                         │
│      PIC.EXE         -  Program Integrity Check                    │
│      UNVIRUS.EXE     -  Virus Check and Remove                     │
│      VSCOPY.EXE      -  Virus-Free Copy                            │
│      PCC.EXE         -  PC Checkup Program                         │
│      READ.ME         -  Last minute updates                       │
│      VIRUSAFE.ICO    -  Windows 3.0 icon file                     │
│      VSMENU.PIF      -  Windows 3.0 PIF file                       │
│                                                                   │
│   All ViruSafe(tm) programs successfully copied, press <Enter ⏎> ...│
│                                                                   │
│                                                                   │
│ Copyright (C) 1991 XTree Company            All rights reserved   │
└─────────────────────────────────────────────────────────────────┘
```

Fig. 7-12

appropriate lines. You can find samples of these lines in the program documentation, but they must be modified to suit your system. They are also more numerous and complex than the lines you manually add to AUTOEXEC.BAT in other anti-virus software, so with ViruSafe, you are probably well-advised to let the program automatically alter your AUTOEXEC.BAT file.

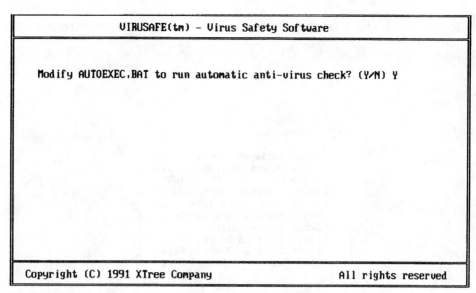

```
┌──────────────────────────────────────────────────────────────────┐
│              VIRUSAFE(tm) - Virus Safety Software                  │
├──────────────────────────────────────────────────────────────────┤
│                                                                    │
│                                                                    │
│   Modify AUTOEXEC.BAT to run automatic anti-virus check? (Y/N) Y   │
│                                                                    │
│                                                                    │
│                                                                    │
│                                                                    │
│                                                                    │
│                                                                    │
│                                                                    │
│                                                                    │
│                                                                    │
│                                                                    │
│                                                                    │
├──────────────────────────────────────────────────────────────────┤
│   Copyright (C) 1991 XTree Company            All rights reserved  │
└──────────────────────────────────────────────────────────────────┘
```

Fig. 7-13

After you either do or don't let the program modify your AUTOEXEC.BAT file, you'll have the opportunity to create an Emergency Rescue Disk to use in the event your boot sector, partition table, or CMOS setup information is damaged by a virus.

ViruSafe is consistent in its user interface so there are only a few commands you need to know to properly use what the program calls VSMENU. The up and down arrow keys position a highlight (move the mouse up and down to accomplish the same thing). Press <Enter> to select an option (click the left mouse button). The <Esc> key backs you out of a menu to the previous menu (click the right mouse button). While running VSMENU, available key commands are always displayed at the bottom of the screen. And there is help available for every menu option by highlighting that option and pressing F1. The PgUp and PgDn keys move you backward and forward by page. The Home key returns you to the first screen, the End key takes you to the last, and <Esc> or a right button click on the mouse returns you to the VSMENU screen.

When you first run ViruSafe, you are asked to configure your virus-monitoring activity using the menu shown in Fig. 7-14. Figure 7-15 is the Main Menu, and Fig. 7-16 shows the submenu for the Virus Protection option. The program is menu-driven in this manner throughout, making it one of the most complete and yet easiest to operate. For those of you who want to work harder, the program can be run from the command line, and can then be configured with all sorts of advanced options to optimize it exactly the way you want it. Figure 7-17 is an example of a help screen that was called up by pressing F1 to get help on a highlighted option.

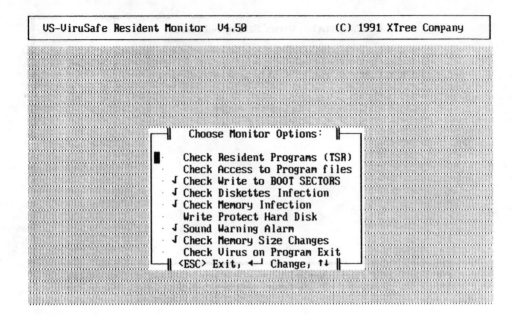

Fig. 7-14

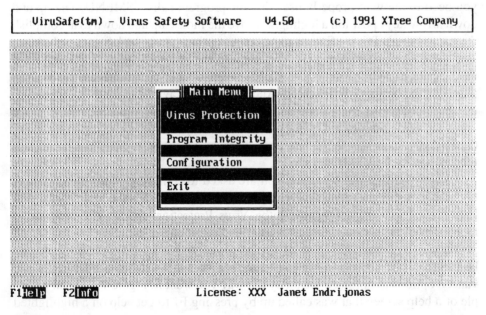

Fig. 7-15

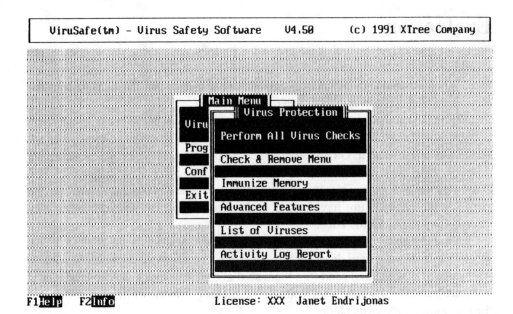

Fig. 7-16

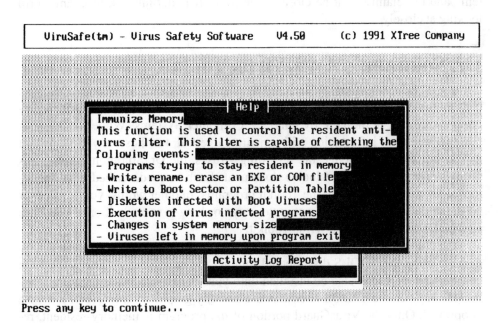

Fig. 7-17

Evaluation

There are no surprises with this program. It does everything a virus program should do and does it with an easily understood and followed menu-driven interface. When in doubt, there is excellent context-sensitive on-line help to complement very well-written and complete documentation.

While the program can detect as yet unknown viruses, it cannot remove them, but that is not a serious drawback in that you know you always can remove an infected file and replace it. On the other hand, the program does "learn" to recognize this new virus and stores its signature so it will recognize any further infection caused by the new pest. This, in essence, provides instant program updates for the virus list rather than your having to download a new list or—as with some programs—pay to obtain the latest list.

XTree Company requests that if you find a new virus, before you delete the infected file from your hard drive (or wherever it is located) you copy the file onto a well-marked diskette and send it to them so that they can find a way to eradicate it in future versions. By doing so, you will be making a worthwhile contribution in the continuing anti-virus battle.

You can operate VirusSafe in one of three ways: automatically; manually (running each program within the package separately from the DOS command line); or on a time-scheduled basis for your own convenience. If you are an advanced user, you can optimize the program by selecting many options using command line operation. In short, this program claims to be "The Most Complete Virus Safety System" and the claim might be close to the truth. It is definitely a program worth looking at closely.

Dr. Solomon's Anti-Virus Toolkit

For one of the most thorough discussions of each individual virus and virus type, pick up the operating manual for Dr. Solomon's Anti-Virus Toolkit, a British program distributed in the U.S. by OnTrack Computer Systems. While for many of you this wealth of information will constitute overkill, for those of you who want to become really knowledgeable regarding viruses, the Dr. Solomon's Anti-Virus Toolkit manual is a very valuable document. Each virus described also has removal instructions geared to the Toolkit programs. In other words, you need never be in the dark about a known computer virus or how to remove it once you have opened Dr. Solomon's Anti-Virus Toolkit.

The Toolkit can be run automatically from a floppy drive, or from a floppy diskette using the TOOLS diskette and running the individual programs from the command line. It may also be installed onto your hard disk. System requirements include any version of DOS later than 2.1 and any graphics card. Use of a mouse is optional. Only the VirusGuard portion of the program is memory-resident, requiring a hard disk or network access.

Installation

Installation is completely menu-driven. Boot your computer using a clean, write-protected floppy diskette that contains the same version of DOS as your system, and then place the Dr. Solomon's Anti-Virus Toolkit in a floppy drive. Log to that drive and at the DOS prompt, type INSTALL and press <Enter>.

The procedure is familiar: First, you select the drive on which to install the program, as shown in Fig. 7-18. Next you are asked to name the directory to install the Toolkit to, as shown in Fig. 7-19. When you press <Enter> the screen in Fig. 7-20 appears with the default directory name; to accept the default, just press <Enter>. The Toolkit is then automatically loaded onto your hard drive.

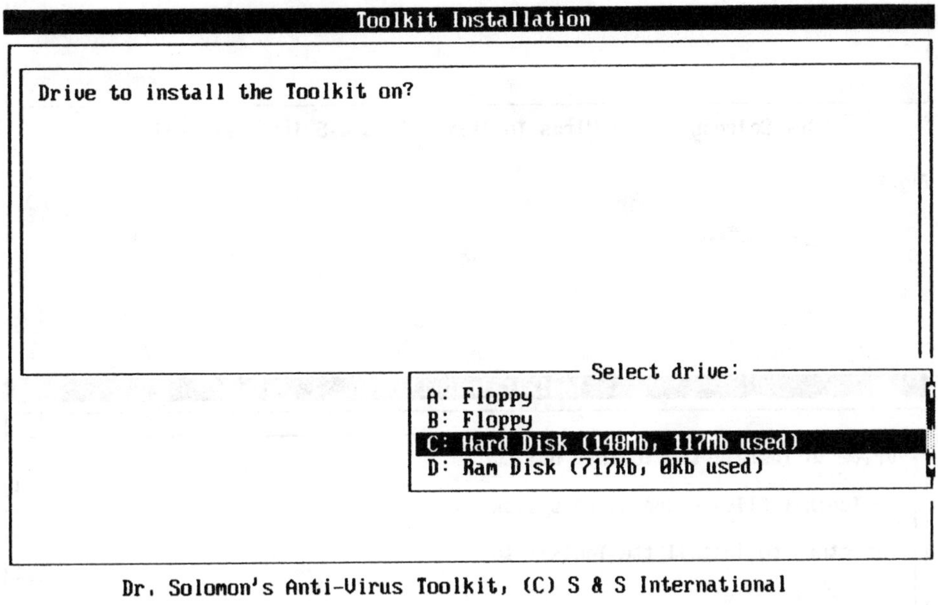

```
╔══════════════════════════════════════════════════════════╗
║                    Toolkit Installation                  ║
╠══════════════════════════════════════════════════════════╣
║                                                          ║
║  Drive to install the Toolkit on?                        ║
║                                                          ║
║                                                          ║
║                                                          ║
║                                                          ║
║                                                          ║
║                                                          ║
║                                                          ║
║                              ┌─ Select drive: ──────┐    ║
║                              │ A: Floppy            │    ║
║                              │ B: Floppy            │    ║
║                              │ C: Hard Disk (148Mb, 117Mb used) │
║                              │ D: Ram Disk (717Kb, 0Kb used)  │
║                              └────────────────────────┘   ║
║                                                          ║
╚══════════════════════════════════════════════════════════╝
      Dr. Solomon's Anti-Virus Toolkit, (C) S & S International
```

Fig. 7-18

Next, as seen in Fig. 7-21, you can install Toolkit into your AUTOEXEC.BAT file so that it becomes memory-resident and scans each time you boot up your computer. Or, if you prefer, you can elect not to put the program into AUTOEXEC.BAT (replace the Y with an N on the screen shown in Fig. 7-21), and run each component of the package on its own from the DOS command line. If you say yes to the AUTOEXEC.BAT installation, you see the screen shown in Fig. 7-22. As usual, unless you have a special need, the defaults shown should be accepted; press F10.

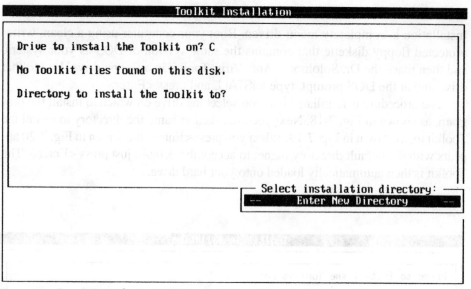

```
┌──────────────────── Toolkit Installation ────────────────────┐
│                                                               │
│ ┌───────────────────────────────────────────────────────────┐ │
│ │ Drive to install the Toolkit on? C                        │ │
│ │                                                           │ │
│ │ No Toolkit files found on this disk.                      │ │
│ │                                                           │ │
│ │ Directory to install the Toolkit to?                      │ │
│ │                                                           │ │
│ │                                                           │ │
│ │                                                           │ │
│ │                                                           │ │
│ │                                                           │ │
│ │                          ┌─ Select installation directory: ─┐
│ │                          │═══     Enter New Directory    ═══│
│ │                          └──────────────────────────────────┘
│ └───────────────────────────────────────────────────────────┘ │
│                                                               │
│                                                               │
│                                                               │
└───────────────────────────────────────────────────────────────┘
      Dr. Solomon's Anti-Virus Toolkit, (C) S & S International
```

Fig. 7-19

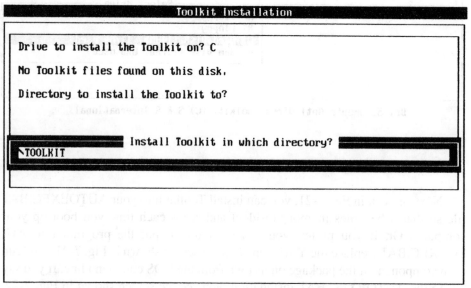

```
┌──────────────────── Toolkit Installation ────────────────────┐
│                                                               │
│ ┌───────────────────────────────────────────────────────────┐ │
│ │ Drive to install the Toolkit on? C                        │ │
│ │                                                           │ │
│ │ No Toolkit files found on this disk.                      │ │
│ │                                                           │ │
│ │ Directory to install the Toolkit to?                      │ │
│ │                                                           │ │
│ │                                                           │ │
│ │          ████ Install Toolkit in which directory? ████    │ │
│ │ ┌───────────────────────────────────────────────────────┐ │ │
│ │ │\TOOLKIT                                               │ │ │
│ │ └───────────────────────────────────────────────────────┘ │ │
│ │                                                           │ │
│ └───────────────────────────────────────────────────────────┘ │
│                                                               │
│                                                               │
│                                                               │
└───────────────────────────────────────────────────────────────┘
      Dr. Solomon's Anti-Virus Toolkit, (C) S & S International
```

Fig. 7-20

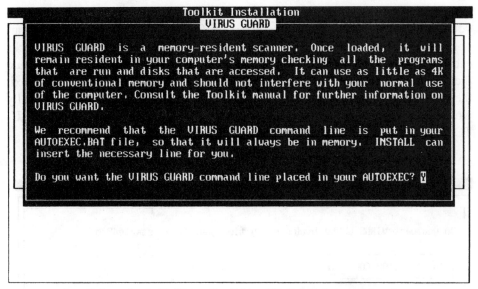

Fig. 7-21

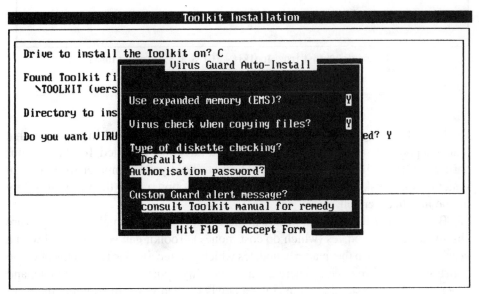

Fig. 7-22

Even if you say no to the AUTOEXEC.BAT question, you might assume that you can still ask the Toolkit to load the VirusGuard portion each time you start your PC, as shown in Fig. 7-23. VirusGuard is the part of the package that checks each program you load for all currently known viruses (except V2P2, V2P6, and their variants). The problem is, to change the N to Y to make this election, you exit the installation program and you can't tell for certain that VirusGuard is actually working. As always, the best solution is to load the program into your AUTOEXEC.BAT and take advantage of all of its capabilities automatically.

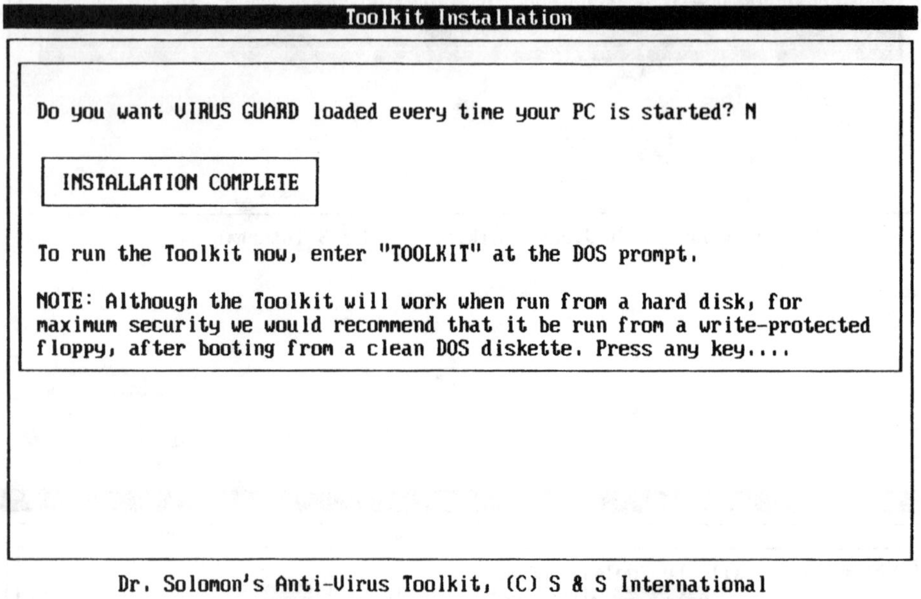

```
                        Toolkit Installation


    Do you want VIRUS GUARD loaded every time your PC is started? N

      ┌─────────────────────┐
      │ INSTALLATION COMPLETE │
      └─────────────────────┘

    To run the Toolkit now, enter "TOOLKIT" at the DOS prompt.

    NOTE: Although the Toolkit will work when run from a hard disk, for
    maximum security we would recommend that it be run from a write-protected
    floppy, after booting from a clean DOS diskette. Press any key....
```

Dr. Solomon's Anti-Virus Toolkit, (C) S & S International

Fig. 7-23

It is interesting to note that this is the first program covered in this book that makes a point of saying that even though you have just installed Toolkit on your hard drive, it is still a better idea to continue to boot your computer from a clean system floppy disk and run the program from a floppy, rather than relying solely on the installed version.

Be sure to use the registration card in the Toolkit package to make certain you are eligible to receive updates (which do cost money). Toolkit can be purchased with a year's subscription to the quarterly updates which you receive for 12 months after the registration card is received. There are also monthly update diskettes available, and Emergency Service should you uncover a newly created virus. In addition, there are faxed advisories to let you know when an immediate virus outbreak might threaten, as happened in March of 1992 with the Michelangelo scare.

Running the Toolkit programs

Most of you will be running the VirusGuard portion of the program automatically from the AUTOEXEC.BAT file and won't bother with the virus removal portions. To run the various programs within the Toolkit, on the command line at the DOS prompt (C:\TOOLKIT), type TOOLKIT and press <Enter> to start up the Toolkit and display the main menu shown in Fig. 7-24. Figure 7-25 shows the same screen after you move the highlight to "Misc. Tools" on the menu, press <Enter> to get the pull-down menu, make a selection on that menu, and then—rather than starting the operation by pressing <Enter>—you press F1 to get more information on your choice.

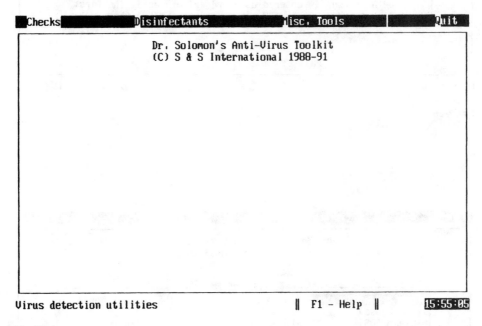

Fig. 7-24

You can also get information on any choice in the system from the menu shown in Fig. 7-26. This is the index that you get through F1 either from the Main Menu without pulling down a submenu, or by pressing F1 a second time after you have read the help screen as shown back in Fig. 7-25. When you highlight a topic and press <Enter>, you get the help screens for that topic. Since Toolkit is made up of a much larger number of programs than most of the anti-virus software you have been reading about up until now, you might need to refer to this help quite often (you can easily find the same information in greater detail in the documentation if you are one of the rare individuals who is patient enough to read the manual).

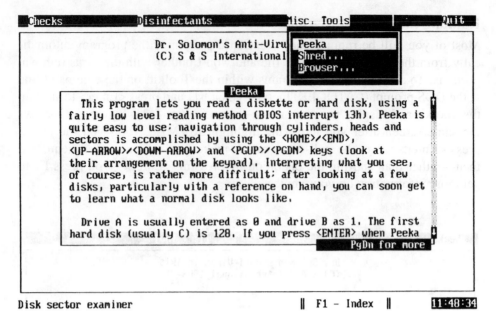

Fig. 7-25

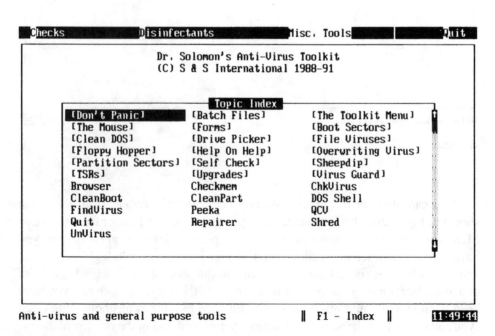

Anti-virus and general purpose tools ‖ F1 - Index ‖ 11:49:44

Fig. 7-26

Evaluation

This program is about as complete as they come and is easily run using the menu-driven interface. The manual, with its wealth of information on viruses and anti-virus protection and prevention techniques is in many ways worth the cost of the program. Since only the VirusGuard portion of the program is memory-resident, Toolkit does not take up an inordinate amount of precious RAM (about 4.5K).

For those of you who want to install and forget it until there is a problem, Toolkit is as automatic as any anti-virus program available once added to AUTOEXEC.BAT. When there is a problem, a full spectrum of tools is available to handle it, along with plenty of clearly written instruction to help you make the right choices and take care of the problem. You can choose to run all the other parts through the graphical menus or, for those of you who are DOS command line addicts, directly from the command line. It is the only program that offers the opportunity to load into high memory (386 systems and above) with just the push of a key.

VirusGuard—the automatic detection program—is virus-specific and requires constant updates, adding to the overall cost of using this program. However, you might consider this a small price to pay for the valuable information and thoroughness of this anti-virus package.

8
CHAPTER

Viruses can happen to anyone, anytime

Viruses can strike any computer anytime. Unless you are looking for a virus, you might very well not discover that your computer has been hit until damage has been done. When the pronoun "you" is used here, it can mean an individual, a network administrator, even an MIS director in a large corporation—no one's DOS-based computer system is immune to the possibility of a virus infection, and everyone needs to take every possible precaution, and provide for the possibility that in the face of even the most vigilant care, a virus might invade your system. There is no need to feel like the obvious victim, the most vulnerable and unprotected link in the computer-using chain when it comes to virus infections. Even the mighty have fallen prey to unexpected blindside attacks from one or more viruses.

There are a lot of virus stories around that many of you have read or heard. Here are some stories that should be totally new to you. Most of these stories are anonymous because many of the folks involved are too embarrassed by what they allowed to happen to let their names be used. Each of them realizes that simple protection efforts could have prevented what happened if only they had been aware of these prevention tactics before their computers were infected—or if they were aware, had taken the time to put the preventive measures into use. In only one case was someone infected twice, at two different times, and only because he didn't bother to take proper precautions after the first infection. You can bet that he is taking the proper precautions today, religiously.

These are not mainly stories about computer makers who sent out systems with infected hard disks, though that has been known to happen and does form a part of several of the stories. These are not just tales about major software manufacturers discovering an infection in their product, which has also happened, and illustrates that software publishers can be just as negligent as anyone. These are stories about how everyday users' computers can contract (and have contracted) virus infections—it can truly happen to anyone anytime unless you are always on the lookout and always taking proper precautions.

An example from Europe

In its January 1992 issue, Virus News International (VNI) published the following "Stop Press" item.

> Welcome to 1992. The cover disk of a magazine called *PC Fun* has Stoned virus on the boot sector. The magazine is dated January 1992 and has the slogan "Only 4.99 (UKP) For An Action Packed Disc." We purchased a copy to verify the information submitted by a VNI reader.
>
> The magazine is available via news agents, mostly in the UK, but also to some extent in the rest of Europe. It is published by MC Publications, Ltd; their phone number is 0494 444821. We spoke to them, and they told us that the diskette had been mastered in Germany, and duplicated by Copytec Software Solutions. Clearly none of the German company, the UK associate or the diskette duplicator checked the diskette for viruses. Stoned is a very old virus, and we would expect that any virus checker at all would detect it. The masthead of the magazine states "every effort is made to thoroughly check the programs on the discs." It would appear that this does not include a virus check of the master.
>
> MC Publications inform us that 18,000 copies were distributed, and they expected that perhaps 7,000 would be sold.
>
> We're sure that you are already checking all incoming diskettes. Let us repeat once more, though. Check all incoming diskettes with your virus scanner.

If you had been the victim of this virus mini-epidemic, whose fault would you have considered it to be—yours or that of the disk maker and seller? While there is more than one point of view, you might have to take at least some of the blame because you failed to take proper precautions, even a precaution as simple as scanning the diskette before turning its contents loose in your system. As a victim, however, you would not have been alone—fortunately, out of the anticipated sale of 7,000 copies, at least one person not only checked the disk but reported the problem. Yet perhaps only a small percentage of people who obtained that disk either checked it or read the warning in VNI. Viruses are not an individual problem, but their detection and removal is an individual activity—the burden is unfortunately yours. The moral of the story is that you cannot rely on the integrity of disk makers and sellers, and this will become more evident as the stories continue.

The European example also shows how viruses do not respect national boundaries and are definitely not a localized problem. This story involves at least two—and probably quite a few more—European countries where even a single copy of the diskette was distributed.

These disk producers should have known better—they should not have released an unchecked diskette. Had the virus on the diskette been something new and exotic, there might have been some excuse for not catching it. The Stoned virus, on the other hand, is on every virus definition list and easily detected by every commercially available anti-virus software package.

Software developers aren't always wary

It is amazing how many people who should know better when it comes to viruses don't. Even companies that develop software are not always very savvy in this regard. For example, one such company that shall remain nameless was caught bragging about the fact that they had developed an operating system for personal computers with an architecture that prevented all the DOS viruses from attacking. Hence, they proclaimed, it was better to use their operating system (which emulates DOS in its user interface) than to continue to fight the virus problem in the world of DOS. This might be true—for the moment.

The company's top executives seemed amazed when it was pointed out to them that there were plenty of clever folks out there eager to try their hands at "inventing" viruses to infect the new architecture, and that once their product was widely distributed, they could be as vulnerable as everyone else. They could not deny this fact and could not cite anything about their architecture that might prevent programmers from creating a virus to infect it. The result, scratch one selling point that back-fired.

The case of twice bitten, finally wise

How about a case of one person with two boot sector viruses, Stoned and Michelangelo? No, his computer didn't have them both at the same time; Stoned came first and after removing Stoned, several months later Michelangelo turned up, in February 1992 to be exact, only weeks before the Michelangelo activation date. This story is one of those "if it can happen, it will" tales.

The computer user in this case is a "program collector"—he buys many of his programs in shrink wrap from what he thinks are reputable dealers, and he also accepts pirated copies from friends, especially to try a program before investing in the package. He doesn't try to fix his own equipment when it goes down—he takes it to a reputable repair facility. He hasn't been particularly vigilant in the past but today, nothing gets onto his computer without a careful scan.

He acquired the Stoned virus in 1991 as a "gift" from his computer repair facility. He took his system in because the monitor was flickering and in the process of using a diagnostic diskette, the repairman infected the system. Once home, he booted the computer and saw the well-known "legalize marijuana" message that indicates the Stoned virus and had to get help removing the virus. This removal was done by someone using their own copy of the Norton AntiVirus.

It is hard to say why, after having had one virus, he didn't install an anti-virus program with a scanner right away, but he didn't. Perhaps it was the "lightning never strikes twice" theory or something as simple as the odds against a second infection . . .. Well, the odds weren't as good as he thought. He went to his local computer dealer and bought a memory utility package for his system. The package contained a bit of extra unwanted value—the Michelangelo virus. Further investigation indicated that the store from which he bought the program accepted returns and probably re-shrink-wrapped them and resold them as new, not as uncommon a practice as one might wish. This time, the McAfee ViruScan program was used to find and identify the virus and McAfee Clean-Up was used to remove it.

Several program diskettes were damaged in these two infections and this user finally decided it was time to add virus protection to his computer system. He has since installed PC-RX and now says that he checks absolutely every diskette that comes his way, even his repairman's diagnostic disk.

Virus replications in geometric proportions

The fellow in the previous story had a run-in with a computer repairman's diagnostic disk, but when he reads this next example, he'll feel better about what happened to him. These are real stories although the old adage about truth being stranger than fiction might seem to apply to this tale of virus woe.

Many computer users have found that having a computer buddy, someone who knows as much or more than they do about computers can be very handy. A buddy is someone who can be called on the telephone for assistance on even the most trivial problems—you know, the ones that can keep you up all night and that once solved, make you scratch your head and wonder why you didn't think of that . . .. Computer buddies can be a great boon but they can also be dangerous, as the following virus odyssey attests.

A computer buddy (unofficial consultant) in Southern California had a job that took him from city to city throughout the Southern California area. In his travels, over the years, he met many people, some of whom he was able to engage in conversation on his favorite topic—computer hardware and software maladies. He carried one of those "Flip File" boxes filled with assorted software-laden floppy disks, including diagnostic software so, as a buddy, he could help his computer friends with problems as he passed through their vicinity. One day, while making a call at a major metropolitan police station, one of his police computer buddies told him that the departmental system was experiencing some anomalies. They were having trouble using their data base. For example sometimes record access became erratic. Other times the keyboard would freeze up.

The good buddy whipped out his trusty DOS system diskette, rebooted the computer system, and proceeded to use his diagnostic diskettes to check the system. Everything appeared perfectly normal, yet, when he ran the application the police were using, he thought he might have detected some of the symptoms about which they had complained. He wasn't sure about this, however, and since the diagnostics had checked out perfectly, there was no cause for alarm. Or so he thought. He even went so far as to transfer the DOS system files from his diskette to overwrite the DOS system files on the hard drive to ensure that if there was a problem in the system files, it had been eliminated. As you shall soon see, it's a good thing he left his telephone number with the police before he went on to his next appointment.

Several days later, he called on another computer buddy, a professor at a branch of the Cal State University system, where he helped with the installation of a new genealogy program and went on to clean up the computer's CONFIG.SYS and AUTOEXEC.BAT files as a favor to the professor. In return, the professor let him copy a great shareware game program onto the floppy disk he was using to edit the CONFIG.SYS and AUTOEXEC.BAT files. The diskette containing the editing program, to which he now copied the shareware game program, was one he had used at the police department; it had been infected by the police computer several days earlier.

Now, by using that disk to edit the professor's AUTOEXEC.BAT, the virus had been passed to the professor's computer. As a result, not only was the buddy's copy of the game on an infected diskette, but all subsequent copies of the game would also be infected. Since the professor was unaware of what had happened, he gave a copy of the infected game to the Laboratory Aide in the Mathematics and Science Lab, where there were some 30 or 40 computers.

While the lab doesn't allow game playing, students will be students. One afternoon, when a student had been left in charge of the lab, he and several of his colleagues decided to try the new game and as a result, infected the lab computers. Some of those same students, still not realizing that the game was spreading a virus infection, took copies along to jobs elsewhere on campus, including the college library and the administration office. It wasn't long after the game was played on a computer in the library that the same computer, now infected, was used to generate labels, thus infecting the label program, which was subsequently used by an assistant to the college president and thus moved all the way to the highest echelons at the school. Soon, computers all over the campus were behaving erratically . . ..

You'd think that by this point, the story would come to an end, but there is more. While the infection was spreading throughout the university campus, the police were continuing to pass the infection from machine to machine, both in the station and to the policemen's homes. One policeman was using his home computer to do desktop publishing—the invitations to his daughter's wedding. He worked tremendously hard on these invitations, wanting his daughter's special day to be perfect in every way.

Included on the invitation was a map that took him four weeks to create to his satisfaction. When the map suddenly vanished from the file, and he was left with text that resembled Greek, he became very angry; it was this policeman who began to trace the infection back to the source and discovered during this trace the involvement of the well-meaning computer buddy who had sensed the anomalies that were occurring but elected to believe the diagnostic software that said all was well. The policeman alerted a number of other people with whom the buddy had had computer contact. By the time the policeman caught up with the computer buddy, a virtual lynch mob was forming of the people whom the buddy had seen after picking up the infection at the police station.

Alas, the besieged buddy called a friend, began to regale him with this soap opera, and the friend immediately supplied a number of anti-virus programs to the buddy. Three weeks and some 3,000 disinfections later, the buddy had removed all the virus infections but he has never been able to remove the ill will created by this fiasco.

There are a few side notes you might find of interest. The original source of the infection in the police computer was a computer that had been impounded from a neo-Nazi group (one of their members had been collecting viruses and had inadvertently infected the computer).

Toward the end of the story, when the buddy's friend offered the anti-virus programs, the buddy, trying to be nice, offered to bring his friend some diskettes. The friend warned him that he could arrive with an Uzi submachine gun, a hand grenade—just about anything, no matter how lethal—but if he had even one diskette on him, he would be denied entrance. No need to tell all of you why, now that you've read this book.

Last, but not least, the former travelling buddy has a new job and he is definitely NOT working in the computer industry.

If you think this is an extreme story, think again. This actually happened. It shows exactly how easily and rapidly a virus infection can spread. There is no substitute for preventive measures. Considering how little preventive measures cost (some are more or less free of charge; they just take time), and how easy they are to implement (again, just a small investment of time), you would be foolish not to be very careful. How many times have you caught a cold from a friend who didn't realize he was coming down with the disease until after he had left you?

An example of haste makes waste—or does it?

A software developer who shall remain nameless was awarded a large contract to create a programming language and documentation for palmtop computers. The software was developed, seemingly without a hitch, but when it came to the documentation, the picture changed radically. While the software was ready and waiting, the company that the developer had subcontracted with to produce the documentation was already three months late and $40,000 over budget. The palmtop manufacturer was losing hundreds of thousands of dollars in advertising costs for products that weren't shipping when they were supposed to.

The software developer, when they realized the problem, immediately took the documentation part of the project inhouse and hired three technical writers to complete it. The files they received from the subcontractor were in Microsoft Word format. Only one of the writers was able to work with that word processor; the other two were only conversant with WordPerfect. Since the writer who knew Word was also WordPerfect fluent, he was assigned to convert the files from Word to WordPerfect.

Even though there is a conversion program within WordPerfect, the writer elected to use a sophisticated third-party conversion program. Unfortunately, the copy of the conversion program he used was infected, and after this program was executed, the infection spread to the workstation, and from the workstation throughout the company's local area network. Ultimately, all machine-readable copies of the documentation being converted were lost. Fortunately there was a hard copy of the documentation but since it was heavily marked up, they couldn't scan it back into the computer. As a result, they had to retype all of the documentation—the online help screens as well as the hard copy manual—after the system was disinfected.

The story might not have been so devastating if it had ended here, but it didn't. No one realized at the time that the virus infection had reached the software they were developing. After delivery and release date schedules had been readjusted, everything seemed to be back to normal. Then the new software language went haywire. Yes, they had backups. But they didn't know which version had what bugs that required correcting, which meant they had to retrace many steps already taken.

By now, the makers of the palmtop hardware were getting rather anxious. In the interests of getting product to market, the software developer gutted the new language by pulling out dozens of commands. The end result was that the originally agreed-upon compensation to the developer was cut in half not just for the late delivery but also because only a subset of the original product was delivered.

The moral of the story here is that a simple check of the conversion diskette before putting it into the system (or even after copying it but before executing it) could have avoided the entire problem. Instead, countless man-hours were lost, a marginal product was delivered, and a company lost compensation while incurring additional expense; not a way to reap profit.

Don't take shortcuts or else . . .

Briefly, there is the story of the shareware vendor who decided to save some money by accepting returns from end users and putting them back into inventory.

And then there was the shareware vendor who, rather than spend the money to make a second set of masters when someone wanted to buy them, sold his only set.

He began to rely upon copies of the copies he had in stock, some of which were returns and were virus-infected. He then used a personal computer rather than a disk duplicator to make copies of his copies to maintain inventory. He, too, accepted end-user returns, so some of the copies he made had virus infections and passed them into the PC he was using when he copied files into a subdirectory for subsequent copy making. In the end he wound up infecting his own system and his entire library of diskettes.

He advertised that these diskettes were "value-added" because he pretested each one to make sure they worked. Then he sold pretested software for less than his competitors were selling "untested" diskettes. He didn't, however, test these diskettes for virus infection—and as a result, he was selling a virus-added, as well as a value-added package.

No software is sacred or immune

A leading developer of network operating software (NOS) inadvertently shipped a version of the company's product that contained a virus. Fortunately it was one that proved more annoying than deadly and was limited to a certain class of computer.

When it was booted on an EISA-based (Extended Industry Standard Architecture) computer system, no ill effects were immediately apparent. However, when the system was rebooted, whether by the warm boot <Ctrl>–<Alt>–<Del> or by turning the system off and turning it back on again (cold boot), the CMOS and EISA setups for the system were wiped out.

It is confusing enough to most computer users to have to restore their CMOS settings (although most of the newer computers now have the CMOS setting in firmware right on the computer, so that you don't have to hunt through everything in your home or office to find the CMOS setup disk that came with the computer when you bought it who knows how long ago). In the case of both a CMOS and EISA setup disappearing, the problem is a bit worse, especially when it happens out of the blue ("the machine was working fine when I turned it off, and there is no logical reason why these setups should disappear . . .").

When EISA setup is involved, you do have to come up with a bootable floppy disk that contains all the appropriate device drivers, and then an EISA setup disk so you can tell the EISA bus which EISA devices are in the various expansion slots. The EISA software needed for setup is enormous—it generally fills a high density diskette and doesn't leave room for DOS system files, device drivers, and any other information you might need. (Just in case you ever get into a situation like this, there are many computer experts who suggest that you make your 1.4Mb floppy drive (3.5-inch media) Drive A in order to have just a bit more capacity than the 1.2Mb, 5.25-inch media offer.)

This problem might have been a virus and it might have been a bug. On the company's technical support bulletin board, in response to user queries, an indignant technical support specialist insisted that it had to be a bug, not a virus. Of course, this merely points up the fact that where many companies are concerned, when a program misbehaves, causing loss of data and a drop in productivity, if it's intentional, it's a virus, but if it is a result of company negligence or carelessness, it can only be a bug. To the user, the semantics don't matter. Either way it is bad news.

To add to the bad news, this company, except for the comments by the tech specialist on the BBS, never acknowledged the problem officially. When they did come out with a software update that alleviated the problem, they didn't bother to tell their user base. Nothing like paying for a defective product and being hung out to dry by the manufacturer as well.

Sneaker net might still be the safest

Many of you might remember the days when "sneaker net" was the only way to transfer files from one computer to another—in other words, by carrying a diskette from one computer to another. Fortunately, today the file transfer process can be automated using software. The latest version of an ultrapopular file-transfer utility program has an obscure virus-like anomaly that is causing users a lot of problems.

When transferring files that fall within a certain range of sizes, everything seems perfectly normal—the filename is copied over, each block copied appears normal, the file size appears the same in a directory listing, the date is right. This, however, does not reflect the true status of the transferred file because the last block has actually lost a dozen or so characters. If it is a text file, it can still be read, but it will be missing something. If it is a graphics program, it might be missing a small detail that can make or break a design. If it is an executable file, it might or might not run, and if it does run, might or might not crash the system in the process.

Once again, as with the network operating system example above, the company never publicly acknowledged the problem, and when a maintenance upgrade release was made available, didn't notify the user base.

This again brings up the question mentioned briefly earlier in this chapter that many of you are probably mentally asking yourselves right now. At what point is a software company obligated to notify users of a known problem they might not yet have encountered. Now, a companion question also comes to mind—is a software company obligated to provide an upgrade to fix the problem and if they do, should it be given to registered users free or should those folks have to pay for the upgrade?

Sometimes it pays to hire the right consultant

When it's time to install a network in your company, large or small, often you hire a consultant or a system integrator to put together and install just the right system. Hiring a virus-conscious network integrator/consultant can also be to your advantage, as one very successful engineering company found out not too long ago.

The engineering firm was highly automated, often exchanging diskettes rather than hard copy of documents (including proposals) with their long list of clients. When it came time to put in a local area network, the company hired a system integrator who began by scanning the workstations that would be part of the system.

Early in the process, the integrator discovered the Stoned virus in a workstation. They immediately suspended the network implementation plans and consulted with the engineering firm on how they should proceed. The engineering people decided to have the integrator check for additional infection and sure enough, further scans indicated that the Stoned virus had spread throughout the company.

There was no way to determine the origin of the infection, but there was no doubt that it was being spread within the company and probably to clients with whom disk exchanges were taking place. From there, of course, it was also being spread into the computers of each of those client companies, and on and on. The engineering firm had to go humbly to all of their clients and explain what had been discovered, and what the consequences to each of their clients might be. Fortunately, the clients took the news in stride—it is reliably reported that no lawsuits ensued, although the possibility certainly existed for such suits.

Before any network installation work could begin, the integrator had to set the clean-up wheels in motion, in this case using the McAfee programs. They scanned every single machine in the company, and wherever the virus was found, they set about cleaning it out. This isn't an easy task with a virus like Stoned that "nests." In some cases they found as many as 40 to 50 copies of the virus on a machine.

Unfortunately there is no quick way to know how many copies exist. All you can do is scan and clean, scan and clean, scan and clean until the scan shows no remaining copies, and a cold boot followed by another scan agrees. This was a costly process to say the least. In this instance, it took two technicians working full time just over a week to get all the copies of the Stoned virus cleaned out. This not only delayed the installation of a much-needed network, therefore reducing productivity during that time, it also cost the engineering firm a great deal of money to pay for the clean-up effort, even though they used their own personnel to do the actual scan and clean work. In addition, the integrator had to scan every diskette they brought back to their office, write-protected or not, to make certain they didn't bring any unwanted guests along from home.

This engineering firm and most of their clients now understand just how vulnerable companies involved in data communications and disk exchanges really are, not just on a sometime basis—such as when there is a virus scare in the media like the Michelangelo scare in March 1992—but every day in all their data transactions. This story illustrates a hard way to become a believer.

On the lighter side (if there is one)

One of life's embarrassing virus moments: A technician and salesperson from a network integration company were doing a site-audit prior to a possible installation. While walking through a corridor between a number of offices at the prospective client's facility, they suddenly heard every PC in the area begin to play Yankee Doodle Dandy. Fortunately, Yankee Doodle is not a destructive virus but it does have to be removed none the less. As a result, the integrator knew that this company would have to be disinfected before a network installation could be accomplished, and as a result, the company was first sold a site license on McAfee software, and then—when the computers were clean—it was possible to begin installing the network.

As most virus-conscious computer professionals will tell you, and this book has repeatedly stressed, you can't be too careful. Nor can you check your system too often in the fight against viruses. Viruses are becoming more sophisticated and causing more severe damage than ever before. In the case of networks, the integrators in these stories know they have to educate the network administrators, who in turn must educate the network users. It is the network administrators who must maintain, for example, a "quarantine workstation" on which any diskette that comes into the company, no matter what the source, is thoroughly scanned before being introduced to the system. For individual computer users, the need to scan incoming media and files is just as great. Though the devastation caused might not make as exciting a horror story on a single-user system as on an extensive multiuser installation, the damage to data and files is no less real to the owner who has to repair or attempt to replace what has been destroyed.

The view from the other end of the hotline

A well-known U.S.-owned diskette manufacturer has taken a very proactive stance when it comes to virus prevention. What was originally the manufacturer's technical hotline for people with disk-related problems now often resembles a virus call-in festival. Many people who think they might have a virus, know they have one, or just fear they might get one aren't that familiar with the various anti-virus software programs and developers, but they do know the name of the manufacturer whose disk they fear carries the infection.

This particular manufacturer, in addition to manning the hotline and giving out information on how to prevent viruses and where to find resources for more detailed information on the subject, also sends out a training force who talk at schools, user-group meetings, and various customer sites about how disks work and how viruses invade them.

The hotline attracts callers at all levels of computer expertise, from the very new beginner to people so advanced they could probably build their own diskettes in the basement if they could afford the equipment. What are some of the more common calls about?

Well, it seems lots of people have purchased diskettes at swap meets, so they have no idea of the source of the disks (what do you want for 15 to 25 cents?). Lo and behold, they bought the diskette because it contained a game program they just couldn't resist, but it also came with a bit of added value—a virus infection. So they call the disk manufacturer's hotline first to find out how to play the game on the disk (those swap meet diskettes don't come with documentation) and then to find out if the problem they are having with it is—could it possibly be—a virus?

Usually it really is a virus infection. These people haven't checked out the disk before or after buying. Perform a scan? What's that? Even with all the publicity that surfaces every time there is a virus scare, many people insist on the "it only happens to the other guy" theory and take ridiculous chances with their computer equipment. The frustrated technicians on the answering end of the hotline can only hope that the infection has not already been spread to the system, but the chances are high that it has.

Frequently, calls come from people who only read half the documentation that came with their anti-virus program, which they bought after they had reason to suspect their computer was infected, and sure enough it was. So they laboriously follow the procedure for detecting and removing that virus, and then continue working and spreading the virus because they didn't read the paragraph that said the virus might be memory-resident and won't be completely out of the system until the system is cold-booted and rescanned. The best anti-virus method is prevention, but if you do have to resort to detection and removal using anti-virus software, be sure to read all about the procedure, not just the part you want to read.

Then there are the folks who are sure the only way they could possibly have a virus is if the diskette manufacturer sent it along with the original disk. A large East Coast firm was positive it was not the source of the virus that suddenly began appearing on its disks. The firm called the disk manufacturer's technical support hotline and insisted the disks were responsible for the virus infection at their facility. Careful checking by the hotline technical personnel revealed that the control numbers on all the disks from their manufacturing operation that were being used by this East Coast firm predated the discovery (and as far as anyone knows, the invention) of the virus in question, so it couldn't have come from the diskette factory.

Eventually, they were proven correct when the East Coast company realized that while the building they were in on the corporate campus had never had a virus problem before, the next building over had had such problems, and since there was a sneaker net moving diskettes from the other building to theirs . . . well, you can figure out the rest.

When these technicians get away from the telephones and out into the field to talk to people, they continue to run into unusual experiences with viruses. In one case, a technician was lecturing to a group of high school teachers, who were working during their summer vacation on continuing education credits at a local university.

In the course of the lecture, the technician had occasion to talk about the Stoned virus and its "legalize marijuana" message. Suddenly, everyone in the room raised his or her hand, and they blurted out almost in unison that the message was familiar. Just that morning they had seen it on all the computers in a university computer lab.

When the technician visited the lab, he found the story to be true, and the lab personnel totally unaware of what was going on. Oh yes, they had seen the message, but it didn't mean anything to them—a student prank? Needless to add, the technician told them what they had and why they should get rid of it; he also suggested they alert their MIS director (or whoever was in charge of the computers) as to its presence, to start the director looking around campus to see how many other computers had been infected by diskettes carried from the lab to other computers. Here is a perfect example of the casual attitude some people, many of whom should know better, take toward virus activity—between media-covered virus events.

By the way, these hotline technicians have also discovered that there is a computer retailer in the Midwest who has hit upon a virus protection scheme to rival the "pet rock." It seems that for around $2.00, this store will sell you a "computer condom," in a little package. When you open the package, all you find is a write-protect tab, just like the write-protect tabs that come with every box of blank 5.25-inch diskettes you buy. Apparently people do like a good laugh because the gimmick is selling well . . .

A painting by Michelangelo
that the artist never envisioned

The following piece, written by science fiction author Rick Cook, is intended to amuse as well as educate. While it reiterates many points that have been made throughout this book, and even takes mild issue with some of the advice presented, it also gives you an interesting perspective on the news media and its involvement in keeping or not keeping the problem of virus infection in the public eye. The piece also recounts more virus experiences, and again raises the question of software seller responsibility to customers.[1-2]

I just touched off a stampede.

Oh, I had help. There were really a few of us who did it. Quite innocently, with the best intentions in the world and through actions which were eminently sensible at every step, we turned a fairly ordinary event into a mild national panic and a six-day wonder.

The worst of it is that thinking back on it, I can't see what we could have done very differently. We did what we were supposed to do, some others did what they were supposed to do and—BLAM! So herewith is my mea culpa and, perhaps, a cautionary tale about the way the techies, the media and the techie media interact and what you can expect from the brew.

For me, it all started with a letter. It was from a man I had talked to at the big Comdex computer trade show in Las Vegas in late October. He had been showing

[1]1992 by Rick Cook. Reprinted by permission.

[2]*Virus News International*, January 1992, Virus News International, LTD., Berkley Court, Mill Street, Berkhamsted, Hertfordshire HP4 2HB, UK, p.56.

a very nice graphics program at a table in an upstairs room of an Italian restaurant which was feeding a sort-of-Italian buffet lunch to anyone who wandered in off the street with a Comdex press pass. (At Comdex, unlike the real world, there is such a thing as a free lunch.)

Since the company was only a minor player in the saga, and since this thing has already hurt their business, I'll just call them Company X.

Anyway, here's the president of Company X along with one of his techies, crammed into a little room at the top of a narrow winding staircase with a dozen other companies, all demonstrating their products to any food-bloated member of the press corps who made the arduous effort to climb a flight of stairs to see them. I climbed, I saw, I complimented and he offered to send me a copy of the program for evaluation.

A couple of weeks later I got my evaluation copy. Then a couple of weeks after that, toward the end of November, came the fateful letter.

The letter informed me that a few copies of their product had left the factory infected with the Michelangelo virus. It told me that a disinfectant program would follow in a few days and what steps to take to avoid infection if my computer was not already infected.

At this point I suppose I should take a short detour into techno-babble to try to explain what the heck was going on. A computer virus is a small program that attaches itself to other programs to spread from computer to computer. When it reaches a new computer, it makes copies of itself and attaches them to still other programs to infect still other computers. Like a true virus, a computer virus is spread passively. Unlike a worm, which is another kind of computer pest, it cannot move from computer to computer on its own. It must be carried by an infected program.

Viruses are the work of computer nerds with too much time and far too little moral sense. There are probably a couple of thousand of them out there right now. All of them are spread by infected programs.

Because of the virus problem, there is a healthy trade in programs to detect and eliminate computer viruses. Some of them are free or available for a few dollars over the computer bulletin boards (which are also one of the main vectors for spreading viruses). Some of them are commercial products. Almost all of them have to be updated regularly because sickos are constantly creating new viruses.

Not all viruses are malignant. Some of them don't do much of anything except spread. Some flash messages on your screen demanding legalizing of marijuana, reuniting Gondwanaland or whatever. Some do bizarre things like making the letters on your screen drop into a disordered heap, or produce rude noises. A few are nasty, destroying data, making your computer crash or wiping out whatever information is on your hard disk.

Michelangelo is one of the nasty ones. It triggers when the computer's internal clock hits March 6 and proceeds to write over everything on the computer's hard disk. Since the virus writes over the data, it is unrecoverable.

I'd heard of this beast. Michelangelo (so named because March 6 is the artist's birthday) is what is known as a "boot block virus". That means it is only spread if you start your computer up using the copy of the operating system on an infected disk. Since most computer owners with hard disks start their systems from the operating system on the hard disk, and since boot block viruses can't be spread just by running a copy of the program, Michelangelo wasn't even particularly virulent as viruses go.

I thought of all this as I read the letter from Company X. The only thing that was even slightly unusual here was that this virus had gotten into a commercial software package. Normally commercial software is considered safe from viruses because the companies that write software and the companies that duplicate the disks for the software companies check carefully for viruses.

On the other hand, it isn't completely unknown for a virus to slip into a commercial program. The result is a hurried recall like the one Company X was instituting. Even though as a computer journalist my job is to be on the lookout for stories, I didn't think much about this. When my copy of the anti-virus program arrived a few days later I didn't even bother to check for the virus.

Then a few weeks later one of the other reporters on the Microbytes electronic news service I write for mentioned that another software company had shipped a few infected disks. I responded to his message on the computer network by mentioning my experience with company X. There still wasn't a lot of interest in Michelangelo as a story.

The reason is that almost everyone in the computer press got burned out on viruses years ago. There was a brief period when we tried to report on every new virus and every significant infection. We quit because A) there were just too many of them, and B) the story was always basically the same. "There's a new virus, here's what it does and the anti-virus programs have been upgraded to deal with it. Make sure you have a current release." Old hat and everyone who did much serious computing knew how to protect themselves anyway.

The other thing was the taint of commercialism that hung over virus stories. Anti-virus programs represent a healthy segment of the software market and the stories always quoted one or more makers of anti-virus software. In fact usually the source of information on the new viruses was the anti-virus companies. At what point, we asked ourselves, did this stop being a legitimate story and become unpaid advertising for anti-virus software?

The thing that tipped the scales for us in this case was when Microbytes got a message from a reader. He had followed up with Company X and discovered that Company X had been infected by a computer they had purchased from a mail-order house in New Jersey. What's more, the mail-order company apparently had shipped a number of infected computers and seemingly had no intention of telling anyone about it!

That was news. First because of the irresponsibility of the computer company and second because the virus was being spread by hardware. Most computers sold today come with the basic software already loaded on their hard disks, but this was the first time I'd heard of that software being infected with a virus.

A painting by Michelangelo that the artist never envisioned   **149**

After the Microbytes editor made a couple of attempts to contact the hardware company, he turned the story over to me and I took my first fateful step toward starting a stampede.

A quick check with the reader, an anti-virus company, company X and an attempt to talk to the mail-order house confirmed the story. Company X had failed to catch the infected computer because Michelangelo was too new for its in-house anti-virus program. More unusually, it was too new for the revision of the virus checker used by the disk duplicating house at the start of the production run. So less than a hundred infected disks were shipped and then caught, apparently before they could infect anything. The mail-order house wasn't talking but there was no sign they intended to tell their customers they had sold infected hardware.

I wrote all this up into a medium-long (500-word) story for Microbytes and once again I thought that was the end of it.

Which simply goes to show that us far-sighted professional prognosticators can be as deeply wrong as anyone else.

All through January a sprinkling of infected commercial software and hardware turned up. A company called Leading Edge shipped a few computers infected with Michelangelo. A couple of software companies announced infections.

Parenthetically, one of the reasons Michelangelo was so successful was that it apparently entered the U.S. computing mainstream just before fall Comdex. The autumn version of Comdex is the biggest computer trade show in the U.S. and the most popular time to release new and upgraded programs. It just so happened that the window of vulnerability before people got their virus checkers updated came during the time when everyone was scrambling to get stuff out the door for Comdex.

In any event, it was still no big thing. But Michelangelo was common enough in the very uncommon mediums of commercial software and hardware that the computer press thought it was worth mentioning. There were brief items in magazines like "PC Week" and "Infoworld" which are written for computer professionals. All of them mentioned Michelangelo and advised readers to make sure their anti-virus programs were up to date. Most of these stories were written out of a sense of obligation rather than the feeling they were breaking news, much like the stories that appear in newspapers just before a holiday reminding people that banks and city offices will be closed.

In late February the Microbytes staff kicked around the idea of doing a heads-up for our readers about the virus, reminding them to make sure to check their systems. I did another short story for Microbytes pointing out that Michelangelo's trigger date was coming and suggesting that readers check their systems.

By this time the Michelangelo story was taking on a momentum of its own. Small stories appeared in newspapers, mostly in the computer column or the technology and business section briefly describing the virus and how it could be combated. Some of these stories quoted makers of anti-virus software about the problem, including some wildly inflated figures on how many computers had become infected.

The technical press had pretty much ignored those numbers because we all know how speculative they were. Most of them were based on the sort of reasoning that starts "if you have X infected computers and each one infects Y more computers . . ." Which is to say the numbers were no better than the assumptions and the assumptions were pure moonshine.

We were gratified but a little bemused by the attention Michelangelo was generating. After all, it wasn't that big a deal. Just one more virus, right?

One more virus wrong. The story kept building until finally about ten days before M-Day when the popular media latched on to the story in a big way.

At this point another factor became obvious. Unlike most viruses, Michelangelo had a fixed trigger date. That gave the whole thing the air of a countdown. "X days from March 6 and counting." That added an air of excitement that most viruses lacked. Even if the idea of a virus was arcane, the target date wasn't. It added anticipation that anyone could understand.

Of course by this time the nuances were being lost. The stories in the popular press painted Michelangelo as a new and especially dangerous threat. They didn't quite call it the first virus but they managed to leave the impression that this was the first time computers at large were in danger. Michelangelo was now right up there with killer bees and holes in the ozone as something we all had to worry about.

And worry we all did. By the time the message had filtered through the popular media it sounded like the end of Civilization As We Know It. The distinctions had been lost and all a lot of people got was that if they didn't do something right now their computer was in dire jeopardy.

One result was that Michelangelo was the first computer virus a lot of people had ever heard of. Another was that there was a mad, frantic scramble to get protection. Several of the commercial software companies offered anti-virus or even anti-Michelangelo programs for free to anyone who would call in and ask for them. It sounded like a fairly inexpensive way to build good will but it backfired when the companies were buried under the tide of requests.

The week before I tried to call Symantec, one of the companies making such an offer, to talk about their new C compiler. The place was a madhouse. The phones were jammed by people wanting copies of the anti-Michelangelo utility Symantec was giving away.

This was not only out of proportion with the seriousness of the threat, it was also obviously out of proportion to the spread of the virus. Because it was a boot-block virus, Michelangelo wasn't very infective. Checks of computer systems across the country showed that only a very few were infected and those infections were rooted out as fast as they were found.

The techies and the computer press were learning a hard lesson about the mainstream media: They are an enormously powerful amplifier, but the granularity isn't very fine. Outside the areas where they concentrate—politics, government and crime—it is very hard for the media to make small distinctions, no matter how important.

One of the reasons is the nature of the business. Reporters are not, in general, technically oriented. Further, the system of assigning reporters to areas of specialization, or beats, breaks down when you move away from the issues where the media concentrate attention. Every paper has at least one police reporter but not many of them have computer reporters and the ones that do usually have reporters who specialize in covering the business side of the computer industry, not the technology. As a result most of these reporters failed to understand the nuances of the situation, especially since one of their major sources of information were the companies selling anti-virus software. The caveats and disclaimers got lost in the process.

In general, media are reluctant to exercise independent judgment in technical stories. It isn't just that the reporters and editors don't know enough to evaluate stories involving computers, molecular biology or other arcana—although that is usually the case. It is that they don't or won't talk to people who are knowledgeable about whether something is worth pursuing.

The result is that the general media are blown hither and yon on technical stories in ways that would be totally unacceptable on police, politics or any of the other core subjects the media cover.

The other problem is the demand for definitive answers to indeterminate questions. Since no one in their right mind would claim that the Michelangelo virus was harmless, it was obviously deadly.

Of course the mass media couldn't very well ignore Michelangelo either. With 70 million personal computers out there, it was a sure bet that at least some of their audience hadn't gotten the word through the computer press. Besides, if all these techies were worried about it, it had to be a problem, didn't it?

What could you say? Of course the Michelangelo virus was real. Of course it would do damage to an infected system. Of course you needed to have an up-to-date virus checker on your computer.

The thing you couldn't convey was how ordinary this all was. You always needed to guard against viruses. Michelangelo was no worse than hundreds of others which infected people's systems all the time. But that wasn't what the popular media wanted to hear and it seldom became part of the story.

The result was a neat little example of pack journalism. Since other media were carrying the story, no one felt they could afford to ignore it. And of course since everyone was carrying the story, obviously it had to be important enough to get on and stay on.

Those of us in the technical press watched in horrified fascination as a simple little "heads up" turned into a self-reinforcing sensation.

In the two or three days before March 6 we were treated to the bizarre spectacle of TV news personalities, who obviously didn't know which side of the floppy disk was up, interviewing bewildered computer store owners and trying to get them to explain a boot block virus in words of .75 syllables.

By now the situation was taking on surrealistic overtones. Anyone who knew anything about computers was well-advised to carry a disk with an anti-virus program in pocket or purse because they would be asked repeatedly to check computers. Several such gurus took to carrying disks for Macintoshes and Unix systems as well even though they were immune to the virus. It was easier to perform unnecessary checks than explain why they were unnecessary.

One of the people on the net reported he was approached by a near-hysterical graduate student who was afraid his pregnant wife might have contracted the virus while working with an infected computer. The man wanted to know if the virus could harm the baby.

One technician reported his company had decided not to install a new telephone switch until after March 6 rather than "take a chance" on having the virus infect the company's telephone system. Never mind that the switch didn't even use a hard disk. Never mind that it couldn't possibly be infected. Why take chances?

Another story, possibly apocryphal, had a medical office "protecting" itself by autoclaving its collection of floppy disks on the theory that autoclaving was how you killed viruses. (It kills floppy disks too.)

This was funny, but it was also a little scary. The response seemed completely illogical.

Then I remembered something I had heard on a panel at World Fantasy Convention about the time I got the first fateful letter. The subject of the panel was myths for the modern world. One of the panelists pointed out that because myths represent archetypical stories, each age tends to recast them in its own terms.

The example he offered was the trickster, the figure who appears in Norse mythology as Loki and in many Native American legends as Coyote. He pointed out that in today's world, the cognate is the system breaker—the clever amoral person who uses his special knowledge to romp through the world's computers, playing pranks, stealing secrets, unleashing viruses and raising all kinds of hell. Perhaps the reason for the Michelangelo Panic was that it fit so neatly into the matrix expressed by myth.

I don't know. I'm just a techie computer journalist who turns out science fiction and fantasy on the side. I'm also a former newspaper reporter and editor and looking at the situation from that dual perspective, I can understand completely how it happened. Everyone did what he or she was supposed to do, all the parts functioned perfectly predictably. Yet the result was something both unpredictable and sub-optimal.

I suppose the best lesson from all this is that you have to read or listen carefully. If the mainstream media come up with something that looks like it might affect you, it's probably a good idea to try to get information from a specialized source before taking drastic action.

I don't know. I only know I'm writing this shortly after midnight, March 7 and I am beginning to understand how Orson Welles must have felt after his War of the Worlds broadcast.

A

APPENDIX

Integrity Master

Integrity Master, a shareware program by Wolfgang Stiller, is included on the diskette that comes with this book. This program, known as IM, can detect and remove known viruses as well as those still unknown. When it finds a known virus, IM tells you its name and describes what it does.

In addition to virus detection and removal, IM finds possible file corruption due to hardware or software problems—problems Stiller says are at least 100 times more likely to cause you trouble than a virus infection. IM can supplement or replace any computer security programs you are using, and also check files as they are decompressed or brought back into your system from a backup copy to make sure they are okay. The program helps you restore accidently erased files, and track changes on your hard disk to enable you to find out where all the space is going. IM can also diagnose problems on your hard drive and reload your boot sector and partition table.

In other words, Integrity Master is not just an anti-virus product. It is a complete data integrity system. Integrity Master requires a PC with 195K of memory available running DOS 2.0 or higher. It supports super large disks and files, and a maximum of 2,621 files in a single directory.

Setup and installation

When you use the installation process for the diskette that comes with this book, Integrity Master is installed first, before the McAfee programs. You might have already installed the McAfee programs alone, as explained at the beginning of chapter 6. If so, when the programs are being extracted, you have the choice of overwriting the previous installation of McAfee (type Y) or not overwriting them (type N).

The opening screen for Integrity Master setup is shown in Fig. A-1. This is an information-only screen. Press any key to move on to the installation program. The screen shown in Fig. A-2 is self-explanatory. "Yes" is the highlighted default, since most of you will not have another copy of Integrity Master on your hard drive; press <Enter>. If you have already installed another copy of the program, type N and then <Enter>.

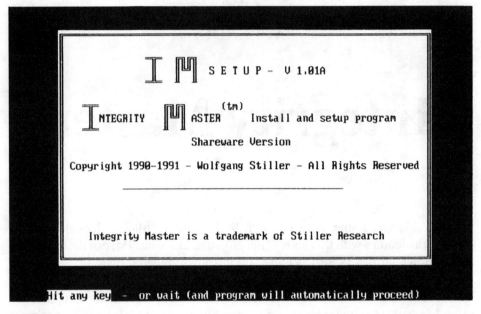

Fig. A-1

The screen that appears next (if this is a first-time installation) deals with Integrity Master's warranty disclaimer and license terms. Please take a moment to read and understand this information, then press any key to continue. You have several screens of information to read regarding these matters, and at the end, you are given the opportunity to agree, disagree, or go back and reread the information. If you do not agree to the terms you have read, installation of the program is terminated. Highlight the "Yes" line or type Y to indicate agreement when you have read the information and are ready to proceed.

More information screens (this program takes a lot of reading to get into) follow. As you finish each information screen, press any key to move on. When you reach the screen shown in Fig. A-3, it might be time for a side trip into Integrity Master in order to understand how the program works, so it is a good idea to take the tutorial. When you finish this tutorial, you should be an expert in navigating the ins and outs of Integrity Master. After you complete this tutorial, you are offered an overview of what Integrity Master does and what it can do for you.

You have finally reached an interactive point in Integrity Master setup; you tell

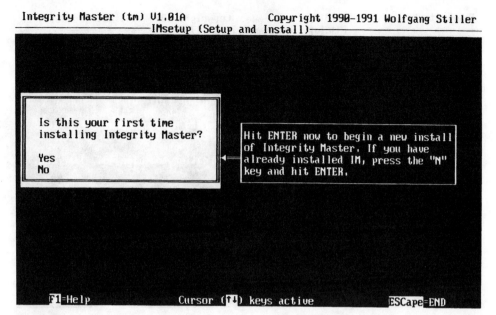

Fig. A-2

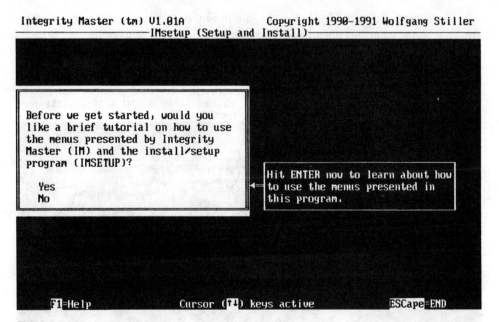

Fig. A-3

the program about your needs, and program parameters are installed accordingly. As usual, I advise you to let the program set up your defaults. However, if you are an advanced computer user and want to make other arrangements, this can be done as indicated in Fig. A-4.

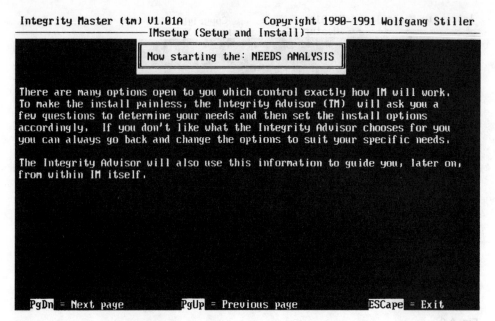

──────────────IMsetup (Setup and Install)──────────────

┌───┐
│ Now starting the: NEEDS ANALYSIS   │
└───┘

There are many options open to you which control exactly how IM will work.
To make the install painless, the Integrity Advisor (TM) will ask you a
few questions to determine your needs and then set the install options
accordingly. If you don't like what the Integrity Advisor chooses for you
you can always go back and change the options to suit your specific needs.

The Integrity Advisor will also use this information to guide you, later on,
from within IM itself.

PgDn = Next page   PgUp = Previous page   ESCape = Exit

Fig. A-4

The screen shown in Fig. A-5 and again in Fig. A-6 should make you feel comfortable about what lies ahead in determining your needs. The program asks you about your computing expertise or lack of it, and even defines each level (compare the description box in Fig. A-5 for a "Brand new user" with the box in Fig. A-6 for

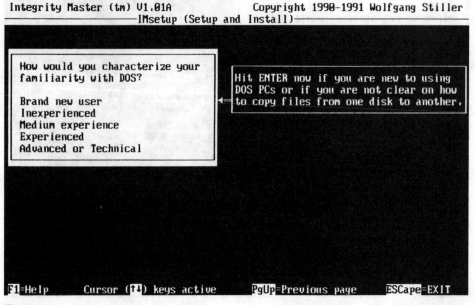

──────────────IMsetup (Setup and Install)──────────────

┌─────────────────────────────┐   ┌─────────────────────────────────┐
│ How would you characterize your │   │ Hit ENTER now if you are new to using │
│ familiarity with DOS?   │   │ DOS PCs or if you are not clear on how │
│   │ ◄── │ to copy files from one disk to another. │
│ Brand new user   │   └─────────────────────────────────┘
│ Inexperienced   │
│ Medium experience   │
│ Experienced   │
│ Advanced or Technical   │
└─────────────────────────────┘

F1=Help   Cursor (↑↓) keys active   PgUp=Previous page   ESCape=EXIT

Fig. A-5

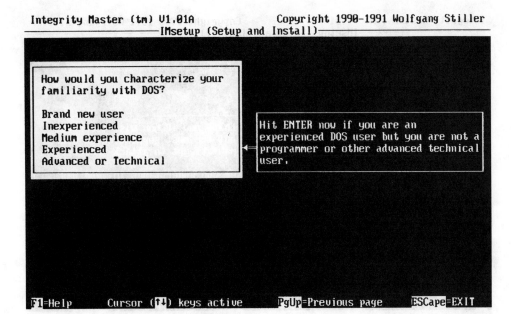

How would you characterize your
familiarity with DOS?

Brand new user
Inexperienced
Medium experience
Experienced
Advanced or Technical

Hit ENTER now if you are an
experienced DOS user but you are not a
programmer or other advanced technical
user.

F1=Help   Cursor (↑↓) keys active   PgUp=Previous page   ESCape=EXIT

Fig. A-6

an "Experienced" one). Using the arrow keys, run up and down the list until you find the description that best fits your level, and press <Enter>. In this discussion, we will follow the path for an Experienced user. Read through the rest of this section before you go further. If you are confused about some of the things we do, then be sure to choose a lower level for your installation process.

Integrity Master offers three alternative levels of security for your computer. In Fig. A-7, Typical Security Protection has been chosen. Each choice has its own description box (as is the case throughout Integrity Master) so you can consider each level on its own merits before making your choice.

The next screen (Fig. A-8) asks you for what purposes you plan to use Integrity Master. As you highlight each option, the description box on the right tells you about that option, so that you can make the best choice for your needs. For the purposes of this book, the "Both other reasons and viruses" option will be chosen.

The default option in speed versus virus protection is the one illustrated in Fig. A-9, probably the one at least 99 percent of you will choose. Press <Enter> to select this option and move to the next screen.

Figure A-10 shows a screen that bears some thought. If you are working with an older computer, one that is running at less than 25 MHz clock speed, you probably want Integrity Master to run its check in background, and print a report for you to read at your convenience. If your machine is running at 25, 33 or even 50 MHz, you might not mind having the work on screen. Of course, the other factor is the size and contents of your hard disk. The bigger the disk, the more time it will take to check. Only you know how much time you have to devote to Integrity Master.

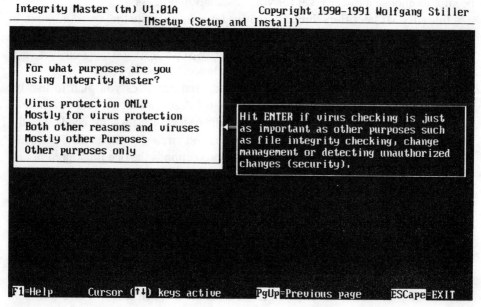

Integrity Master (tm) V1.01A   Copyright 1990-1991 Wolfgang Stiller
─────────────────IMsetup (Setup and Install)─────────────────

Integrity Master can be used as a
security checker to detect any
unauthorized file changes.
If someone changed something while
you were gone, you can find out!

How much security do you need?

ABSOLUTE security required
Typical security protection
Security is not vital

Hit ENTER now if you wish to detect
all but the most sophisticated users
who may attempt to attack your PC.

A user who understands IM, and has
access to this program could sneak in
and change your files, and then run
IM to hide any changes. This is only
a threat if IM.EXE is accessible to
the user. (Keep IM.EXE on diskette)

F1=Help   Cursor (↑↓) keys active   PgUp=Previous page   ESCape=EXIT

Fig. A-7

Integrity Master (tm) V1.01A   Copyright 1990-1991 Wolfgang Stiller
─────────────────IMsetup (Setup and Install)─────────────────

For what purposes are you
using Integrity Master?

Virus protection ONLY
Mostly for virus protection
Both other reasons and viruses
Mostly other Purposes
Other purposes only

Hit ENTER if virus checking is just
as important as other purposes such
as file integrity checking, change
management or detecting unauthorized
changes (security).

F1=Help   Cursor (↑↓) keys active   PgUp=Previous page   ESCape=EXIT

Fig. A-8

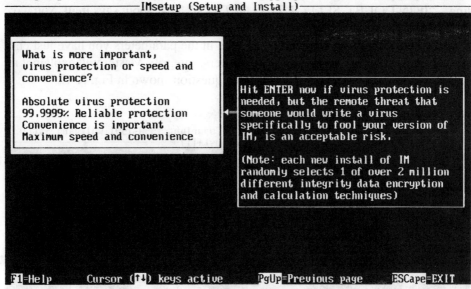

What is more important,
virus protection or speed and
convenience?

Absolute virus protection
99.9999% Reliable protection
Convenience is important
Maximum speed and convenience

Hit ENTER now if virus protection is
needed, but the remote threat that
someone would write a virus
specifically to fool your version of
IM, is an acceptable risk.

(Note: each new install of IM
randomly selects 1 of over 2 million
different integrity data encryption
and calculation techniques)

F1=Help   Cursor (↑↓) keys active   PgUp=Previous page   ESCape=EXIT

Fig. A-9

Integrity Master can be used in a fully interactive manner or it can be
run in an unattended environment. There are many variations between these
two extremes.

Depending upon your type of PC and the speed and size of your disk, it may
take while to check or initialize all your files. This is why you might
want to run IM unattended and then read the report file or printout. On the
other hand, "quick integrity update" checking, is usually very fast. A full
integrity initialize on 273mb of 7,920 files on our 386/33 (15 ms ESDI disk)
takes 15 minutes; a full integrity check of all files takes 10 minutes and
quick integrity update takes 10 to 20 seconds.   On a PC/XT (70ms disk), the
times are identical, except only 31mb (1750 files) are checked.

To give Integrity Advisor an idea of how to set things up please select the
best answer to the following question:

Do you intend to sit and watch Integrity Master run?

I like to see Everything on my screen; I do not want reports to read later.
I like to see everything on my Screen; but I'll want to see the reports also.
I Generally prefer to read written reports.
I only read Written reports; I'll never sit and watch IM check my disk.

F1=Help   Cursor (↑↓) keys active   PgUp=Previous page   ESCape=EXIT

Fig. A-10

The nice part about the options given on the screen in Fig. A-11 is its middle line—"IF IN DOUBT, SELECT THIS OPTION." That about says it all. You have now reached the end of the Needs Analysis portion of installing Integrity Master. In the event that you want to make a change in the parameters you have just chosen, or are merely curious about the parameters, Integrity Master will explain it all in detail if you answer Yes to the on-screen question shown in Fig. A-12.

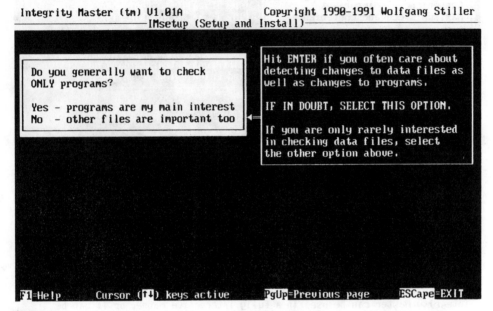

Fig. A-11

When you are finished with the parameter setup, Integrity Master performs a simple hardware analysis of your system, giving you an on-screen report as illustrated in Fig. A-13. Press <Enter>. The next screen gives you two choices: complete the install and exit, or manually go back and change one or more install parameters. For most of you, it is time to complete the install and exit. Highlight that option on the screen and press <Enter>.

Before you can exit to DOS and go on to install the McAfee Virus Central program, there are a few more installation screens to look at and absorb. Figure A-14 tells you how to continue to print or view the files that have been written to help you work with your now customized version of Integrity Master, while Fig. A-15 (after all this time) tells you how to "Quick Install" Integrity Master. When you press <PgDn> to continue, you see successive screens that ask you to do certain things (such as make a copy of Integrity Master on a diskette that also contains your DOS system files; you are also told how to format the disk so it will have the system files).

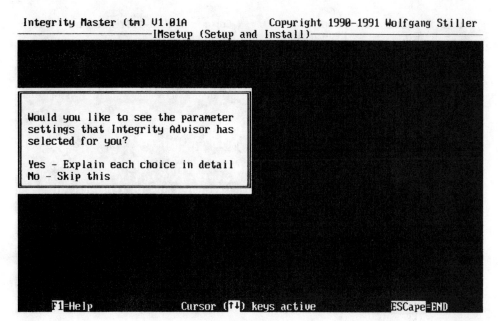

```
Integrity Master (tm) V1.01A          Copyright 1990-1991 Wolfgang Stiller
─────────────────────IMsetup (Setup and Install)─────────────────────



    ┌──────────────────────────────────────────┐
    │                                          │
    │  Would you like to see the parameter     │
    │  settings that Integrity Advisor has     │
    │  selected for you?                       │
    │                                          │
    │  Yes - Explain each choice in detail     │
    │  No - Skip this                          │
    │                                          │
    └──────────────────────────────────────────┘




    F1=Help              Cursor (↑↓) keys active        ESCape=END
```

Fig. A-12

```
Integrity Master (tm) V1.01A          Copyright 1990-1991 Wolfgang Stiller
─────────────────────IMsetup (Setup and Install)─────────────────────


     ┌──────────────────────────────────────────────┐
     │             Hardware analysis done!          │
     │                                              │
     │   Highest usable drive: D                    │
     │                                              │
     │   Floppy drives: A B                         │
     │                                              │
     │   Hard drives  : C                           │
     │                                              │
     │   No DOS boot sector on:                     │
     │                                              │
     │   No partition sector on: A B D              │
     │                                              │
     └──────────────────────────────────────────────┘

                        Hit any key
```

Fig. A-13

The Integrity Advisor has prepared a list of a few steps you will need to do
to finish installation of IM. It is based upon your needs analysis, and any
options which you changed.

We have also prepared a checklist of steps for using
IM on a day to day basis (based on a similar analysis).

Both of these procedures have been customized specially for your needs. In
addition to presenting them here, we will write them to file "IMPROC.TXT"
on your current disk. We have included two .BAT files to allow you to
view or print these procedures at any time. After you finish IMSETUP, you
may type:

          IMPRINT IMPROC.TXT   for a printout or

          IMVIEW IMPROC.TXT   to see the procedures on your screen.

Hit any key

Fig. A-14

```
**********************************************************************
**                                                                  **
**   S P E C I A L     Q U I C K     I N S T A L L     P R O C E D U R E   **
**                                                                  **
**********************************************************************
** Since you may be wanting to do a quick evaluation of Integrity Master **
** to see how it meets your needs, we offer a short-cut install procedure. **
** The full procedure which follows is intended to guard against unknown **
** viruses already infecting your system and is not necessary for a quick **
** evaluation.                                                       **
**********************************************************************
** Quick install:                                                   **
**  1) Simply copy your IM files IM.EXE and IM.PRM to a convenient  **
**     location.   ("COPY IM.* A:" would copy them to a floppy)     **
**                                                                  **
**  2) Enter the command: "IM /IE /Dc"  Substitute for "c", in the "/Dc" **
**     parameter, the disk you wish to check.  That's it!           **
**                                                                  **
** To execute IM, just enter "IM".  The menus will guide you from there. **
**                                                                  **
**********************************************************************
      PgDn = Next page                    ESCape = Last Menu
```

Fig. A-15

Much of this is elementary DOS and will not be new to you (especially after reading this book). Just read each screen and follow the instructions and eventually you see a screen that finishes with the comforting words: "This completes the list of additional steps to finish the install." Congratulations.

You still won't be quite finished, as the system now gives you a customized checklist for day-to-day use of Integrity Master based on the choices you made during the installation. It is probably worth your while to print each of these screens to keep as documentation at your elbow when using Integrity Master, at least until you become really proficient.

How Integrity Master works

Integrity Master is started from the DOS command line [C:\PC-VIRUS] by typing IM and pressing <Enter>.

Integrity Master's developer has written in the documentation that most people should never have to read the User's Guide—certainly not to learn how to use the program—because the tutorials within the program should be self-explanatory. Take a look at the screen shown in Fig. A-16, the first screen that comes up when you start to run Integrity Master. While you can't see the highlight bar, the arrow from this description box is pointing at the submenu selection. When you select Options from the Main Menu (the choices across the top), your screen resembles Fig. A-17. A different submenu appears with an appropriate description box for the item highlighted.

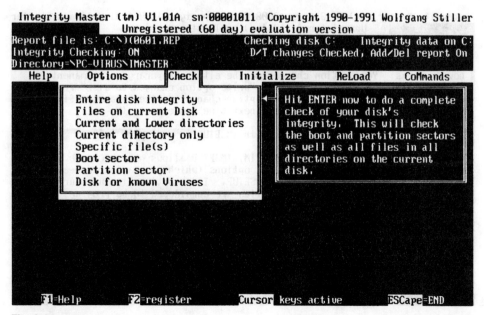

Fig. A-16

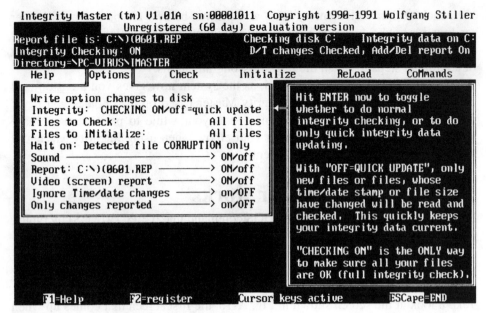

Fig. A-17

So far, it's easy enough. Now, if you want more information on the item highlighted on the screen in Fig. A-17, for example, press F1, and the Options menu help screen appears, as shown in Fig. A-18. Use the up and down arrow keys to scroll through all of this help since it goes on for more than a single page. If this

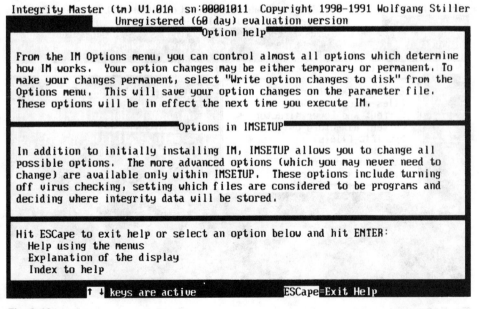

Fig. A-18

isn't enough, you find on the help screen(s) that certain words have a different color or bold letter at the beginning—or somewhere within. Press one of those letters and even more help appears. To get to the screen in Fig. A-19, for example, I typed E for "Explanation of the Display" (see the lowest box in Fig. A-18).

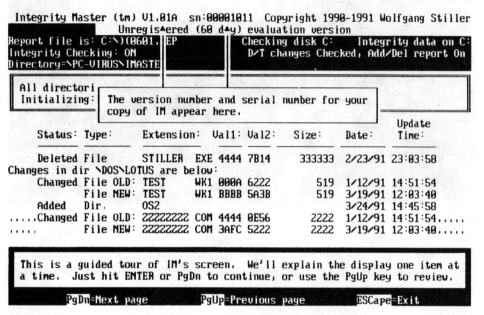

Fig. A-19

When you press <PgDn> on this menu, description boxes for each item on the IM screen are displayed, one at a time. You simply can't go wrong inside Integrity Master with all the help and description opportunities. Using the PgUp key, the up and down arrow keys, and the Escape key, you can back out to the Options submenu where you started and go on from there.

Initializing integrity data   This is your first step, the first time you use Integrity Master. On the Main Menu, choose the Initialize option. The screen in Fig. A-20 appears. From this submenu, you initialize or create the integrity data that describes your files and system sectors. Stiller suggests that you choose Entire disk integrity to initialize when you first start up IM. Unless you turned off virus checking, IM checks for viruses while initializing these files. IM also saves reload information for your boot sector and partition table, so that you can use the reload option later to restore it should this become necessary. Save these files on floppy disk for later use.

There is no place here to go into all the options and submenus available, but since the explanations and help are so thorough, you should be able to figure out everything for yourself with no trouble. As with any other anti-virus program, you

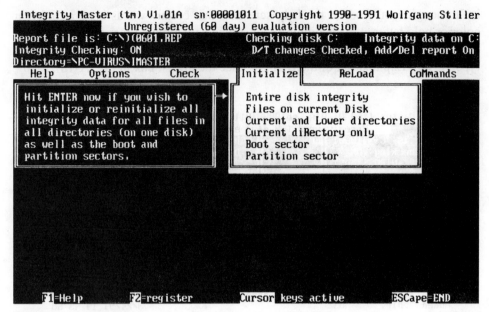

Fig. A-20

should use IM to check every program you put onto your hard drive before you run it, and you should run regular checks of all your executable files (you do this from the Check submenu) to make certain there have been no unexpected changes.

Evaluation

Shareware might generally be "no frills" software, but Integrity Master can be considered an exception. It might not have the fanciest graphics, but it has such wonderful depth of explanation and help in an easy-to-use format that even those of you who have no knowledge of the DOS command line can manage. Of course, those of you who are DOS fanatics can run the entire program from the command line, but you'll need to talk to Wolfgang Stiller and acquire his documentation to get that right unless you want to spend hours experimenting.

This is not a program that does automatic checking at bootup; you do not enter it into your AUTOEXEC.BAT or CONFIG.SYS file. You will have to remember to run it to safeguard your computer. Since it is so easy to run and so well-defined, this should not be a hardship.

B
APPENDIX

The McAfee Virus List

Each program reviewed in this book has been able to handle "X" number of viruses and strains. The largest number is quoted by the McAfee programs, and many of the programs rely on the McAfee list for their virus definitions. The list is included here for quick reference to the current crop of known viruses, their variants, and what they infect.

VIRUS CHARACTERISTICS LIST V89
Copyright 1989, 1990, 1991, 1992 McAfee Associates
All Rights Reserved.
(408) 988-3832

The following list outlines the major characteristics of the known IBM PC and compatible virus strains identified by SCAN. The number of known variants of each virus is also listed. This number is listed in parentheses beside the name of the strain. The total number of known viruses is summed at the end of the list. The Clean-Up virus I.D. code is included in brackets.

```
A Infects Fixed Disk Partition Table-A-------------------+
9 Infects Fixed Disk Boot Sector-----9---------------+   |
8 Infects Floppy Diskette Boot-------8-------------+  |  |
7 Infects Overlay Files--------------7-----------+ |  |  |
6 Infects EXE Files------------------6---------+ | |  |  |
5 Infects COM files------------------5-------+ | | |  |  |
4 Infects COMMAND.COM----------------4-----+ | | | |  |  |
3 Virus Installs Self in Memory------3---+ | | | | |  |  |
2 Virus Uses Self-Encryption---------2-+ | | | | | |  |  |
1 Virus Uses STEALTH Techniques------1-+| | | | | | |  |  |
```

A Infects Fixed Disk Partition Table
9 Infects Fixed Disk Boot Sector
8 Infects Floppy Diskette Boot
7 Infects Overlay Files
6 Infects EXE Files
5 Infects COM files
4 Infects COMMAND.COM
3 Virus Installs Self in Memory
2 Virus Uses Self-Encryption
1 Virus Uses STEALTH Techniques

Virus	Disinfector	1	2	3	4	5	6	7	8	9	A	Increase in Infected Program's Size	Damage
1008 [1008]	Clean-Up	.	x	x	x	x	.	.	.	.	.	1008	O,P,D,L
1014 [Vienna]	Clean-Up	.	.	x	x	x	.	.	.	.	.	1014	O,P,L
1024 (2) [Alf]	Clean-Up	.	.	x	x	x	.	.	.	.	.	1024	O,P
1033 [1033]	Clean-Up	.	.	x	.	.	x	x	.	.	.	1033	O,P,L
1024PSRC [PS10]	Clean-Up	.	.	x	x	x	.	.	.	.	.	1024	O,P
1067 [1067]	Clean-Up	.	.	x	x	x	.	.	.	.	.	1067	O,P,L
1210 [1210]	Clean-Up	.	.	x	.	x	.	.	.	.	.	1210	O,P,L
1241 [1241]	Clean-Up	.	.	x	x	x	.	.	.	.	.	1241	L,O,P
1244 [1244]	Clean-Up	.	.	x	.	x	x	x	.	.	.	1244	L,O,P
1253 - Boot [1253]	M-Disk	.	.	x	.	.	.	.	x	x	x	N/A	B,O,P,D,L
1253 - COM [1253]	Clean-Up	.	.	x	x	x	.	.	.	.	.	1253	O,P,D,L
1260 (4) [V2P2]	Clean-Up	.	x	.	x	x	.	.	.	.	.	1260	P
1280 [Crime-B]	Clean-Up	.	x	.	.	x	.	.	.	.	.	1168	P,F
1376 [1376]	Clean-Up	.	.	x	x	x	x	x	.	.	.	1376	O,P,L
1381 [1381]	Clean-Up	.	.	.	.	.	x	x	.	.	.	1381	O,P
1385 [1385]	Clean-Up	.	.	x	x	x	.	.	.	.	.	1385	O,P,L
1392 [1392]	Clean-Up	.	.	x	x	x	x	.	.	.	.	1392	O,P,L
1559/1554 (2) [1559]	Clean-Up	.	x	x	x	x	x	.	.	.	.	1554	O,P,L
1575/1591 (5) [15xx]	Clean-Up	.	.	x	x	x	x	.	.	.	.	varies	O,P,L
1605 (2) [Jeru]	Clean-Up	.	.	x	x	x	x	.	.	.	.	1605	L,O,P,D
1661 [1661]	Clean-Up	.	.	x	x	x	.	.	.	.	.	1661	O,P,L
1677 [1677]	Clean-Up	.	.	x	x	x	.	.	.	.	.	1677	O,P,L
1720 (4) [1720]	Clean-Up	.	.	x	.	x	x	x	.	.	.	1720	F,O,P,L
1840 [Alf]	Clean-Up	.	.	x	.	.	x	x	.	.	.	1840	O,P,L,D
191 [Tiny]	Clean-Up	.	.	.	x	x	.	.	.	.	.	191	L,O,P
1963 [1963]	Clean-Up	x	.	x	x	x	x	x	.	.	.	1963	O,P,L,D
1971/8 Tunes (2) [1971]	Clean-Up	.	.	x	.	x	x	x	.	.	.	1971	O,P
2330 [2330]	Clean-Up	.	.	x	x	x	x	x	.	.	.	2330	O,P,L
2559 [2559]	Clean-Up	.	.	.	.	.	x	.	.	.	.	2559	L,O,P
262 [262]	Clean-Up	.	.	x	x	x	.	.	.	.	.	262	O,P,L
2622 [2622]	Clean-Up	.	.	x	x	x	x	x	x	x	x	2622	O,P,L D
2930 [Spain]	Clean-Up	.	.	x	.	x	x	.	.	.	.	2930	P
310 [310]	Clean-Up	.	.	x	x	x	.	.	.	.	.	310	O,P,L
337 [337]	Clean-Up	.	.	x	x	x	.	.	.	.	.	337	O,L
3445 [3445]	Clean-Up	x	x	x	.	x	x	.	.	.	.	3445	O,P,D,L
365 [365]	Clean-Up	.	.	x	x	x	.	.	.	.	.	365	O,P,L
370-B [370]	Clean-Up	.	.	.	.	x	.	.	.	.	.		
382 (2) [382]	Clean-Up	.	.	.	x	x	x	.	.	.	.	Overwrites	L,O,P
405 [Burger]	Clean-Up	.	.	.	.	x	.	.	.	.	.	Overwrites	
408 [408]	Clean-Up	.	.	x	x	x	.	.	.	.	.	408	L,O,P
4096 (9) [4096]	Clean-Up	x	.	x	x	x	x	x	.	.	.	4096	D,O,P,L
482 [482]	Clean-Up	.	.	x	x	x	.	.	.	.	.	482	O,P
487 [487]	Clean-Up	.	.	.	.	x	.	.	.	.	.		
510 [VHP]	Clean-Up	.	.	x	x	.	.	.	.	.	.	510	O,L
512 (5) [512]	Clean-Up	x	.	x	x	x	.	.	.	.	.	N/A	O,P,L
5120 (3) [5120]	Clean-Up	.	.	x	x	x	x	.	.	.	.	5120	O,P,D,L
555 [BWish]	Clean-Up	.	.	x	x	x	x	x	.	.	.	555	O,P,L
560 [560]	Clean-Up	.	.	x	x	x	.	.	.	.	.	560	O,P,L
621 [621]	Clean-Up	.	.	x	x	x	.	.	.	.	.	621	O,P,D
651 [Alf]	Clean-Up	.	.	x	.	x	.	.	.	.	.	651	O,P,D
709 [709]	Clean-Up	.	.	x	x	x	.	.	.	.	.	709	O,P
733 [733]	Clean-Up	.	.	x	x	.	.	.	.	.	.	733	O,P,D,L
737 [737]	Clean-Up	.	.	x	x	x	x	.	.	.	.	737	O,P,L

Name	Tool	Markers	Size	Codes
748 [748]	Clean-Up	. . x x x	748	O,D,L
765 [765]	Clean-Up	. . x . . x x . . .	765	O,P,L
777 [777]	Clean-Up	. . x x x	777	O,P
7808 [7808]	Clean-Up	. . x x x x x . . .	7808	O,P,L,D
789 [789]	Clean-Up	. . x x x	789	O,L
7th Son (4) [7S]	Clean-Up	. . . x x	350	O,P
812 (2) [812]	Clean-Up	. . x x x x x . . .	812	O,D
834/Arab Virus [Ar]	Clean-Up	. . x . x	834	O,P
855 [855]	Clean-Up	. . x x x x x . . .	855	O,P,L
903 [903]	Clean-Up	. . x x x	903	O,P
905 [905]	Clean-Up	. . . . x		
923 [923]	Clean-Up	. . x x x x x . . .	923	O,P,L,D
Ada [Ada]	Clean-Up	. . x x x	2600	O,P,L
AGI-Plan [AGI]	Clean-Up	. . . x x	1536	O,P,L
Ah [Alf]	Clean-Up	. . x x x	1173	B,L,O,P
AIDS Trojan (13) [Aids]	Clean-Up	. . . x	Overwrites	
AirCop (3) [AirCop]	Clean-Up	. . x . . . . . x .	N/A	B,O
Akuku (2) [Akuku]	Clean-Up	. . . x x x	891	L,O,P
Alabama (3) [Alabama]	Clean-Up	. . x . . x	1560	O,P,L
Alfa (2) [Alf]	Clean-Up	. . x x x x x . . .	1150	L,O,P
Amstrad (7) [Amst]	Clean-Up	. . . . x	847	P
Anthrax - Boot (2) [Atx]	M-Disk	. . x x	N/A	B,O,P,D
Anthrax - File (4) [Atx]	Clean-Up	. . x x x x	1206	O,P,D
Anti-D [AD]	Clean-Up	. . x x x	945	O,P,L
Anti-Pascal II (4) [AP-2]	Clean-Up	. . . x x	400	B,L,O,P
Anti-Pascal (3) [AP]	Clean-Up	. . . x x	605	L,O,P
Anti-Tel [A-Vir]	Clean-Up	x x x . . . . x . x	N/A	B,F,L,O
Argentina [Arg]	Clean-Up	. . x x x	1249	O,P,D
Armagedon (3) [Arma]	Clean-Up	. . x x x	1079	O,P
ASP-472 [472]	Clean-Up	. . x x x x x . . .	472	L,O,P
AT144 [144]	Clean-Up	. . . x x	144	O,P
August 16 [A16]	Clean-Up	. . . x x	631	O,P
Australia [Aust]	Clean-Up	. . x x x x x . . .	1433	O,P,L,D
Azusa (2) [Azusa]	Clean-Up	. . x . . . . x . x	N/A	D,O,B,L
A-403 [A-403]	Clean-Up	. . x x x	Overwrites	L,O,P
BackTime [BT]	Clean-Up	. . x x x	528	L,O,P
Bad Boy (4) [BB]	Clean-Up	. . x x x	1000	O,P,D
BadGuy (3) [IB]	Clean-Up	. . . x x	265	O,L
Bandit [Ban]	Clean-Up	. . x x x x x . . .	988	O,D
Barcelona [Barc]	Clean-Up	. . x . x	1792	L,O,P
Beast [Bea]	Clean-Up	. . . x x	429	O,P,L
BeBe [BeBe]	Clean-Up	. . . x x	1004	O,P,D
Beeper (2) [Beep]	Clean-Up	. . x . x	482	O,P,D
Best Wishes [BWish]	Clean-Up	. . . x x x x . . .	1024	O,P,D
Beta [Bet]	Clean-Up	. . . . x	1117	L,O,P
Black Monday (3) [BMon]	Clean-Up	. . x x x x x . . .	1055	L,O,P,D
Bljec (8) [Blj]	Clean-Up	. . . x x	369	O,P
Blood (2) [Blood]	Clean-Up	. . . x x	418	L,O,P
Bloody! [Bloody]	Clean-Up	. x x . . . . x . x	N/A	B,O
Blood-2 [Blood]	Clean-Up	. . . . x	427	O,P,D
Bob [Bob]	Clean-Up	. . x x x	718	O,P,L
Boys (3) [Boys]	Clean-Up	. . x x x	500	O,D
Brothers [Bro]	Clean-Up	x . x . x x x . . .	2045	L,O,P
Burger (28) [Burger]	Clean-Up	. . . x x x	Overwrites	
Burghofer [Bgh]	Clean-Up	. . x x x	525	L,O,P
Busted	Clean-Up	. . . . x	Overwrites	O,P,L
CADKill [CK]	Clean-Up	. . x x x x x . . .	1163	O,P,D
Cancer [Pix]	Clean-Up	. . . . x	1480	O,P,D
Cannabis (2) [CB]	Clean-Up	. ? x . . . x . . .	N/A	B,L,O
Cara [Cara]	Clean-Up	. . x x x	1024	F,L,O,P
Carioca (6) [Carioca]	Clean-Up	. . x . x	951	O,P
Cascade/170x (14) [170x]	Clean-Up	. x x . x	1701	O,P
Casino [Casino]	Clean-Up	. . x x x		O,P,L
Casper (2) [Casper]	Clean-Up	. x . x x	1200	L,O,P,D
Caz [Caz]	Clean-Up	. . x x x x x . . .	1204	L,O,P
CB-1530 [1530]	Clean-Up	. . . x x x x . . .	1530	L,O,P
CD [CD]	Clean-Up	. x x . x x x . . .	2161	O,L,D,P
Chaos [GenB]	M-Disk	. . x . . . . x x .	N/A	B,O,D,F
Cheeba (2) [CHB]	Clean-Up	. x x x x x x . . .	1683	L,O,P
Chemist [Chm]	Clean-Up	. . x x x	650	O,P,L
Christmas Tree [XA1]	Clean-Up	. x . x	1539	F,O,P,L
Christmas Violator[Vienna]	Clean-Up	. . . x x		O,P,D

Virus	Tool	Type pattern	Size	Class
Cinderella [Cind]	Clean-Up	. . x x x	390	O,P,L
Color [Col]	Clean-Up	. . x x x	802	O,P,D
Copyright [1193]	Clean-Up	. . x x x	1193	L,O,P
Cop-Mpl [COP]	Clean-Up	. . . x x x	1113	L,O,P
Cossiga [Cos]	Clean-Up	. . x . . x x . . .	899	O,P,L
Cracker Jack [CRJ]	Clean-Up	. . . . x	varies	L,O,P
Crash [Crash]	Clean-Up	. . . . . x	See Note	
Crazy Eddie [Crazy]	Clean-Up	. . x ? x x . . . x	varies	F,L,O,P
Crazy Imp [Imp]	Clean-Up	x . x x x	1445	O,P,L
Cree4per [Cre]	Clean-Up	. . x x x	475	O,P,L
Crew-2480 [2480]	Clean-Up	. . . x x	2480	L,O,P
CRF [CRF]	Clean-Up	. . x x x	270	O,P
CSL (2) [CSL]	Clean-Up	. . x x x	457	L,O,P
Curse Boot [Curse]	M-Disk	. . x . . . . x x .	N/A	B,O
Dada [Dd]	Clean-Up	. . x . . x x . . .	1363	O,P,D
Damage [Alf]	Clean-Up	. . x x x x x . . .	1063	O,D,P
Dark Avenger (11) [Dav]	Clean-Up	. . x x x x x . . .	1800	O,P,L
Darth Vader (6) [512]	Clean-Up	. . x x x	varies	O,L,P
Datacrime II-B [Crime-2B]	Clean-Up	. x . x x x	1917	P,F
Datacrime-2 [Crime-2]	Clean-Up	. x . . x x	1514	P,F
Datacrime/1168 (3) [Crime]	Clean-Up	. x . . x	1280	P,F
DataLock [Data]	Clean-Up	. . x x x x x . . .	920	O,P
Day10 [D10]	Clean-Up	. . . x x	674	F,L,O,P
DBASE [Dbase]	Clean-Up	. . x . x	1864	D,O,P
Dedicated [Dame]	SCAN /D	x x x x x	Varies	O,P,L
Define [Def]	Clean-Up	. . . x x x	Overwrites	L,O,P
Deicide [Dei]	Clean-Up	. . . x x x	Overwrites	F,L,O,P
Demolition [Dmo]	Clean-Up	. . x x x	1585	L,O,P
Demon (5) [Dem]	Clean-Up	. . . x x	Overwrites	F,L,O,P
Den Zuk (5) [GenB]	Clean-Up	. x . . . . x . . .	N/A	O,B
Destructor [Dest]	Clean-Up	. x x x x x x . . .	1150	O,P
Devil's Dance (2) [Dance]	Clean-Up	. x . x	941	D,O,P,L
Dir Virus [Dir]	Clean-Up	x . x x x	691	O,P,D
Dir-2/CD 1x (3) [D2]	Clean-Up	x x x x x x x . . .	1024	O,L,D,P
Disk Killer (4) [Killer]	Clean-Up	. . x . . . . x x .	N/A	B,O,P,D,F
DM (3) [DM]	Clean-Up	. . x x x	400	L,O,P
Dodo [Dod]	Clean-Up	. . x x	408	O,P,L
Do Nothing [Nothing]	Clean-Up	. . x . x	608	P
Doodle (14) [Doodle]	Clean-Up	. . x . x x	2885	O,P
Doom II [Dm2]	Clean-Up	. . x . x x	2504	O,P,D,L
Dot Killer [Dot]	Clean-Up	. . x x x	944	O,P
Dutch [Dt]	Clean-Up	. . x x x x x . . .	555	D,O,P
D-Tiny (4) [D-T]	Clean-Up	. . x x x x	124	L,O,P
EDV (2) [EDV]	Clean-Up	x . x . . . . x x x	N/A	B,O
Einstein [Ein]	Clean-Up	. . . x . x	878	L,O,P
Eliza [El]	Clean-Up	. . . x x	1193	L,O,P
EMF [EMF]	Clean-Up	. . . x x	404	O,P,L
Empire (3) [Emp]	Clean-Up	. x x . . . . x x .	N/A	O,P
Enemy [Enm]	Clean-Up	. . x x x x x . . .	1285	O,P,D
Enigma [Enigma]	Clean-Up	. x x . . x x . . .	1755	O,P
Error [Arma]	Clean-Up	. . . . . x x . . .	628	O,P
ETC [ETC]	Clean-Up	. . x x x	572	O,D,L,P
Exterminator [M45]	Clean-Up	. . x x x x	451	O,L,D
E-92 [E92]	Clean-Up	. . x x x	728	O,D,L
Farcus [Farc]	Clean-Up	. . x . . . x x x .	N/A	B,O,P,L
Father Christmas [VHP]	Clean-Up	. . x x	1881	O,P
Fear [Dame]	SCAN /D	. x x x x	Varies	O,P,L
Feist [Fst]	Clean-Up	. . x x x x x . . .	670	O,P,L
Fellowship (4) [Fellow]	Clean-Up	. . x . . x	1022	O,P,D,L
FichV2 [Fv2]	Clean-Up	. . x x x		O,P,L
Filler [Filler]	Clean-Up	x . x . . . . x . x	N/A	B,F,L,O
Fingers [Fing]	Clean-Up	. . x x x x x . . .	1322	O,P,D
Fish (2) [Fish]	Clean-Up	x x x x x x x . . .	3584	O,P,L
Flash [Flash]	Clean-Up	. . x x x x	688	O,P,D,L
Flip (5) [Flip]	Clean-Up	. x x x x x x . . .	2343	O,P,D,L
Form (4) [Form]	Clean-Up	. . x . . . . x x .	N/A	B,O,D
Frere Jacques [Mule]	Clean-Up	. . x . x x x . . .	1811	O,P
Friday 13th COM [Fri13]	Clean-Up	. . . . x	512	P
Frogs [Frogs]	Clean-Up	. . x x x	1500	O,P
Fu Manchu (4) [Fu]	Clean-Up	. . x . x x x . . .	2086	O,P
F-Word [FW]	Clean-Up	. . x x x	417	O,P,D

Name	Tool	Characteristics	Size	Codes
Generic Boot [GenB]	Clean-Up	. . x . . . . . x x .	N/A	B,L,O
Generic MBR [GenP]	Clean-Up	? . x x	See Note	F,L,O
Gergana (9) [Gerg]	Clean-Up	. . . x x	varies	L,O,P
Get Password 1 [Jeru]	Clean-Up	. . x . x x x . . .	1914	O,P,L
Ghost Boot [Ghost]	Clean-Up	. . x . . . . x x .	N/A	B,O
Ghost COM [Ghost]	Clean-Up	. . . . x	2351	B,P
Goblin [CRJ]	Clean-Up	. . x x x	1951	O,P,L
Gosia [Gs]	Clean-Up	. . x x x	466	L,O,P
Gotcha (4) [Gtc]	Clean-Up	. . x x x x x . . .	806	O,P,L
Got-you [GY]	Clean-Up	. . . . . x	3052	L,O,P
Grapje [Gr]	Clean-Up	. . . . x	1039	L,O,P
Greemlin [Arf]	Clean-Up	x . x x x x x . . .	1146	O,P,L,D
Growing Block [Grb]	Clean-Up	. . x x x x x . . .	1446	O,P,L,D
Guppy [Guppy]	Clean-Up	. . x x x	152	O,P
Haifa [Hf]	Clean-Up	x x x x x x x . . .	2351	L,O,P
Halloechen [Hal]	Clean-Up	. . x x x x x . . .	2011	L,O,P
Halloween [HW]	Clean-Up	. . x x x	10000	L,O,P
Happy N. Y. [HNY]	Clean-Up	. . x x x x x . . .	1865	O,P
Happy [Happy]	Clean-Up	. . . x x	453	O,P
Hary [Hary]	Clean-Up	. . x x x x	997	O,L,P
Hastings [Hst]	Clean-Up	. . . . x	N/A	O,L
Hero (2) [Hero]	Clean-Up	. . x x x x x . . .	506	O,L,P
Hero-394 [HrB]	Clean-Up	. . x	394	L,O,P
Hitchcock [Hitc]	Clean-Up	. . . x x	1121	O,P
Holland Girl (6) [Sylvia]	Clean-Up	. . . . x	1332	P
Holo/Holocaust (3) [Hl]	Clean-Up	x . x x x	3784	O,P,L,D
Horse Boot [DRP]	Clean-Up	. . x x x . . x x .	N/A	B,P
Horse (7) [Hrs]	Clean-Up	. . x x x x x . . .	1154	O,P,L
HS [HS]	Clean-Up	. . x x x x x . . .	4103	O,P,L
Hungarian [Hng]	Clean-Up	. . x x x x x . . .	695	O,L
Hybrid [Hyb]	Clean-Up	. . . x x	1306	O,P,L
Hydra (12) [Hyd]	Clean-Up	. . . x x	varies	L,O,P
Hymn (3) [Hymn]	Clean-Up	. . x x x x x . . .	642	O,P,D
H-2 [H-2]	Clean-Up	. . x x x x x . . .	1962	O,P,L
Icelandic II [Ice-3]	Clean-Up	. . x . . x	661	O,P
Icelandic (3) [Ice]	Clean-Up	. . x . . x	642	O,P
Icelandic-3 [Ice-3]	Clean-Up	. . x . . x	853	O,P
IKV528 [I528]	Clean-Up	. . . x x	528	O,P
Incom [Inc]	Clean-Up	. . . . x	648	O,P
Infinity [Inf]	Clean-Up	. . . x x	732	O,P
Invader (8) [Invader]	Clean-Up	. x x . x x x x x .	4096	B,L,O,P,D
Invol Virus [Inl]	Clean-Up	. . . . . x x . . .	1413	O,P,L,D
Iraqi Warrior [Lisbon]	Clean-Up	. . . x x	777	O,P,L,D
Israeli Boot [Iboot]	Clean-Up	. . x . . . . x . .	N/A	B,O
Italian Pest (3) [Murphy]	Clean-Up	. . x . x	1910	L,O,P
ItaVir (3) [Ita]	Clean-Up	. . . . x	3880	O,P,L,B
I-B (5) [IB]	Clean-Up	. . . x x	varies	F,L,O,P
Japan [C-J]	Clean-Up	. . x x x	600	O,P
Jeff (3) [Jeff]	Clean-Up	. . x x x	828	O,P,D,F
Jerk (2) [Jrk]	Clean-Up	. . x x x	1077	L,O,P
Jerusalem (48) [Jeru]	Clean-Up	. . x . x x x . . .	1808	O,P
JoJo (3) [JoJo]	Clean-Up	. . x . x	1701	O,P
Joke [JK]	Clean-Up	. . . . x		
Joker (3) [Joke]	Clean-Up	. . x x x		O,P
Joshi (4) [Joshi]	Clean-Up	x . x . . . x x x .	N/A	B,O,D
July 13th [J13]	Clean-Up	. x . . . x	1201	O,P,D,L
June 16th [June16]	Clean-Up	. . x x	1726	F,O,P,L
Justice [Justice]	Clean-Up	. . x x x	1242	O,P
JW2 (2) [Jab]	Clean-Up	. . x x x x	1812	L,O,P
K [K]	Clean-Up	. . x x x x x . . .	4928	O,P,L
Kalah [Kl]	Clean-Up	. . x x x	390	O,P,L,D
Kamikaze [Kami]	Clean-Up	. . . . . x	Overwrites	
Karin [Kar]	Clean-Up	. . . x x	1090	L,O,P
Kemerov (3) [Keme]	Clean-Up	. . . x x	257	L,O,P
Kemerov (5) [Keme]	Clean-Up	. . x x x	varies	O,L,P,D
Kennedy (4) [Tiny]	Clean-Up	. . x . x	308	O,P
Keypress (4) [Key]	Clean-Up	. . x x x x	1232	O,P,D
Kiev [Kiev]	Clean-Up	. . . x x	483	L,O,P
Kiev-1 [Kl]	Clean-Up	. . . x x x		
Klaeren [Kla]	Clean-Up	. x x x x x x . . .	981	O,P,L,D
Korea (4) [Korea]	Clean-Up	. . . . . . x x .	N/A	B,O

Virus	Tool	Flags	Size	Platforms
Kukaturbo [Kakt]	Clean-Up	. . x x	Overwrites	
KU-448 [KU]	Clean-Up	. . x x	448	L,O,P
Label [Label]	Clean-Up	. . x x	Overwrites	
Lazy [Lazy]	Clean-Up	. . x x	720	O,P
LCV [LCV]	Clean-Up	. . . x		
Leapfrog Virus (3) [Leap]	Clean-Up	. . x x x	516	O,P,D
Leech [Leech]	Clean-Up	x x x x x	934	O,P,L,D
Lehigh (2) [Lehigh]	Clean-Up	. . x x	N/A	P,F
Leprosy (7) [Vip]	Clean-Up	. . x x x x . . .	Overwrites	
Leprosy-3 (4) [Lep3]	Clean-Up	. . . x x	Overwrites	L,O,P
Leprosy-B [Vip]	Clean-Up	. . . x x	Overwrites	
Lib1172 (2) [1186]	Clean-Up	. . x x x	1172	L,O,P
Liberty (13) [Liberty]	Clean-Up	. x x x x x . . .	2862	O,P
Lisbon (2) [VHP]	Clean-Up	. . . . x	648	P
Little Pieces [LPC]	Clean-Up	. . x . x x . . .	1374	O,P
Loa Duong [Loa]	Clean-Up	. . x . . . . x x x	N/A	B,O,P,L
Love Child (3) [LC]	Clean-Up	. . x x x	488	O,D
Lozinsky (4) [Loz]	Clean-Up	. . . x x	1023	O,P,D
Lucifer [Alf]	Clean-Up	x . x x x x x . .	1086	O,P,D,L
Macedonia [Mce]	Clean-Up	. . x . x	400	L,O,P
Malage [Mlg]	Clean-Up	. x x x x x x x x	2626	O,P,L
Maltese Amoeba [Irs]	Clean-Up	. x x x x x x . .	2505	O,P,L
Mannequin [Mn]	Clean-Up	. x x x x x . . .	778	O,P,L,D
Manoal [Mno]	Clean-Up	. . x x x	957	L,P
Manta [Mant]	Clean-Up	. . . x x	1077	L,O,P
Marauder [Mar]	Clean-Up	. . . x x	860	O,P,L
Mardi Bros. (3) [Mardi]	Clean-Up	. x . . . . x x .	N/A	B,O
Mface [Mfc]	Clean-Up	. . x x x	1441	O,P,L
MG (4) [MG]	Clean-Up	. . x x x	500	L,O,P
MGTU Virus (4) [MGTU]	Clean-Up	. . . x x	273	O,P,D
Michaelangelo [Mich]	Clean-Up	. . x . . . x x x	N/A	B,O
Microbes [Micro]	M-Disk	. . x . . . x x .	N/A	B,O,D
Miky [Miky]	Clean-Up	. . x x x x x . .	2350	O,P,L
Mini Virus (4) [M45]	Clean-Up	. . . x x	varies	O,P
Mir (2) [DAV]	Clean-Up	. . x x x x x . .	1745	O,P,L
Mirror (2) [Mirror]	Clean-Up	. . x . . x . . .	928	O,P
MIX1 (4) [Ice]	Clean-Up	. . x . . x . . .	1618	O,P
Mix2 [MX2]	Clean-Up	. . x x x x x . .	2280	O,P
Moctezuma [MC]	Clean-Up	. . x x x x x . .	2208	L,O,P
Mono [Mo]	Clean-Up	. . x x x	1063	L,O,P
Monxla (3) [VHP]	Clean-Up	. . . x x	939	O,P
Monxla-B [VHP]	Clean-Up	. . . x x	535	O,P,L
Mosquito [Mosq]	Clean-Up	. x x . . x x . .	1028	O,D,P
MPC [MPC]	Clean-Up	. . x . . x x . .	689	O,P,L
MPS 1.1 [M11]	Clean-Up	. . . x x	469	L,O,P
MPS 3.1 (3) [MPS]	Clean-Up	. . . x x	640	L,O,P
MSTU [MSTU]	Clean-Up	. . . x x x . . .	531	L,O,P
Mule (2) [Mule]	Clean-Up	. x x x x	4171	O,P,D
Multi [M-123]	Clean-Up	. . . x x	123	L,O,P
Mummy [Mum]	Clean-Up	. x x . . x x . .	1374	L
Munich [Mun]	Clean-Up	. . . x x		O,P
Murphy (6) [Murphy]	Clean-Up	. x x x x x x . .	1277	O,P
Music Bug (11) [MBug]	Clean-Up	. . x . . . . x . x	N/A	B,O
Mutant (8) [Mut]	Clean-Up	. . . x x	123	L,O,P
Mutation Engine [DAME]	Clean-Up	x x x x x	VARIES	
M-128 [M128]	Clean-Up	. . x x x	128	L,O,P
Necrophilia [Nec]	Clean-Up	. . x x x	varies	O,P,L,D
New Sunday [Su2]	Clean-Up	. . x . x x x . .	1636	O,P,L,D
Newcom [Alf]	Clean-Up	. . x x x	3045	O,P,L
New-1701 [1701]	Clean-Up	. . x x x	1701	L,O,P
Nina [Nina]	Clean-Up	. . x x x	256	O,P,D
Nines Compliment [Nns]	Clean-Up	. . x x x	705	O,P,L
Nobock [Nbk]	Clean-Up	. . . . . x . . .	440	L,O,P
Nomenclature (4) [Nom]	Clean-Up	. . x x x x x . .	1024	O,P,D
NOP [NOP]	M-Disk	. . x . . . . x . x	N/A	O,B,L
No-Int [Stoned]	Clean-Up	x . x . . . . x . x	N/A	O,B,L
Off Stealth [SVC50]	Clean-Up	x . x x x x x . .	1689	O,P,D
Ohio [Ohio]	Clean-Up	. . x . . . x . .	N/A	B,O
Ontario [Ont]	Clean-Up	. x x x x x . . .	varies	O,P,D
Oropax (5) [Oro]	Clean-Up	. . x . x	2773	P,O
P1 (7) [P1r]	Clean-Up	. x x . x	varies	O,P,D,L
P529 [529]	Clean-Up	. . x x x	529	O,P,D

```
Pest (8) [Murphy]          Clean-Up    . . x x x x x . . .   1910        O,P,L
Phantom [Phant]            Clean-Up    . . x x x . . . . .   2253        O,P
Pig [Pig]                  Clean-Up    . . x x x . . . . .   407         O,P,L
Ping Pong-B (7) [Ping]     Clean-Up    . . x . . . . x x .   N/A         O,B
Pirate [Pir]               Clean-Up    . . . x x . . . . .   Overwrites  L,O,P
Pixel (5) [Pix]            Clean-Up    . . . x x . . . . .   779         O,P
Plague (3) [Plague]        Clean-Up    . . . . x x . . . .   Overwrites
Plastique (9) [Plq]        Clean-Up    . . x x x x x . . .   3012        O,P,D
Platinum [Plt]             Clean-Up    . x . . x x . . . .   1489        O,P,L,D
Plov [Plov]                Clean-Up    . . x x x x x . . .   1000        L,O,P
Poem [Pm]                  Clean-Up    . . x x x . . . . .   1825        F,L,O,P
Pogue [Dame]               Clean-Up    . x x . x . . . . .   varies      L,O,P
Polimer [Polimer]          Clean-Up    . . . x x . . . . .   512         O,P,D
Polish 217 [P-217]         Clean-Up    . . . x x . . . . .   217         O,P,D
Polish-2 [Pol-2]           Clean-Up    . . x x x . . . . .   512         O,P,D
Possessed (6) [Poss]       Clean-Up    . . x x x x x . . .   2443        L,O,P
Pregnant [Prg]             Clean-Up    . . x x x . . . . .   1199        L,O,P
Print Screen (2) [PrtScr]  M-Disk      . . x . . . . x x .   N/A         B,O,D
Prism [Flip]               Clean-Up    . . x x x x x x . x   2153
B,F,L,O,P
Psycho [Psc]               Clean-Up    . . . . x . . . . .   N/A         O
QMU [QML]                  Clean-Up    . . x x x . . . . x   1513        F,L,O,P
QP3 [QP3]                  Clean-Up    . . x x x x x . . .   1028        L,O,P
Quiet [Qt]                 Clean-Up    . . x x x . . . . .   2063        O,P
Rage [Rag]                 Clean-Up    . . x x . . . . . .   575         L,O,P
Ram [Ram]                  Clean-Up    . . x . x x x . . .   varies      L,O,P
Raubkopi [Raub]            Clean-Up    . . x x x . . . . .   varies      L,O,P
RedX (2) [Redx]            Clean-Up    . . . x x . . . . .   796         O,P
Relzfu [233]               Clean-Up    . . x x x . . . . .   233         O,P,L
Reset [RST]                Clean-Up    . . x x . . . . . .   440         O,P
RMIT [RMIT]                Clean-Up    . . x x x . . . . .   Overwrites  L,O,P
RNA [RNA]                  Clean-Up    . . x x x x x . . .   7296        O,P,L
RPVS [453]                 Clean-Up    . . x x x . . . . .   453         O,P
R-10 [R10]                 Clean-Up    . . x x x . . . . .   500         O,P
R-11 [R-11]                Clean-Up    x . x x x . . . . .   700         O,L,D
Saddam [Saddam]            Clean-Up    . . x x x . . . . .   919         O,P,D,L
Saturday 14th (3) [Arma]   Clean-Up    . . x . x x x . . .   685         F,O,P,L
SBC [SBC]                  Clean-Up    . . x . x x x . . .               L,O,P
Scott's Valley [2133]      Clean-Up    . x x . x x x . . .   2133        L,O,P,D
Scream 2 [Sc2]             Clean-Up    . x x x x x x . . .   1324        O,P,L
Screaming Fist [Scr]       Clean-Up    . . x x x x x . . .   711         O,P,L
SCT [SCT]                  Clean-Up    . . . . x . . . . .
Semtex [Set]               Clean-Up    . . x x x . . . . .   1000        L,O,P
Sentinel (3) [Sent]        Clean-Up    . . x x x x x . . .   4625        L,O,P,D
Sentinel-X [BCV]           Clean-Up    . . x x x x x . . .   4625        L,O,P,D
Sh [Sh]                    Clean-Up    . . . x x x x . . .   Overwrites  L,O,P
Shadow (3) [Sha]           Clean-Up    . . . x x . . . . .   723         O,P
Shake (2) [Shake]          Clean-Up    . . x . x . . . . .   476
```

Virus [ID]	Tool	Pattern	Size	Flags
Spanish April Fool [D28]	Clean-Up	. . x . . x x . . .	1400	O,L,P
Spanish [Spain]	Clean-Up	. . x x x x x . . .	2930	O,P,L,D
Spanz [Spz]	Clean-Up	. . x x x	663	O,D
Spar [Spar]	Clean-Up	. . x x x x	1255	O,P
Spyer (3) [Spyer]	Clean-Up	. . x . x x x . . .	1181	O,P
Squawk [Sqa]	Clean-Up	. . x x x x x . . .	852	O,P,L
Squeaker [Sqe]	Clean-Up	. . x x x x x . . .	1091	L,O,P
Staf [Staf]	Clean-Up	. . x x x	2083	O,P,L
Star Dot (4) [Sdot]	Clean-Up	. . x . x		O,P,L
Stardot-801 (3) [I-F]	Clean-Up	. . . x x x	604	D,F,L,O,P
Stink [Sti]	Clean-Up	. . . x	1254	L,O,P
Stoned (26) [Stoned]	Clean-Up	. . x . . . . x . x	N/A	O,B,L
Stone-90 [VHP]	Clean-Up	. . . x x	961	O,P
Striker [STR]	Clean-Up	. . x x x	461	D,O,P,F
Subliminal (3) [Sub]	Clean-Up	. . x x x	1496	O,P
Sunday (6) [Sunday]	Clean-Up	. x . x x x . . .	1636	O,P
Sunday-2 [Su2]	Clean-Up	. . x x x x x . . .	2877	L,O,P
Suriv 402 [S-4]	Clean-Up	. . x x x	897	L,O,P
Suriv A (2) [SurivA]	Clean-Up	. . x . x	897	O,P
Surrender [Sur]	Clean-Up	. . x x x x x . . .	513	O,P,L
SVC 5.0/6.0 (2) [SVC50]	Clean-Up	x x x x x x x . . x	3103	B,L,O,P
Sverdlov (2) [Sv]	Clean-Up	. . x x x x x . . .	1962	O,P
SVir (4) [Svir]	Clean-Up	. . x . . x	512	L,O,P
Swap Boot [Iboot]	M-Disk	. . x . . . x . .	N/A	B
Swiss 143 [S143]	Clean-Up	. . x x	143	O,P,D
SX [SX]	Clean-Up	. . x x x	800	L,O,P
Sylvia [Sylvia]	Clean-Up	. . x . x	1332	L,O,P
Sys Virus [Sys]	Clean-Up	x x x x x x x . . .	N/A	O,P,D
Syslock/3551 [Syslock]	Clean-Up	. x . . x x	3551	P,D
S-847 [Pix]	Clean-Up	. . x . x	850	O,P
Taiwan (11) [Taiwan]	Clean-Up	. . . . x	708	P
Taiwan3 [T3]	Clean-Up	. . x x x x x . . .	2905	O,P,D,L
Taiwan4 [T4]	Clean-Up	. . x x x x x . . .	2576	O,P,D
Telecom Boot [Tele]	M-Disk	. x x . . . . x x	N/A	B,P
Telecom File [Tele]	Clean-Up	. x x . x	3700	B,P,O,D
Tequila [Teq]	Clean-Up	x x x . . x . . . x	2468	O,P,F,L
Terror (3) [Ter]	Clean-Up	. . x x x x x . . .	1085	O,P,F
Tester [TV]	Clean-Up	. . x x x	1000	O,P
Timid [Tmd]	Clean-Up	. . x x	306	L,O,P
Tiny 133 [T133]	Clean-Up	. . x x	133	O,P
Tiny (31) [Tiny]	Clean-Up	. . x x	163	O,P
Tokyo [Tokyo]	Clean-Up	. . x . . x	1258	L,O,P
Tony [Tn]	Clean-Up	. . x x	200	L,O,P
Topo [Topo]	Clean-Up	. . x . . x	1542	L,O,P
Traceback (3) [3066]	Clean-Up	. . x . x x	3066	P
Traveller [Trv]	Clean-Up	. . x x x x	1220	L,O,P
Troi [Troi]	Clean-Up	. . x x x	322	O,P,L
Tuesday (2) [Alf]	Clean-Up	. . x . x x x . . .	1163	O,P,L,P
Tumen V0.5 [Tum5]	Clean-Up	. . x x x	1663	O,P,L,D
Tumen V2.0 [Tum2]	Clean-Up	. . x x x	1092	O,P,L,D
Turbo (2) [Pol-2]	Clean-Up	. . x x x	448	L,O,P
Twin-351 [Twin]	Clean-Up	x . x . x x	351	L,O,P
Typo Boot (2) [TBoot]	Clean-Up	. . x . . . . x x .	N/A	O,B
Typo/Fumble/712 (2) [712]	Clean-Up	. . x . x	867	O,P
Ucender [Uce]	Clean-Up	. . x x x x x . . .	1783	O,P,L
USSR 1049 [Alf]	Clean-Up	. . x x x x	1049	O,P,L
USSR 2144 (8) [U2144]	Clean-Up	. x x x x x x . . .	2144	L,O,P,D
USSR 256 (5) [U256]	Clean-Up	. x . x x	256	P,D
USSR 257 [U257]	Clean-Up	. x . x x	257	P,D
USSR 3103 [SVC]	Clean-Up	x x x x x x x . . x	3103	B,L,O,P
USSR 311 [U311]	Clean-Up	. . . . x	321	O,P
USSR 394 [U394]	Clean-Up	. x . x x	394	P,D
USSR 492 [U492]	Clean-Up	. . . . x	492	O,P
USSR 516 (4) [Leap]	Clean-Up	. . x x x	516	O,P
USSR 600 [U600]	Clean-Up	. x . x x	600	P,D
USSR 696 [U696]	Clean-Up	. x . x x	696	P,D
USSR 707 [U707]	Clean-Up	. x . x x	707	P,D
USSR 711 [U711]	Clean-Up	. x . . x	711	P,D
USSR 830 [U830]	Clean-Up	. . x x x	830	O,P
USSR 948 [U948]	Clean-Up	. x . . x x x . . .	948	O,P,D
USSR (11) [USSR]	Clean-Up	. x . . . x	575	O,P

Virus	Disinfector		Size Increase	Characteristics
V1028 [QP2]	Clean-Up	. . x x x x . . .	1028	O,P,L
V125 [M128]	Clean-Up	. . x x x	125	P
V1463 [1452]	Clean-Up	. . . x x	1463	O,P
V2000 (3) [2000]	Clean-Up	. . x x x x . . .	2000	O,P,L
V2100 (5) [2100]	Clean-Up	. . x . x x . . .	2100	O,P,D,L
V270X [268P]	Clean-Up	. . . x x	270	O,P,L,D
V299 [V299]	Clean-Up	. . . . x	299	O,P,D
V2P2 [v2p2]	Clean-Up	. x . . x	varies	L,O,P
V2P6 [V2P6]	Clean-Up	. x . . x	varies	L,O,P
V400 (5) [MCE]	Clean-Up	. . x . x	varies	O,P,D
V483 [B483]	Clean-Up	. . x x x	483	O,P
V5 [V-5]	Clean-Up	. . . x x x	547	O,D
V800 (3) [V800]	Clean-Up	x x x . x	800	O,P,L
V801 [V801]	Clean-Up	. . x x x x x . . .	801	O,P,L
V82 [V82]	Clean-Up	. x . . x x x x x	2000	O,P,L
V961 [V961]	Clean-Up	. . x x x	961	O,P
Vacsina (19) [Vacs]	Clean-Up	. . x . x x x . . .	1206	O,P
Vcomm (5) [Vcomm]	Clean-Up	. . . . . x	1074	O,P,L
VHP (7) [VHP]	Clean-Up	. . . x x	varies	L,O,P
Victor (2) [Victor]	Clean-Up	. . x x x x x . . .	2458	P,D,L
Vienna/648 (49) [Lisbon]	Clean-Up	. . . . x	648	P
Violator (5) [Vienna]	Clean-Up	. . . . x	1055	O,P,D
Viper [Vip]	Clean-Up	. . x x x	Overwrites	L,O,P
Virus-101 [101]	Clean-Up	. x x x x x x x . .	2560	P
Virus-90 [90]	Clean-Up	. . x . x	857	P
Voronezh (2) [Vor]	Clean-Up	x x x x x x . . .	1600	O,P,D
VP [VP]	Clean-Up	. . . x x	913	L,O,P
Vriest [Vrst]	Clean-Up	. . x x x	1280	L,O,P
VTS [VTS]	Clean-Up	. . . . x		
V-Label [Label]	Clean-Up	. . x x x x . . .	Overwrites	L,O,P
W13 (4) [W13]	Clean-Up	. . . . x	532	O,P
Warrior 2 [war2]	Clean-Up	. . . . x		
Warrior [War]	Clean-Up	. . x . x	1024	O,P,D
Whale (34) [Whale]	Clean-Up	x x x x x x x . .	9216	L,O,P,D
Wisconsin (3) [Wisc]	Clean-Up	. x . x x	825	O,P,D
Wolfman (3) [Wolf]	Clean-Up	. . x x x x	2064	O,P
Wonder [Wond]	Clean-Up	. . . . x x	Overwrites	L,O,P
Wordswap (4) [Ws]	Clean-Up	. . x x x x . . .	varies	D,F,L,O,P
WWT (3) [WWT]	Clean-Up	. . . x x	varies	L,O,P
Xabaras [Xab]	Clean-Up	. . . . . x . . .	Overwrites	L,O,P
Xuxa [xu]	Clean-Up	. . x x x	1413	O,P,L
Yale/Alameda (3) [Alameda]	Clean-Up	. . x . . . . x . .	N/A	B
Yankee - 2 [Enigma]	Clean-Up	. . . . x x	1961	O,P
Yap [Yap]	Clean-Up	. x x x x	6258	L,O,P
Zaragosa [Zar]	Clean-Up	. . x x x x x . . .	1159	L,O,P
Zero Bug/1536 [Zero]	Clean-Up	. . x . x	1536	O,P
ZeroHunt [Hunt]	Clean-Up	x x x . x	N/A	O,P,D
ZK900 [Z900]	Clean-Up	. . x x x x	900	L,O,P
ZRK (3) [ZRK]	Clean-Up	. . x x x x x . . .	2968	O,L,P
# 1 [N1]	Clean-Up	. . x x x	11240	O,L,P

Unique Known Viruses   — 534
Known Variants of Viruses — 729
Total Known Viruses   — 1263

LEGEND:

Size Increase:

N/A	— Virus does not attach to files
None	— Virus does not change file size (attaches to tag end of file)
Overwrites	— Virus overwrites beginning of file, no file size change
All Others	— The length in bytes by which a file will increase when infected

Damage Fields:

B — Corrupts or overwrites the boot sector
D — Corrupts data files
F — Formats or overwrites all/part of disk
L — Directly or indirectly corrupts file linkage
O — Affects system run-time operation
P — Corrupts program or overlay files

Characteristics:

x — Yes
. — No

Disinfectors:

CLEAN-UP — CLEAN-UP universal virus disinfector
SCAN /D — VIRUSCAN with /D option
SCAN /D/A — VIRUSCAN with /D and /A options
MDISK /P — MDISK with "P" option
All Others — The name of disinfecting program

NOTES

SCAN /D OPTION

The SCAN /D options will overwrite and then delete the entire infected program. The program must then be replaced from the original program diskette. If you wish to try and recover an infected program, then use the above-named disinfector if available.

OVERLAY-INFECTING VIRUSES AND THE /A OPTION

If a virus infects Overlay Files (Item 7) Clean-Up should be used with the /A option when removing the virus.

CRASH VIRUS

The "Crash" virus (in all implementations we have encountered) crashes when run. It is included since it is possible that under other architectures than those tested, it might flourish.

GENERIC BOOT SECTOR [GENB] AND MBR [GENP] VIRUSES

The Generic Boot Sector and Master Boot Record (or partition table) ID code is a routine used to detect unknown viruses—it is not the name of a specific virus. If you have found such a virus on your system, please forward a copy to McAfee Associates for analysis by our technical staff prior to removal with the CLEAN-UP program.

Glossary

access Gain entry to a system or program. (See read access; write access.)

application Software programs that perform a specific task such as word processing, database management, or accounting.

backup The process of duplicating data and programming stored in memory. Through this process, one or more copies are created and held in reserve in case a system has to be restored after a virus infection has been cleared up.

bit Abbreviation for *binary digits*, the ones and zeros that are the basic building blocks of data stored in a computer.

boot To boot a computer is to start it. During the startup process, system instructions come from a hard-wired chip, a hard disk, or a floppy disk. (Originally *bootstrap*.)

boot infector A virus that gets into the boot sector of either a hard or floppy disk.

boot sector The section of a disk (or diskette) that holds the code used to get the operating system up and running.

bug An electronic fault in a hardware system, or an error in a program, that prevents either the system or the program from properly carrying out assigned tasks or functions.

bulletin board system (BBS) An electronic mail system through which you can send or receive messages, and from which program updates and other timely virus information can be made available for downloading.

byte A collection of bits (binary digits), usually eight, that make a single character of text. Usually used as a measure of a computer's memory capacity, or of the memory capacity of any computer storage medium.

checksum The result of a procedure used to verify the integrity and accuracy of sectors on a disk by calculating the number of bits in each sector and comparing current to previous counts. (Often referred to as *CRC*.)

cold boot To clear, reload, and restart the system by turning the computer off, counting to at least 20 to let the fans cease turning, and then turning the system back on.

.COM A file extension that indicates a command program used to carry out DOS commands.

crash What happens when a program or a system fails (often referred to as a *program crash* or *disk crash*).

data The raw information that is processed by a computer. Data files contain information to be processed, as opposed to executable files that contain system or program instructions to be run.

directory A sort of "table of contents" (or list) that tells you what is on a hard or floppy disk. The main directory is called the root directory and each root directory can contain numerous subdirectories. The structure is that of a tree.

disk The medium for electromagnetic storage of data and program files. It can be a hard or floppy disk, internal or external to the computer. No matter its configuration, any disk is vulnerable to virus infection.

disk drive The hardware that reads files and records data to disk, either hard or floppy format.

documentation Information about a program, including how to install, run, and optimize the program. It can be in hard copy, on-line format, or both.

DOS Disk operating system.

.EXE A file extension that indicates an executable file containing programs that DOS can run. It is generally more complex and includes more features than a .COM program.

execution Using an instruction file to make a computer run.

file A collection of data, usually related; can be text, graphics, or machine language instructions.

fixed disk Also called a hard disk, the fixed disk is built into a computer. It has a larger capacity than a floppy diskette, and the information stored can be more quickly accessed than with a floppy.

hacker A computer enthusiast, often known for illegal activities that result from perceived challenges presented by computer systems and telecommunications.

hard copy Printed data or information.

hardware Computer equipment, components, or machinery. (See software.)

host computer In the world of viruses, a host computer is any computer that has a virus in residence.

host program Any program to which a virus attaches itself, and from which it spreads to other programs. Host programs can be executable files in applications programs or in the operating system.

kilobyte 1,000 bytes, abbreviated as K or KB logic bomb. A software program that is destructive when certain conditions that activate it are met; not a true virus because it does not replicate.

megabyte A million bytes, abbreviated as M or MB memory. The ability and devices that enable a computer/machine to store information subject to recall.

modem A modulator/demodulator device that allows electronic signals to be transmitted via telephone line.

monitor The video screen on which you see information

network A system of computers linked by direct connection, or over telephone lines (or other electronic transmission methods).

operating system A series of programs that enable you to interact with your computer and that manage computer functions. The operating system that hosts the viruses discussed in this book (and which runs the anti-virus software discussed) is *DOS* (disk operating system), either MS-DOS (Microsoft) or PC-DOS (IBM).

output Information that is displayed on the screen, stored on disk, or sent to the printer.

piracy Making (and selling or just giving away) an illegal copy of a commercial copyrighted software program.

RAM Acronym for *random-access memory*. Storage area for information and programs that is wiped out when the computer is turned off.

read Access data or program instructions from storage on a disk or chip.

read access Ability to read a file (but not write to it).

reboot To reload the operating system software and give your computer a fresh start.

replication The process of self-isolation by a virus from its current host program, and its attachment to a new host; the mechanism by which infection is spread.

ROM Acronym for *read-only memory*. ROM contains permanently stored information, usually programming code, which cannot be altered, and remains in memory when you turn off your computer.

sector A portion of a disk that contains sections of the tracks on which information is stored.

shareware Programs that are readily available to you that you can try for a limited time before actually buying them.

software The instructions that tell a computer what to do, what tasks to perform. (See hardware.)

sysop The abbreviation used to denote the system operator of a bulletin board system.

system A computer, including both hardware and software (operating system).

system files Files containing programming code (information) used by the operating system.

terminal The combination of a keyboard (mouse) and monitor through which you communicate with your computer.

time bomb A damaging program set to activate at a specific time.

Trojan horse A damaging program that is disguised as an innocent program. It is not a virus because it cannot replicate, but it may be playing host to a hidden virus within.

virus A segment (string) of self-replicating code that attaches itself to executable files in the operating system or application programs. A virus can replicate itself an infinite number of times (limited only by its design).

virus creation The act of designing, structuring, or coding a virus.

warm boot To press the <Ctrl>, <Alt>, and <Del> keys simultaneously (or to press your computer's reset button) to clear the system, restart it, and reload the operating system.

worm A program that destroys data but does not replicate itself, and is therefore not a true virus.

write access Ability to add or change data within a file.

write protection Prevention against alteration of information on a disk. When a disk is write-protected, the information on it can only be read, not altered. This offers some protection from viruses. You can write-protect a 5.25-inch disk by covering its square notch with one of the tabs that comes in the disk package. You can write-protect a 3.5-inch disk by moving its plastic tab from the default (open) position to the closed, write-protect position.

Index